Tangents

GREG BEAR

# Tangents

VGSF

VGSF is an imprint of Victor Gollancz Ltd
14 Henrietta Street, London WC2E 8QJ

First published in Great Britain 1989
by Victor Gollancz Ltd

First VGSF edition 1990

*British Library Cataloguing in Publication Data*
Bear, Greg, *1951–*
  Tangents.
  I. Title
  813'.54 [F]

ISBN 0-575-04775-5

Printed and bound in Great Britain
by Cox & Wyman Ltd, Reading

# Acknowledgements

"Blood Music" appeared in ANALOG. Copyright © 1983 by Greg Bear.

"Sleepside Story" was originally published by Cheap Street Press in a limited edition in 1988. Copyright © 1988 by Greg Bear.

"Webster" appeared in ALTERNITIES, edited by David Gerrold. Copyright © 1973 by Greg Bear.

"A Martian Ricorso" appeared in ANALOG. Copyright © 1976 by Greg Bear.

"Dead Run" appeared in OMNI. Copyright © 1985 by Greg Bear.

"Schrödinger's Plague" appeared in ANALOG. Copyright © 1982 by Greg Bear.

"Through Road No Whither" appeared in FAR FRONTIERS, edited by Jerry Pournelle and Jim Baen. Copyright © 1985 by Greg Bear.

"Tangents" appeared in OMNI. Copyright © 1986 by Greg Bear.

"Sisters" appears in this anthology for the first time. Copyright © 1989 by Greg Bear.

"The Machineries of Joy" was first published by Nesfa Press in EARLY HARVEST. Copyright © 1987 by Greg Bear.

*This book is for Erik*
*More wonderful by far than anything*
*contained herein.*

# Contents

# Tangents

# INTRODUCTION

**W**hat is so fascinating about science fiction? Why do so many feel an attraction to its subjects, and a persistent few continue to think of it as (on the whole) worthless garbage?

The answer, I think, lies in a basic American dichotomy. America has always been a land set firmly not in the past, but in the future. On a recent visit to England, I found dozens of wonderful bookstores chock full of the past—ancient history, rooms full of it, and great literature in such monumental stacks as to be overwhelming. In the usual American bookstore, history might occupy a few bookcases; great literature has its honored place, but this year's paperbacks dominate. The past is not disregarded, but neither does it loom so large and run so deep in our blood.

America is suspended in a continuous *grand jeté* into the future. People who live in the future have different sophistications than those who are ever looking backward. But many Americans seem to feel this is a disordered way of living and thinking. They yearn for the relatively unchanging pleasures of history, of stories familiar and well told, of nuance over broad sweep; they yearn for an investigation of the problems of the past, still far from solved, but at least giving the appearance of being solvable.

For many, the future is much more frightful than the past. The future is not only filled with problems; the problems cannot be solved because most of them are unknown. The future is not a well-thumbed leather-bound book read before a cozy glowing fireplace. The wisdom of the past tells us that bad things are bound to happen, and our newly acquired powers point to bad things becoming worse. Optimism is a difficult frame of mind when one reads history.

Some Americans pretend that nothing will change, then, or that the best has already been, and what's to come is best ignored, if only out of politeness. This condition is not unknown elsewhere; but in America, among people so afflicted, the severity is even more pronounced. Having so little past— only a few centuries, as opposed to thousands of years—a few Americans cling to what there is, and in their provincial reactionism outdo the citizens of nations with millennia behind them.

But for those many who embrace the future, who feel— however naively—that there might be wonder and greatness there, a literature has arisen at once young and full of energy, brash and often unsophisticated, commercial and designed to appeal to a broad if discerning public.

For decades now, we have dwelled in a ghetto largely of

our own making. But the walls have been reinforced from the outside by a dwindling yet still influential intellectual elite for whom the forms and subjects of the past are all that can be discussed. Science fiction writers have blithely skipped on, retaining their essential childlike character, but at the same time displaying a remarkable ability to entertain those very people who are making the future.

Engineers. Scientists. Computer programmers and designers. Astronauts and the men and women who build their rockets. Motion picture directors. Dreamers for whom the past, however interesting, is a kind of prison from which we must all break free.

Revolutionaries. Thomas Jefferson, Alexander Hamilton, Benjamin Franklin, Thomas Paine, imagined a republic, and it came to be. Jules Verne, H. G. Wells, Arthur C. Clarke, Robert A. Heinlein, imagined a space program, and it came to be. Writers today envision hundreds of futures a year, thousands a decade, of which most are playful, for the sake of an evening's thoughtful entertainment; and a few are more than that, are serious extrapolations to be seriously and soberly considered.

Science fiction has now grown far beyond its ghetto walls. It has supplied names for history books, clichés for television advertising, shapes for architecture. The extremes of science cross-fertilize with the imagined technologies of SF. It has enraged, shaped, and enlivened world literature. It is truly international, and becoming more so year by year.

But why do *I* write science fiction?

Instinct, I suppose. I began writing it when I was eight, after thinking and drawing and telling stories to friends. After seeing a Ray Harryhausen monster from Venus eat sulphur and almost eat Rome. That monster gave me nightmares, and I knew where my particular future lay. I glued myself on to various writers, starting out with the Tom Swift, Jr., adventure novels and moving on to Edgar Rice Burroughs and then to

Robert A. Heinlein and Arthur C. Clarke, and through Clarke to Olaf Stapledon, and through Ray Bradbury to Edgar Allan Poe and Thomas Wolfe and Nikos Kazantzakis, and through James Blish to James Joyce, and through Robert Silverberg to Joseph Conrad, spreading out roots, always adhering to the path of science fiction until in my growth I peeped beyond the branching pathways and saw the wonders of the past mixing with the future.

I suppose this all sounds a little breathless, a little naive. So be it. I do not willingly give up my past, for in it are visions of the future that I continue to cherish, however crude and inadequate. They come to me from men who cared, men with genuine vision. I will not cut myself loose from them simply to be pasted with the label of sophistication.

So here's my challenge. We're big now. Grown-up. Almost mature. Judge all of science fiction by your most knowing, discerning mental yardstick: you'll inch and foot and yard (and oh, yes, *meter*) yourself past authors who can satisfy most of your demands and requirements. There are great books being written.

We're in the middle of a literary revolution. But this is not a vicious historical tragedy of a revolution; it is a joyous celebration. We celebrate what we fear, as well as what we desire. Science fiction writers, and writers of that all-inclusive category, fantasy, adore strong emotions. Fear. Love. Revulsion. Obsession.

I classify *sense of wonder* as a strong emotion. The modern scientific equivalent of epiphany is what I call the "intellectual high," when a revelation has been handed down so magnificent, so mind-expanding, that exaltation is the only reasonable response. Science fiction, then, sometimes has the trappings of a modern religion—a cult religion for the skeptical, for the unfettered thinker.

It has enthusiasm. All this appealed to me when I was very young, and it still does.

The stories in this book range from the beginning of my career to the present, and cover a broad variety; that's the way I like it. While my greatest success has been with large, sprawling science fiction novels of the type loosely described as "hard," I'm fond of short stories, and of fantasy and magic realism.

Perhaps the most famous story collected here is "Blood Music," first published in 1983. The idea occurred to me within ten minutes of reading an article in *New Scientist* on biochips, theoretical organic computers that might be as small as a single cell. Even before the story won its share of awards, I realized that it needed expansion, and was working on a novel-length version of the same name. The novel departs substantially from the short story. Both have been reprinted and translated all over the world; I remain a faithful reader of *New Scientist*.

I'm very fond of "Sleepside Story," perhaps because it differs so greatly from most of my writing. Quite often, between my science fiction novels, I feel the urge to explore a different territory, something I've never done before . . . In this case, an urban fairy tale.

"Dead Run," another fantasy, was turned into a *Twilight Zone* television episode, brilliantly scripted by Alan Brennert. Because Alan and I are good friends, a rare opportunity arose. For a period of several weeks, Alan called me with updates on his script, advising me on the limitations he had to work around and the changes necessary for filming. (Interestingly, CBS was not at all reluctant to air the subject matter.) I was able to throw in more than two cents' worth of my own advice, and so in a way, without reducing Alan's role one whit, the screenplay became a kind of collaboration. Alan worked out an ending that was better than the ending in the original, I think; so in revising the story for this collection, I've made some changes. In a way, without reducing my role one whit, Alan has now collaborated on this printed version.

"Sisters" is hard SF with a strong social slant. It's also a preliminary working out of themes and ideas I'll be developing more fully in my novel, *Queen of Angels*. "Sisters" appears for the first time in this collection.

"Tangents" was originally written for a computer magazine that decided not to run fiction. I thought of it as an homage to the mathematical fantasies collected by Clifton Fadiman in the 1950s, in particular Martin Gardner's "The No-Sided Professor," which introduced me to Möbius strips when I was eleven or twelve. Rudy Rucker's *The Fourth Dimension* provided additional fuel. The story gathered more awards, perhaps because, behind the mathematics, there is an angry parable based on the life of the English mathematician Alan Turing . . . Or perhaps because science fiction readers truly appreciate mathematical fantasies.

"Schrödinger's Plague" is a jape on physics, something of an in-joke. In fact, the situation described therein—or at least the outcome—is not possible, so several physicists whom I trust have informed me. But finding out *why* it's not possible could involve the reader in a solid undergraduate course in quantum mechanics. To my delight, science (and science fiction) writer John Gribbin cited the story as one of several that motivated him to write his book, *In Search of Schrödinger's Cat*.

"Webster" and "A Martian Ricorso" were first printed earlier in my career, and still, I think, have their charms.

And what else is so attractive about science fiction, especially to younger writers?

Here, mired in the future, the short story is alive and well.

# Blood Music

There is a principle in nature I don't think anyone has pointed out before. Each hour, a myriad of trillions of little live things—bacteria, microbes, "animalcules"—are born and die, not counting for much except in the bulk of their existence and the accumulation of their tiny effects. They do not perceive deeply. They do not suffer much. A hundred billion, dying, would not begin to have the same importance as a single human death.

Within the ranks of magnitude of all creatures, small as microbes or great as humans, there is an equality of "elan," just as the branches of a tall tree, gathered together, equal the bulk of the limbs below, and all the limbs equal the bulk of the trunk.

That, at least, is the principle. I believe Vergil Ulam was the first to violate it.

It had been two years since I'd last seen Vergil. My memory of him hardly matched the tan, smiling, well-dressed gentleman standing before me. We had made a lunch appointment over the phone the day before, and now faced each other in the wide double doors of the employees' cafeteria at the Mount Freedom Medical Center.

"Vergil?" I asked. "My God, Vergil!"

"Good to see you, Edward." He shook my hand firmly. He had lost ten or twelve kilos and what remained seemed tighter, better proportioned. At university, Vergil had been the pudgy, shock-haired, snaggle-toothed whiz kid who hot-wired doorknobs, gave us punch that turned our piss blue, and never got a date except with Eileen Termagent, who shared many of his physical characteristics.

"You look fantastic," I said. "Spend a summer in Cabo San Lucas?"

We stood in line at the counter and chose our food. "The tan," he said, picking out a carton of chocolate milk, "is from spending three months under a sunlamp. My teeth were straightened just after I last saw you. I'll explain the rest, but we need a place to talk where no one will listen close."

I steered him to the smoker's corner, where three diehard puffers were scattered among six tables.

"Listen, I mean it," I said as we unloaded our trays. "You've changed. You're looking good."

"I've changed more than you know." His tone was motion-picture ominous, and he delivered the line with a theatrical lift of his brows. "How's Gail?"

Gail was doing well, I told him, teaching nursery school. We'd married the year before. His gaze shifted down to his food—pineapple slice and cottage cheese, piece of banana cream pie—and he said, his voice almost cracking, "Notice something else?"

I squinted in concentration. "Uh."

"Look closer."

"I'm not sure. Well, yes, you're not wearing glasses. Contacts?"

"No. I don't need them anymore."

"And you're a snappy dresser. Who's dressing you now? I hope she's as sexy as she is tasteful."

"Candice isn't—wasn't responsible for the improvement in my clothes," he said. "I just got a better job, more money to throw around. My taste in clothes is better than my taste in food, as it happens." He grinned the old Vergil self-deprecating grin, but ended it with a peculiar leer. "At any rate, she's left me, I've been fired from my job, I'm living on savings."

"Hold it," I said. "That's a bit crowded. Why not do a linear breakdown? You got a job. Where?"

"Genetron Corp.," he said. "Sixteen months ago."

"I haven't heard of them."

"You will. They're putting out common stock in the next month. It'll shoot off the board. They've broken through with MABs. Medical—"

"I know what MABs are," I interrupted. "At least in theory. Medically Applicable Biochips."

"They have some that work."

"What?" It was my turn to lift my brows.

"Microscopic logic circuits. You inject them into the human body, they set up shop where they're told and trouble-shoot. With Dr. Michael Bernard's approval."

That was quite impressive. Bernard's reputation was spotless. Not only was he associated with the genetic engineering biggies, but he had made news at least once a year in his practice as a neurosurgeon before retiring. Covers on *Time, Mega, Rolling Stone*.

"That's supposed to be secret—stock, breakthrough, Bernard, everything." He looked around and lowered his voice. "But you do whatever the hell you want. I'm through with the bastards."

I whistled. "Make me rich, huh?"

"If that's what you want. Or you can spend some time with me before rushing off to your broker."

"Of course." He hadn't touched the cottage cheese or pie. He had, however, eaten the pineapple slice and drunk the chocolate milk. "So tell me more."

"Well, in med school I was training for lab work. Biochemical research. I've always had a bent for computers, too. So I put myself through my last two years—"

"By selling software packages to Westinghouse," I said.

"It's good my friends remember. That's how I got involved with Genetron, just when they were starting out. They had big money backers, all the lab facilities I thought anyone would ever need. They hired me, and I advanced rapidly.

"Four months and I was doing my own work. I made some breakthroughs"—he tossed his hand nonchalantly—"then I went off on tangents they thought were premature. I persisted and they took away my lab, handed it over to a certifiable flatworm. I managed to save part of the experiment before they fired me. But I haven't exactly been cautious . . . or judicious. So now it's going on outside the lab."

I'd always regarded Vergil as ambitious, a trifle cracked, and not terribly sensitive. His relations with authority figures had never been smooth. Science, for him, was like the woman you couldn't possibly have, who suddenly opens her arms to you, long before you're ready for mature love—leaving you afraid you'll forever blow the chance, lose the prize. Apparently, he did. "Outside the lab? I don't get you."

"Edward, I want you to examine me. Give me a thorough physical. Maybe a cancer diagnostic. Then I'll explain more."

"You want a five-thousand-dollar exam?"

"Whatever you can do. Ultrasound, NMR, thermogram, everything."

"I don't know if I can get access to all that equipment. NMR full-scan has only been here a month or two. Hell, you couldn't pick a more expensive way—"

"Then ultrasound. That's all you'll need."

"Vergil, I'm an obstetrician, not a glamour-boy lab-tech. OB-GYN, butt of all jokes. If you're turning into a woman, maybe I can help you."

He leaned forward, almost putting his elbow into the pie, but swinging wide at the last instant by scant millimeters. The old Vergil would have hit it square. "Examine me closely and you'll . . ." He narrowed his eyes. "Just examine me."

"So I make an appointment for ultrasound. Who's going to pay?"

"I'm on Blue Shield." He smiled and held up a medical credit card. "I messed with the personnel files at Genetron. Anything up to a hundred thousand dollars medical, they'll never check, never suspect."

He wanted secrecy, so I made arrangements. I filled out his forms myself. As long as everything was billed properly, most of the examination could take place without official notice. I didn't charge for my services. After all, Vergil had turned my piss blue. We were friends.

He came in late at night. I wasn't normally on duty then, but I stayed late, waiting for him on the third floor of what the nurses called the Frankenstein wing. I sat on an orange plastic chair. He arrived, looking olive-colored under the fluorescent lights.

He stripped, and I arranged him on the table. I noticed, first off, that his ankles looked swollen. But they weren't puffy. I felt them several times. They seemed healthy but looked odd. "Hm," I said.

I ran the paddles over him, picking up areas difficult for the big unit to hit, and programmed the data into the imaging system. Then I swung the table around and inserted it into the enameled orifice of the ultrasound diagnostic unit, the hum-hole, so-called by the nurses.

I integrated the data from the hum-hole with that from the paddle sweeps and rolled Vergil out, then set up a video frame. The image took a second to integrate, then flowed into a pattern showing Vergil's skeleton. My jaw fell.

Three seconds of that and it switched to his thoracic organs, then his musculature, and, finally, vascular system and skin.

"How long since the accident?" I asked, trying to take the quiver out of my voice.

"I haven't been in an accident," he said. "It was deliberate."

"Jesus, they beat you to keep secrets?"

"You don't understand me, Edward. Look at the images again. I'm not damaged."

"Look, there's thickening here"—I indicated the ankles—"and your ribs—that crazy zigzag pattern of interlocks. Broken sometime, obviously. And—"

"Look at my spine," he said. I rotated the image in the video frame.

Buckminster Fuller, I thought. It was fantastic. A cage of triangular projections, all interlocking in ways I couldn't begin to follow, much less understand. I reached around and tried to

16

feel his spine with my fingers. He lifted his arms and looked off at the ceiling.

"I can't find it," I said. "It's all smooth back there." I let go of him and looked at his chest, then prodded his ribs. They were sheathed in something tough and flexible. The harder I pressed, the tougher it became. Then I noticed another change.

"Hey," I said. "You don't have any nipples." There were tiny pigment patches, but no nipple formations at all.

"See?" Vergil asked, shrugging on the white robe, "I'm being rebuilt from the inside out."

In my reconstruction of those hours, I fancy myself saying, "So tell me about it." Perhaps mercifully, I don't remember what I actually said.

He explained with his characteristic circumlocutions. Listening was like trying to get to the meat of a newspaper article through a forest of sidebars and graphic embellishments.

I simplify and condense.

Genetron had assigned him to manufacturing prototype biochips, tiny circuits made out of protein molecules. Some were hooked up to silicon chips little more than a micrometer in size, then sent through rat arteries to chemically keyed locations, to make connections with the rat tissue and attempt to monitor and even control lab-induced pathologies.

"*That* was something," he said.

"We recovered the most complex microchip by sacrificing the rat, then debriefed it—hooked the silicon portion up to an imaging system. The computer gave us bar graphs, then a diagram of the chemical characteristics of about eleven centimeters of blood vessel . . . then put it all together to make a picture. We zoomed down eleven centimeters of rat artery. You never saw so many scientists jumping up and down, hugging each other, drinking buckets of bug juice.'' Bug juice was lab ethanol mixed with Dr. Pepper.

Eventually, the silicon elements were eliminated completely in favor of nucleoproteins. He seemed reluctant to explain in detail, but I gathered they found ways to make huge molecules— as large as DNA, and even more complex—into electrochemical computers, using ribosome-like structures as ''encoders'' and ''readers'' and RNA as ''tape.'' Vergil was able to mimic reproductive separation and reassembly in his nucleoproteins, incorporating program changes at key points by switching nucleotide pairs. ''Genetron wanted me to switch over to supergene engineering, since that was the coming thing everywhere else. Make all kinds of critters, some out of our imagination. But I had different ideas.'' He twiddled his finger around his ear and made theremin sounds. ''Mad scientist time, right?'' He laughed, then sobered. ''I injected my best nucleoproteins into bacteria to make duplication and compounding easier. Then I started to leave them inside, so the circuits could interact with the cells. They were heuristically programmed; they taught themselves. The cells fed chemically coded information to the computers, the computers processed it and made decisions, the cells became smart. I mean, smart as planaria, for starters. Imagine an *E. coli* as smart as a planarian worm!''

I nodded. ''I'm imagining.''

''Then I really went off on my own. We had the equipment, the techniques; and I knew the molecular language. I could make really dense, really complicated biochips by compounding the nucleoproteins, making them into little brains. I did some research into how far I could go, theoretically. Sticking with bacteria, I could make a biochip with the computing capacity of a sparrow's brain. Imagine how jazzed I was! Then I saw a way to increase the complexity a thousandfold, by using something we regarded as a nuisance—quantum chit-chat between the fixed elements of the circuits. Down that small, even the slightest change could bomb a biochip. But I developed a program that actually predicted and took advantage of electron tunneling. Emphasized the heuristic aspects of the computer, used the chit-chat as a method of increasing complexity.''

"You're losing me," I said.

"I took advantage of randomness. The circuits could repair themselves, compare memories, and correct faulty elements. I gave them basic instructions: Go forth and multiply. Improve. By God, you should have seen some of the cultures a week later! It was amazing. They were evolving all on their own, like little cities. I destroyed them all. I think one of the petri dishes would have grown legs and walked out of the incubator if I'd kept feeding it.''

"You're kidding." I looked at him. "You're not kidding.''

"Man, they *knew* what it was like to improve! They knew where they had to go, but they were just so limited, being in bacteria bodies, with so few resources.''

"How smart were they?''

"I couldn't be sure. They were associating in clusters of a hundred to two hundred cells, each cluster behaving like an autonomous unit. Each cluster might have been as smart as a rhesus monkey. They exchanged information through their pili, passed on bits of memory, and compared notes. Their organization was obviously different from a group of monkeys. Their world was so much simpler, for one thing. With their abilities, they were masters of the petri dishes. I put phages in with them; the phages didn't have a chance. They used every option available to change and grow.''

"How is that possible?''

"What?" He seemed surprised I wasn't accepting everything at face value.

"Cramming so much into so little. A rhesus monkey is not your simple little calculator, Vergil."

"I haven't made myself clear," he said, obviously irritated. "I was using nucleoprotein computers. They're like DNA, but all the information can interact. Do you know how many nucleotide pairs there are in the DNA of a single bacteria?"

It had been a long time since my last biochemistry lesson. I shook my head.

"About two million. Add in the modified ribosome structures—fifteen thousand of them, each with a molecular weight of about three million—and consider the combinations and permutations. The RNA is arranged like a continuous loop paper tape, surrounded by ribosomes ticking off instructions and manufacturing protein chains . . ." His eyes were bright and slightly moist. "Besides, I'm not saying every cell was a distinct entity. They cooperated."

"How many bacteria in the dishes you destroyed?"

"Billions. I don't know." He smirked. "You got it, Edward. Whole planetsful of *E. coli*."

"But Genetron didn't fire you then?"

"No. They didn't know what was going on, for one thing. I kept compounding the molecules, increasing their size and complexity. When bacteria were too limited, I took blood from myself, separated out white cells, and injected them with the new biochips. I watched them, put them through mazes and little chemical problems. They were whizzes. Time is a lot faster at that level—so little distance for the messages to cross, and the environment is much simpler. Then I forgot to store a file under my secret code in the lab computers. Some managers found it and guessed what I was up to. Everybody panicked. They thought we'd have every social watchdog in the country on our backs because of what I'd done. They started to destroy my work and wipe my programs. Ordered me to sterilize my white cells. Christ.'' He pulled the white robe off and started to get dressed. ''I only had a day or two. I separated out the most complex cells—''

''How complex?''

''They were clustering in hundred-cell groups, like the bacteria. Each group as smart as a four-year-old kid, maybe.'' He studied my face for a moment. ''Still doubting? Want me to run through how many nucleotide pairs there are in a mammalian cell? I tailored my computers to take advantage of the white cells' capacity. Four billion nucleotide pairs, Edward. And they don't have a huge body to worry about, taking up most of their thinking time.''

''Okay,'' I said. ''I'm convinced. What did you do?''

''I mixed the cells back into a cylinder of whole blood and injected myself with it.'' He buttoned the top of his shirt and smiled thinly at me. ''I'd programmed them with every drive I could, talked as high a level as I could using just enzymes and such. After that, they were on their own.''

''You programmed them to go forth and multiply, improve?'' I repeated.

''I think they developed some characteristics picked up by the biochips in their *E. coli* phases. The white cells could talk to each other with extruded memories. They found ways to ingest other types of cells and alter them without killing them.''

'You're crazy.''

''You can see the screen! Edward, I haven't been sick since. I used to get colds all the time. I've never felt better.''

''They're inside you, finding things, changing them.''

''And by now, each cluster is as smart as you or I.''

''You're absolutely nuts.''

He shrugged. ''Genetron fired me. They thought I was going to take revenge for what they did to my work. They ordered me out of the labs, and I haven't had a real chance to see what's been going on inside me until now. Three months.''

"So . . ." My mind was racing. "You lost weight because they improved your fat metabolism. Your bones are stronger, your spine has been completely rebuilt—"

"No more backaches even if I sleep on my old mattress."

"Your heart looks different."

"I didn't know about the heart," he said, examining the frame image more closely. "As for the fat—I was thinking about that. They could increase my brown cells, fix up the metabolism. I haven't been as hungry lately. I haven't changed my eating habits that much—I still want the same old junk—but somehow I get around to eating only what I need. I don't think they know what my brain is yet. Sure, they've got all the glandular stuff—but they don't have the *big* picture, if you see what I mean. They don't know *I'm* in here. But boy, they sure did figure out what my reproductive organs are.''

I glanced at the image and shifted my eyes away.

"Oh, they look pretty normal," he said, hefting his scrotum obscenely. He snickered. "But how else do you think I'd land a real looker like Candice? She was just after a one-night stand with a techie. I looked okay then, no tan but trim, with good clothes. She'd never screwed a techie before. Joke time, right? But my little geniuses kept us up half the night. I think they made improvements each time. I felt like I had a goddamned fever."

His smile vanished. "But then one night my skin started to crawl. It really scared me. I thought things were getting out of hand. I wondered what they'd do when they crossed the blood-brain barrier and found out about *me*—about the brain's real function. So I began a campaign to keep them under control. I figured, the reason they wanted to get into the skin was the simplicity of running circuits across a surface. Much easier than trying to maintain chains of communication in and around muscles, organs, vessels. The skin was much more direct. So I bought a quartz lamp." He caught my puzzled expression. "In the lab, we'd break down the protein in biochip cells by exposing them to ultraviolet light. I alternated sunlamp with quartz treatments. Keeps them out of my skin and gives me a nice tan."

"Give you skin cancer, too," I commented.

"They'll probably take care of that. Like police."

"Okay. I've examined you, you've told me a story I still find hard to believe . . . what do you want me to do?"

"I'm not as nonchalant as I act, Edward. I'm worried. I'd like to find some way to control them before they find out about my brain. I mean, think of it, they're in the trillions by now, each one smart. They're cooperating to some extent. I'm probably the smartest thing on the planet, and they haven't even begun to get their act together. I don't really want them to take over." He laughed unpleasantly. "Steal my soul, you know? So think of some treatment to block them. Maybe we can starve the little buggers. Just think on it." He buttoned his shirt. "Give me a call." He handed me a slip of paper with his address and phone number. Then he went to the keyboard and erased the image on the frame, dumping the memory of the examination. "Just you," he said. "Nobody else for now. And please . . . hurry."

It was three o'clock in the morning when Vergil walked out of the examination room. He'd allowed me to take blood samples, then shaken my hand—his palm was damp, nervous —and cautioned me against ingesting anything from the specimens.

Before I went home, I put the blood through a series of tests. The results were ready the next day.

I picked them up during my lunch break in the afternoon, then destroyed all of the samples. I did it like a robot. It took me five days and nearly sleepless nights to accept what I'd seen. His blood was normal enough, though the machines diagnosed the patient as having an infection. High levels of leukocytes—white blood cells—and histamines. On the fifth day, I believed.

Gail came home before I did, but it was my turn to fix dinner. She slipped one of the school's disks into the home system and showed me video art her nursery kids had been creating. I watched quietly, ate with her in silence.

I had two dreams, part of my final acceptance. In the first, that evening, I witnessed the destruction of the planet Krypton, Superman's home world. Billions of superhuman geniuses went screaming off in walls of fire. I related the destruction to my sterilizing the samples of Vergil's blood.

The second dream was worse. I dreamed that New York City was raping a woman. By the end of the dream, she gave birth to little embryo cities, all wrapped up in translucent sacs, soaked with blood from the difficult labor.

I called him on the morning of the sixth day. He answered on the fourth ring. "I have some results," I said. "Nothing conclusive. But I want to talk with you. In person."

"Sure," he said. "I'm staying inside for the time being." His voice was strained; he sounded tired.

Vergil's apartment was in a fancy high-rise near the lake shore. I took the elevator up, listening to little advertising jingles and watching dancing holograms display products, empty apartments for rent, the building's hostess discussing social activities for the week.

Vergil opened the door and motioned me in. He wore a checked robe with long sleeves and carpet slippers. He clutched an unlit pipe in one hand, his fingers twisting it back and forth as he walked away from me and sat down, saying nothing.

"You have an infection," I said.

"Oh?"

"That's all the blood analyses tell me. I don't have access to the electron microscopes."

"I don't think it's really an infection," he said. "After all, they're my own cells. Probably something else . . . some sign of their presence, of the change. We can't expect to understand everything that's happening."

I removed my coat. "Listen," I said, "you really have me worried now." The expression on his face stopped me: a kind of frantic beatitude. He squinted at the ceiling and pursed his lips.

"Are you stoned?" I asked.

He stood his head, then nodded once, very slowly. "Listening," he said.

"To what?"

"I don't know. Not sounds . . . exactly. Like music. The heart, all the blood vessels, friction of blood along the arteries, veins. Activity. Music in the blood." He looked at me plaintively. "Why aren't you at work?"

"My day off. Gail's working."

"Can you stay?"

I shrugged. "I suppose." I sounded suspicious. I glanced around the apartment, looking for ashtrays, packs of papers.

"I'm not stoned, Edward," he said. "I may be wrong, but I think something big is happening. I think they're finding out who I am."

I sat down across from Vergil, staring at him intently. He didn't seem to notice. Some inner process involved him. When I asked for a cup of coffee, he motioned to the kitchen. I boiled a pot of water and took a jar of instant from the cabinet. With cup in hand, I returned to my seat. He twisted his head back and forth, eyes open. "You always knew what you wanted to be, didn't you?" he asked.

"More or less."

"A gynecologist. Smart moves. Never false moves. I was

different. I had goals, but no direction. Like a map without roads, just places to be. I didn't give a shit for anything, anyone but myself. Even science. Just a means. I'm surprised I got so far. I even hated my folks.''

He gripped his chair arms.

"Something wrong?" I asked.

"They're talking to me," he said. He shut his eyes.

For an hour he seemed to be asleep. I checked his pulse, which was strong and steady, felt his forehead—slightly cool—and made myself more coffee. I was looking through a magazine, at a loss what to do, when he opened his eyes again. "Hard to figure exactly what time is like for them," he said. "It's taken them maybe three, four days to figure out language, key human concepts. Now they're on to it. On to me. Right now."

"How's that?"

He claimed there were thousands of researchers hooked up to his neurons. He couldn't give details. "They're damned efficient, you know," he said. "They haven't screwed me up yet."

"We should get you into the hospital now."

"What in hell could other doctors do? Did *you* figure out any way to control them? I mean, they're my own cells."

"I've been thinking. We could starve them. Find out what metabolic differences—"

"I'm not sure I want to be rid of them," Vergil said. "They're not doing any harm."

"How do you know?"

He shook his head and held up one finger. "Wait. They're trying to figure out what space is. That's tough for them: They break distances down into concentrations of chemicals. For them, space is like intensity of taste."

"Vergil—"

"Listen! Think, Edward!" His tone was excited but even. "Something big is happening inside me. They talk to each other across the fluid, through membranes. They tailor something— viruses?—to carry data stored in nucleic acid chains. I think they're saying 'RNA.' That makes sense. That's one way I programmed them. But plasmidlike structures, too. Maybe that's what your machines think is a sign of infection—all their chattering in my blood, packets of data. Tastes of other individuals. Peers. Superiors. Subordinates."

"Vergil, I still think you should be in a hospital."

"This is my show, Edward," he said. "I'm their universe. They're amazed by the new scale." He was quiet again for a time. I squatted by his chair and pulled up the sleeve to his robe. His arm was crisscrossed with white lines. I was about to go to the phone when he stood and stretched. "Do you realize," he said, "how many body cells we kill each time we move?"

"I'm going to call for an ambulance," I said.

"No, you aren't." His tone stopped me. "I told you, I'm not sick, this is my show. Do you know what they'd do to me in a hospital? They'd be like cavemen trying to fix a computer. It would be a farce."

"Then what the hell am I doing here?" I asked, getting angry. "I can't do anything. I'm one of those cavemen."

"You're a friend," Vergil said, fixing his eyes on me. I had the impression I was being watched by more than just Vergil. "I want you here to keep me company." He laughed. "But I'm not exactly alone."

He walked around the apartment for two hours, fingering things, looking out windows, slowly and methodically fixing himself lunch. "You know, they can actually feel their own thoughts," he said about noon. "I mean, the cytoplasm seems to have a will of its own, a kind of subconscious life counter to the rationality they've only recently acquired. They hear the chemical 'noise' of the molecules fitting and unfitting inside."

At two o'clock, I called Gail to tell her I would be late. I was almost sick with tension, but I tried to keep my voice level. "Remember Vergil Ulam? I'm talking with him right now."

"Everything okay?" she asked.

Was it? Decidedly not. "Fine," I said.

"Culture!" Vergil said, peering around the kitchen wall at me. I said good-bye and hung up the phone. "They're always swimming in that bath of information. Contributing to it. It's a kind of gestalt thing. The hierarchy is absolute. They send tailored phages after cells that don't interact properly. Viruses specified to individuals or groups. No escape. A rogue cell gets pierced by the virus, the cell blebs outward, it explodes and dissolves. But it's not just a dictatorship. I think they effectively have more freedom than in a democracy. I mean, they vary so differently from individual to individual. Does that make sense? They vary in different ways than we do."

"Hold it," I said, gripping his shoulders. "Vergil, you're pushing me to the edge. I can't take this much longer. I don't understand, I'm not sure I believe—"

"Not even now?"

"Okay, let's say you're giving me the right interpretation. Giving it to me straight. Have you bothered to figure out the consequences yet? What all this means, where it might lead?"

He walked into the kitchen and drew a glass of water from the tap then returned and stood next to me. His expression had changed from childish absorption to sober concern. "I've never been very good at that."

"Are you afraid?"

"I was. Now, I'm not sure." He fingered the tie of his robe. "Look, I don't want you to think I went around you, over

28

your head or something. But I met with Michael Bernard yesterday. He put me through his private clinic, took specimens. Told me to quit the lamp treatments. He called this morning, just before you did. He says it all checks out. And he asked me not to tell anybody." He paused and his expression became dreamy again. "Cities of cells," he continued. "Edward, they push tubes through the tissues, spread information—"

"Stop it!" I shouted. "Checks out? What checks out?"

"As Bernard puts it, I have 'severely enlarged macrophages' throughout my system. And he concurs on the anatomical changes."

"What does he plan to do?"

"I don't know. I think he'll probably convince Genetron to reopen the lab."

"Is that what you want?"

"It's not just having the lab again. I want to show you. Since I stopped the lamp treatments, I'm still changing." He undid his robe and let it slide to the floor. All over his body, his skin was crisscrossed with white lines. Along his back, the lines were starting to form ridges.

"My God," I said.

"I'm not going to be much good anywhere else but the lab soon. I won't be able to go out in public. Hospitals wouldn't know what to do, as I said."

"You're . . . you can talk to them, tell them to slow down," I said, aware how ridiculous that sounded.

"Yes, indeed I can, but they don't necessarily listen."

"I thought you were their god or something."

"The ones hooked up to my neurons aren't the big wheels. They're researchers, or at least serve the same function. They know I'm here, what I am, but that doesn't mean they've convinced the upper levels of the hierarchy."

"They're disputing?"

"Something like that. It's not all that bad, anyway. If the lab is reopened, I have a home, a place to work." He glanced out the window, as if looking for someone. "I don't have anything left but them. They aren't afraid, Edward. I've never felt so close to anything before." The beatific smile again. "I'm responsible for them. Mother to them all."

"You have no way of knowing what they're going to do."

He shook his head.

"No, I mean it. You say they're like a civilization—"

"Like a thousand civilizations."

"Yes, and civilizations have been known to screw up. Warfare, the environment—"

I was grasping at straws, trying to restrain a growing panic. I wasn't competent to handle the enormity of what was happening. Neither was Vergil. He was the last person I would have called insightful and wise about large issues.

"But I'm the only one at risk."

"You don't know that. Jesus, Vergil, look what they're *doing* to you!"

"To me, all to me!" he said. "Nobody else."

I shook my head and held up my hands in a gesture of defeat. "Okay, so Bernard gets them to reopen the lab, you move in, become a guinea pig. What then?"

"They treat me right. I'm more than just good old Vergil Ulam now. I'm a goddamned galaxy, a super-mother."

"Super-host, you mean." He conceded the point with a shrug.

I couldn't take any more. I made my exit with a few flimsy excuses, then sat in the lobby of the apartment building, trying to calm down. Somebody had to talk some sense into him. Who would he listen to? He had gone to Bernard . . .

And it sounded as if Bernard was not only convinced, but very interested. People of Bernard's stature didn't coax the

Vergil Ulams of the world along unless they felt it was to their advantage.

I had a hunch, and I decided to play it. I went to a pay phone, slipped in my credit card, and called Genetron.

"I'd like you to page Dr. Michael Bernard," I told the receptionist.

"Who's calling, please?"

"This is his answering service. We have an emergency call and his beeper doesn't seem to be working."

A few anxious minutes later, Bernard came on the line. "Who the hell is this?" he asked. "I don't have an answering service."

"My name is Edward Milligan. I'm a friend of Vergil Ulam's. I think we have some problems to discuss."

We made an appointment to talk the next morning.

I went home and tried to think of excuses to keep me off the next day's hospital shift. I couldn't concentrate on medicine, couldn't give my patients anywhere near the attention they deserved.

Guilty, angry, afraid.

That was how Gail found me. I slipped on a mask of calm and we fixed dinner together. After eating, holding onto each other, we watched the city lights come on in late twilight through the bayside window. Winter starlings pecked at the yellow lawn in the last few minutes of light, then flew away with a rising wind which made the windows rattle.

"Something's wrong," Gail said softly. "Are you going to tell me, or just act like everything's normal?"

"It's just me," I said. "Nervous. Work at the hospital."

"Oh, lord," she said, sitting up. "You're going to divorce me for that Baker woman." Mrs. Baker weighed three hundred and sixty pounds and hadn't known she was pregnant until her fifth month.

"No," I said, listless.

"Rapturous relief," Gail said, touching my forehead lightly. "You know this kind of introspection drives me crazy."

"Well, it's nothing I can talk about yet, so . . ." I patted her hand.

"That's disgustingly patronizing," she said, getting up. "I'm going to make some tea. Want some?" Now she was miffed, and I was tense with not telling.

Why not just reveal all? I asked myself. An old friend was turning himself into a galaxy.

I cleared away the table instead. That night, unable to sleep, I looked down on Gail in bed from my sitting position, pillow against the wall, and tried to determine what I knew was real, and what wasn't.

I'm a doctor, I told myself. A technical, scientific profession. I'm supposed to be immune to things like future shock.

Vergil Ulam was turning into a galaxy.

How would it feel to be topped off with a trillion Chinese? I grinned in the dark and almost cried at the same time. What Vergil had inside him was unimaginably stranger than Chinese. Stranger than anything I—or Vergil—could easily understand. Perhaps ever understand.

But I knew what was real. The bedroom, the city lights faint through gauze curtains. Gail sleeping. Very important. Gail in bed, sleeping.

The dream returned. This time the city came in through the window and attacked Gail. It was a great, spiky lighted-up prowler, and it growled in a language I couldn't understand, made up of auto horns, crowd noises, construction bedlam. I tried to fight it off, but it got to her—and turned into a drift of stars, sprinkling all over the bed, all over everything. I jerked awake and stayed up until dawn, dressed with Gail, kissed her, savored the reality of her human, unviolated lips.

I went to meet with Bernard. He had been loaned a suite in a big downtown hospital; I rode the elevator to the sixth floor, and saw what fame and fortune could mean.

The suite was tastefully furnished, fine serigraphs on wood-paneled walls, chrome and glass furniture, cream-colored carpet, Chinese brass, and wormwood-grain cabinets and tables.

He offered me a cup of coffee, and I accepted. He took a seat in the breakfast nook, and I sat across from him, cradling my cup in moist palms. He wore a dapper gray suit and had graying hair and a sharp profile. He was in his mid sixties and he looked quite a bit like Leonard Bernstein.

"About our mutual acquaintance," he said. "Mr. Ulam. Brilliant. And, I won't hesitate to say, courageous."

"He's my friend. I'm worried about him."

Bernard held up one finger. "Courageous—and a bloody damned fool. What's happening to him should never have been allowed. He may have done it under duress, but that's no excuse. Still, what's done is done. He's talked to you, I take it."

I nodded. "He wants to return to Genetron."

"Of course. That's where all his equipment is. Where his home probably will be while we sort this out."

"Sort it out—how? Why?" I wasn't thinking too clearly. I had a slight headache.

"I can think of a large number of uses for small, superdense computer elements with a biological base. Can't you? Genetron has already made breakthroughs, but this is something else again."

"What do you envision?"

Bernard smiled. "I'm not really at liberty to say. It'll be revolutionary. We'll have to get him in lab conditions. Animal

33

experiments have to be conducted. We'll start from scratch, of course. Vergil's...um...colonies can't be transferred. They're based on his own white blood cells. So we have to develop colonies that won't trigger immune reactions in other animals."

"Like an infection?" I asked.

"I suppose there are comparisons. But Vergil is not infected."

"My tests indicate he is."

"That's probably the bits of data floating around in his blood, don't you think?"

"I don't know."

"Listen, I'd like you to come down to the lab after Vergil is settled in. Your expertise might be useful to us."

Us. He was working with Genetron hand in glove. Could he be objective? "How will you benefit from all this?"

"Edward, I have always been at the forefront of my profession. I see no reason why I shouldn't be helping here. With my knowledge of brain and nerve functions, and the research I've been conducting in neurophysiology—"

"You could help Genetron hold off an investigation by the government," I said.

"That's being very blunt. Too blunt, and unfair."

"Perhaps. Anyway, yes: I'd like to visit the lab when Vergil's settled in. If I'm still welcome, bluntness and all." He looked at me sharply. I wouldn't be playing on *his* team; for a moment, his thoughts were almost nakedly apparent.

"Of course," Bernard said, rising with me. He reached out to shake my hand. His palm was damp. He was as nervous as I was, even if he didn't look it.

I returned to my apartment and stayed there until noon, reading, trying to sort things out. Reach a decision. What was real, what I needed to protect.

There is only so much change anyone can stand: innovation, yes, but slow application. Don't force. Everyone has the right to stay the same until they decide otherwise.

The greatest thing in science since . . .

And Bernard would force it. Genetron would force it. I couldn't handle the thought. "Neo-Luddite," I said to myself. A filthy accusation.

When I pressed Vergil's number on the building security panel, Vergil answered almost immediately. "Yeah," he said. He sounded exhilarated. "Come on up. I'll be in the bathroom. Door's unlocked."

I entered his apartment and walked through the hallway to the bathroom. Vergil lay in the tub, up to his neck in pinkish water. He smiled vaguely and splashed his hands. "Looks like I slit my wrists, doesn't it?" he said softly. "Don't worry. Everything's fine now. Genetron's going to take me back. Bernard just called." He pointed to the bathroom phone and intercom.

I sat on the toilet and noticed the sunlamp fixture standing unplugged next to the linen cabinets. The bulbs sat in a row on the edge of the sink counter. "You're sure that's what you want," I said, my shoulders slumping.

"Yeah, I think so," he said. "They can take better care of me. I'm getting cleaned up, going over there this evening. Bernard's picking me up in his limo. Style. From here on in, everything's style."

The pinkish color in the water didn't look like soap. "Is that bubble bath?" I asked. Some of it came to me in a rush then and I felt a little weaker; what had occurred to me was just one more obvious and necessary insanity.

"No," Vergil said. I knew that already.

"No," he repeated, "it's coming from my skin. They're not telling me everything, but I think they're sending out scouts. Astronauts." He looked at me with an expression that didn't quite equal concern; more like curiosity as to how I'd take it.

The confirmation made my stomach muscles tighten as if waiting for a punch. I had never even considered the possibility until now, perhaps because I had been concentrating on other aspects. "Is this the first time?" I asked.

"Yeah," he said. He laughed. "I've half a mind to let the little buggers down the drain. Let them find out what the world's really about."

"They'd go everywhere," I said.

"Sure enough."

"How . . . how are you feeling?"

"I'm feeling pretty good now. Must be billions of them." More splashing with his hands. "What do you think? Should I let the buggers out?"

Quickly, hardly thinking, I knelt down beside the tub. My fingers went for the cord on the sunlamp and I plugged it in. He had hot-wired doorknobs, turned my piss blue, played a thousand dumb practical jokes and never grown up, never grown mature enough to understand that he was sufficiently brilliant to transform the world; he would never learn caution.

He reached for the drain knob. "You know, Edward, I—"

He never finished. I picked up the fixture and dropped it into the tub, jumping back at the flash of steam and sparks. Vergil screamed and thrashed and jerked and then everything was still, except for the low, steady sizzle and the smoke wafting from his hair.

I lifted the toilet lid and vomited. Then I clenched my nose and went into the living room. My legs went out from under me and I sat abruptly on the couch.

After an hour, I searched through Vergil's kitchen and found bleach, ammonia, and a bottle of Jack Daniel's. I returned to the bathroom, keeping the center of my gaze away from Vergil. I poured first the booze, then the bleach, then the ammonia into the water. Chlorine started bubbling up and I left, closing the door behind me.

The phone was ringing when I got home. I didn't answer. It could have been the hospital. It could have been Bernard. Or the police. I could envision having to explain everything to the police. Genetron would stonewall; Bernard would be unavailable.

I was exhausted, all my muscles knotted with tension and whatever name one can give to the feelings one has after—

Committing genocide?

That certainly didn't seem real. I could not believe I had just murdered a hundred trillion intelligent beings. Snuffed a galaxy. It was laughable. But I didn't laugh.

It was easy to believe that I had just killed one human being, a friend. The smoke, the melted lamp rods, the drooping electrical outlet and smoking cord.

Vergil.

I had dunked the lamp into the tub with Vergil.

I felt sick. Dreams, cities raping Gail (and what about his girlfriend, Candice?). Letting the water filled with them out. Galaxies sprinkling over us all. What horror. Then again, what potential beauty—a new kind of life, symbiosis and transformation.

Had I been thorough enough to kill them all? I had a moment of panic. Tomorrow, I thought, I will sterilize his apartment. Somehow, I didn't even think of Bernard.

When Gail came in the door, I was asleep on the couch. I came to, groggy, and she looked down at me.

"You feeling okay?" she asked, perching on the edge of the couch. I nodded.

"What are you planning for dinner?" My mouth didn't work properly. The words were mushy. She felt my forehead.

"Edward, you have a fever," she said. "A very high fever."

I stumbled into the bathroom and looked in the mirror. Gail was close behind me. "What is it?" she asked.

There were lines under my collar, around my neck. White lines, like freeways. They had already been in me a long time, days.

"Damp palms," I said. So obvious.

I think we nearly died. I struggled at first, but in minutes I was too weak to move. Gail was just as sick within an hour.

I lay on the carpet in the living room, drenched in sweat. Gail lay on the couch, her face the color of talcum, eyes closed, like a corpse in an embalming parlor. For a time I thought she was dead. Sick as I was, I raged—hated, felt tremendous guilt at my weakness, my slowness to understand all the possibilities. Then I no longer cared. I was too weak to blink, so I closed my eyes and waited.

There was a rhythm in my arms, my legs. With each pulse of blood, a kind of sound welled up within me, like an orchestra thousands strong, but not playing in unison; playing whole seasons of symphonies at once. Music in the blood. The sound became harsher, but more coordinated, wave-trains finally canceling into silence, then separating into harmonic beats.

The beats seemed to melt into me, into the sound of my own heart.

First, they subdued our immune responses. The war—and it was a war, on a scale never before known on Earth, with trillions of combatants—lasted perhaps two days.

By the time I regained enough strength to get to the kitchen faucet, I could feel them working on my brain, trying to crack the code and find the god within the protoplasm. I drank until I was sick, then drank more moderately and took a glass to Gail. She sipped at it. Her lips were cracked, her eyes bloodshot and ringed with yellowish crumbs. There was some color in her skin. Minutes later, we were eating feebly in the kitchen.

"What in hell is happening?" was the first thing she asked. I didn't have the strength to explain. I peeled an orange and shared it with her. "We should call a doctor," she said. But I knew we wouldn't. I was already receiving messages; it was becoming apparent that any sensation of freedom we experienced was illusory.

The messages were simple at first. Memories of commands, rather than the commands themselves, manifested themselves in my thoughts. We were not to leave the apartment—a concept which seemed quite abstract to those in control, even if undesirable—and we were not to have contact with others. We would be allowed to eat certain foods and drink tap water for the time being.

With the subsidence of the fevers, the transformations were quick and drastic. Almost simultaneously, Gail and I were immobilized. She was sitting at the table, I was kneeling on the floor. I was able barely to see her in the corner of my eye.

Her arm developed pronounced ridges.

They had learned inside Vergil; their tactics within the two of us were very different. I itched all over for about two hours—two hours in hell—before they made the breakthrough and found me. The effort of ages on their timescale paid off and they communicated smoothly and directly with this great, clumsy intelligence who had once controlled their universe.

They were not cruel. When the concept of discomfort and its undesirability was made clear, they worked to alleviate it. They worked too effectively. For another hour, I was in a sea of bliss, out of all contact with them.

With dawn the next day, they gave us freedom to move again; specifically, to go to the bathroom. There were certain waste products they could not deal with. I voided those—my urine was purple—and Gail followed suit. We looked at each other vacantly in the bathroom. Then she managed a slight smile. "Are they talking to you?" she asked. I nodded. "Then I'm not crazy."

For the next twelve hours, control seemed to loosen on some levels. I suspect there was another kind of war going on in me. Gail was capable of limited motion, but no more.

When full control resumed, we were instructed to hold each other. We did not hesitate.

"Eddie . . ." she whispered. My name was the last sound I ever heard from outside.

Standing, we grew together. In hours, our legs expanded and spread out. Then extensions grew to the windows to take in sunlight, and to the kitchen to take water from the sink. Filaments soon reached to all corners of the room, stripping paint and plaster from the walls, fabric and stuffing from the furniture.

By the next dawn, the transformation was complete.

I no longer have any clear view of what we look like. I suspect we resemble cells—large, flat, and filamented cells, draped purposefully across most of the apartment. The great shall mimic the small.

Our intelligence fluctuates daily as we are absorbed into the minds within. Each day, our individuality declines. We are, indeed, great clumsy dinosaurs. Our memories have been taken over by billions of them, and our personalities have been spread through the transformed blood.

Soon there will be no need for centralization.

Already the plumbing has been invaded. People throughout the building are undergoing transformation.

Within the old time frame of weeks, we will reach the lakes, rivers, and seas in force.

I can barely begin to guess the results. Every square inch

of the planet will teem with thought. Years from now, perhaps much sooner, they will subdue their own individuality—what there is of it.

New creatures will come, then. The immensity of their capacity for thought will be inconceivable.

All my hatred and fear is gone now.

I leave them—us—with only one question.

*How many times has this happened, elsewhere?* Travelers never came through space to visit the Earth. They had no need.

They had found universes in grains of sand.

# Sleepside
Story

Oliver Jones differed from his brothers as wheat from chaff. He didn't grudge them their blind wildness; he loaned them money until he had none, and regretted it, but not deeply. His needs were not simple, but they did not hang on the sharp signs of dollars. He worked at the jobs of youth without complaining, knowing there was something better waiting for him. Sometimes it seemed he was the only one in the family able to take cares away from his momma, now that Poppa was gone and she was lonely even with the two babies sitting on her lap, and his younger sister Yolanda gabbing about the neighbors.

The city was a puzzle to him. His older brothers Denver and Reggie believed it was a place to be conquered, but Oliver did not share their philosophy. He wanted to make the city part of him, sucked in with his breath, built into bones and brains. If he could dance with the city's music, he'd have it made, even though Denver and Reggie said the city was wide and cruel and had no end; that its four quarters ate young men alive, and spat back old people. Look at Poppa, they said; he was forty-three and he went to the fifth quarter, Darkside, a bag of wearied bones; they said, take what you can get while you can get it.

This was not what Oliver saw, though he knew the city was cruel and hungry.

His brothers and even Yolanda kidded him about his faith. It was more than just going to church that made them rag him, because they went to church, too, sitting superior beside Momma. Reggie and Denver knew there was advantage in being seen at devotions. It wasn't his music that made them laugh, for he could play the piano hard and fast as well as soft and tender, and they all liked to dance, even Momma sometimes. It was his damned sweetness. It was his taste in girls, quiet and studious; and his honesty.

On the last day of school, before Christmas vacation, Oliver made his way home in a fall of light snow, stopping in the old St. John's churchyard for a moment's reflection by his father's grave. Surrounded by the crisp, ancient slate gravestones and the newer white marble, worn by the city's acid tears, he thought he might now be considered grown-up, might have to support all of his family. He left the churchyard in a somber mood and walked between the tall brick and brownstone tenements, along the dirty, wet black streets, his shadow lost in Sleepside's greater shade, eyes on the sidewalk.

Denver and Reggie could not bring in good money, money that Momma would accept; Yolanda was too young and not likely to get a job anytime soon, and that left him, the only one who would finish school. He might take in more piano students, but he'd have to move out to do that, and how could he find another place to live without losing all he made to rent? Sleepside was crowded.

Oliver heard the noise in the flat from half a block down the street. He ran up the five dark, trash-littered flights of stairs and pulled out his key to open the three locks on the door. Swinging the door wide, he stood with hand pressed to a wall, lungs too greedy to let him speak.

The flat was in an uproar. Yolanda, rail-skinny, stood in the kitchen doorway, wringing her big hands and wailing. The two babies lurched down the hall, diapers drooping and fists stuck in their mouths. The neighbor widow Mrs. Diamond Freeland bustled back and forth in a useless dither. Something was terribly wrong.

"What is it?" he asked Yolanda with his first free breath. She just moaned and shook her head. "Where's Reggie and Denver?" She shook her head less vigorously, meaning they weren't home. "Where's Momma?" This sent Yolanda into hysterics. She bumped back against the wall and clenched her fists to her mouth, tears flying. "Something happen to Momma?"

"Your momma went uptown," Mrs. Diamond Freeland said, standing flatfooted before Oliver, her flower print dress distended over her generous stomach. "What are you going to do? You're her son."

"Where uptown?" Oliver asked, trying to control his quavering voice. He wanted to slap everybody in the apartment. He was scared and they weren't being any help at all.

"She we-went sh-sh-shopping!" Yolanda wailed. "She got her check today and it's Christmas and she went to get the babies new clothes and some food."

Oliver's hands clenched. Momma had asked him what he wanted for Christmas, and he had said, "Nothing, Momma. Not really." She had chided him, saying all would be well when the check came, and what good was Christmas if she couldn't find a little something special for each of her children? "All right," he said said. "I'd like sheet music. Something I've never played before."

"She must of taken the wrong stop," Mrs. Diamond Freeland said, staring at Oliver from the corners of her wide eyes. "That's all I can figure."

"What happened?"

Yolanda pulled a letter out of her blouse and handed it to him, a fancy purple paper with a delicate flower design on the borders, the message handwritten very prettily in gold ink fountain pen and signed. He read it carefully, then read it again.

*To the Joneses.*

*Your momma is uptown in My care. She came here lost and I tried to help her but she stole something very valuable to Me she shouldn't have. She says you'll come and get her. By you she means her youngest son Oliver Jones and if not him then Yolanda Jones her eldest daughter. I will keep one or the other here in exchange for your momma and one or the other must stay here and work for Me.*

*Miss Belle Parkhurst*
*969 33rd Street*

"Who's she, and why does she have Momma?" Oliver asked.

"I'm not going!" Yolanda screamed.

"Hush up," said Mrs. Diamond Freeland. "She's that whoor. She's that uptown whoor used to run the biggest cathouse."

Oliver looked from face to face in disbelief.

"Your momma must of taken the wrong stop and got lost," Mrs. Diamond Freeland reiterated. "That's all I can figure. She went to that whoor's house and she got in trouble."

"I'm not going!" Yolanda said. She avoided Oliver's eyes. "You know what she'd make me do."

"Yeah," Oliver said softly. "But what'll she make *me* do?"

Reggie and Denver, he learned from Mrs. Diamond Freeland, had come home before the message had been received, leaving just as the messenger came whistling up the outside hall. Oliver sighed. His brothers were almost never home; they thought they'd pulled the wool over Momma's eyes, but they hadn't. Momma knew who would be home and come for her when she was in trouble.

Reggie and Denver fancied themselves the hottest dudes on the street. They claimed they had women all over Sleepside and Snowside; Oliver was almost too shy to ask a woman out. He was small, slender, and almost pretty, but very strong for his size. Reggie and Denver were cowards. Oliver had never run from a true and worthwhile fight in his life, but neither had he started one.

The thought of going to Miss Belle Parkhurst's establishment scared him, but he remembered what his father had told him just a week before dying. "Oliver, when I'm gone—that's soon now, you know it—Yolanda's flaky as a bowl of cereal and your brothers . . . well, I'll be kind and just say your momma, she's going to need you. You got to turn out right so as she can lean on you."

The babies hadn't been born then.

"Which train did she take?"

"Down to Snowside," Mrs. Diamond Freeland said. "But she must of gotten off in Sunside. That's near Thirty-third."

"It's getting night," Oliver said.

Yolanda sniffed and wiped her eyes. Off the hook. "You going?"

"Have to," Oliver said. "It's Momma."

Said Mrs. Diamond Freeland, "I think that whoor got something on her mind."

On the line between dusk and dark, down underground where it shouldn't have mattered, the Metro emptied of all the day's passengers and filled with the night's.

Sometimes day folks went in tight-packed groups on the Night Metro, but not if they could avoid it. Night Metro was for carrying the lost or human garbage. Everyone ashamed or afraid to come out during the day came out at night. Night Metro also carried the zeroes—people who lived their lives and when they died no one could look back and say they remembered them. Night Metro—especially late—was not a good way to travel, but for Oliver it was the quickest way to get from Sleepside to Sunside; he had to go as soon as possible to get Momma.

Oliver descended the four flights of concrete steps, grinding his teeth at the thought of the danger he was in. He halted at the bottom, grimacing at the frightened knots of muscle and nerves in his back, repeating over and over again, "It's Momma. It's Momma. No one can save her but me." He dropped his bronze cat's head token into the turnstile, *clunk-chunking* through, and crossed the empty platform. Only two indistinct figures waited trackside, heavy-coated though it was a warm evening. Oliver kept an eye on them and walked back and forth in a figure eight on the grimy foot-scrubbed concrete, peering nervously down at the wet and soot under the rails. Behind him, on the station's smudged white tile walls hung a gold mosaic trumpet and the number 7, the trumpet for folks who couldn't read to know when to get off. All Sleepside stations had musical instruments.

The Night Metro was run by a different crew than the Day Metro. His train came up, clean and silver-sleek, without a spot of graffiti or a stain of tarnish. Oliver caught a glimpse of the driver under the SLEEPSIDE/CHASTE RIVER/SUNSIDE-46TH destination sign. The driver wore or had a bull's head and carried a prominent pair of long gleaming silver scissors on his Sam Browne belt. Oliver entered the open doors and took a smooth handgrip even though the seats were mostly empty. Somebody standing was somebody quicker to run.

There were four people on his car: two women—one young, vacant, and not pretty or even very alive-looking, the other old and muddy-eyed with a plastic daisy-flowered shopping bag—and two men, both sunny blond and chunky, wearing shiny-elbowed business suits. Nobody looked at anybody else. The doors shut and the train grumbled on, gathering speed until the noise of its wheels on the tracks drowned out all other sound and almost all thought.

There were more dead stations than live and lighted ones. Night Metro made only a few stops congruent with Day Metro. Most stations were turned off, but the only people left standing there wouldn't show in bright lights anyway. Oliver tried not to look, to keep his eyes on the few in the car with him, but every so often he couldn't help peering out. Beyond I-beams and barricades, single orange lamps and broken tiled walls rushed by, platforms populated by slow smudges of shadow.

Some said the dead used the Night Metro, and that after midnight it went all the way to Darkside. Oliver didn't know what to believe. As the train slowed for his station, he pulled the collar of his dark green nylon windbreaker up around his neck and rubbed his nose with one finger. Reggie and Denver would never have made it even this far. They valued their skins too much.

The train did not move on after he disembarked. He stood by the open doors for a moment, then walked past the lead car on his way to the stairs. Over his shoulder, he saw the driver standing at the head of the train in his little cabin of fluorescent coldness, the eyes in the bull's head sunk deep in shade. Oliver felt rather than saw the starlike pricks in the sockets, watching him. The driver's left hand tugged on the blades of the silver shears.

"What do you care, man?" Oliver asked softly, stopping for an instant to return the hidden stare. "Go on about your work. We all got stuff to do."

The bull's nose pointed a mere twitch away from Oliver, and the hand left the shears to return to its switch. The train doors closed. The silver side panels and windows and lights picked up speed and the train squealed around a curve into darkness. He climbed the two flights of stairs to Sunside Station.

Summer night lay heavy and warm on the lush trees and grass of a broad park. Oliver stood at the head of the Metro entrance and listened to the crickets and katydids and cicadas sing songs unheard in Sleepside, where trees and grass were sparse. All around the park rose dark-windowed walls of high marble and brick and gray stone hotels and fancy apartment buildings with gable roofs.

Oliver looked around for directions, a map, anything. Above the Night Metro, it was even possible ordinary people might be out strolling, and he could ask them if he dared. He walked toward the street and thought of Momma getting this far and of her being afraid. He loved Momma very much. Sometimes she seemed to be the only decent thing in his life, though more and more often young women distracted him as the years passed, and he experienced more and more secret fixations.

"Oliver Jones?"

A long white limousine waited by the curb. A young, slender woman in violet chauffeur's livery, with a jaunty black and silver cap sitting atop exuberant hair, cocked her head coyly, smiled at him, and beckoned with a white-leather-gloved finger. "Are you Oliver Jones, come to rescue your momma?"

He walked slowly toward the white limousine. It was bigger and more beautiful than anything he had ever seen before, with long ribbed chrome pipes snaking out from under the hood and through the fenders, stand-alone golden headlights, and a white tonneau roof made of real leather. "My name's Oliver," he affirmed.

"Then you're my man. Please get in." She winked and held the door open.

When the door closed, the woman's arm—all he could see of her through the smoky window glass—vanished. The driver's door did not open. She did not get in. The limousine drove off by itself. Oliver fell back into the lush suede and velvet interior. An electronic wet bar gleamed silver and gold and black above a cool white-lit panel on which sat a single crystal glass filled with ice cubes. A spigot rotated around and waited for instructions. When none came, it gushed fragrant gin over the ice and rotated back into place.

Oliver did not touch the glass.

Below the wet bar, the television set turned itself on. Passion and delight sang from the small, precise speakers. "No," he said. "No!"

The television shut off.

He edged closer to the smoky glass and saw dim streetlights and cab headlights moving past. A huge black building trimmed with gold ornaments, windows outlined with red, loomed on the corner, all but three of its windows dark. The limousine turned smoothly and descended into a dark underground garage. Lights throwing huge golden cat's eyes, tires squealing on shiny concrete, it snaked around a slalom of walls and pillars and dusty limousines and came to a quick stop. The door opened.

Oliver stepped out. The chauffeur stood holding the door, grinning, and doffed her cap. "My pleasure," she said.

The car had parked beside a big wooden door set into hewn stone. Fossil bones and teeth were clearly visible in the matrix of each block in the walls. Glistening ferns in dark ponds flanked the door. Oliver heard the car drive away and turned to look, but he did not see whether the chauffeur drove this time or not.

He walked across a wood plank bridge and tried the black iron handle on the door. The door swung open at the suggestion of his fingers. Beyond, a narrow red-carpeted staircase with rosebush-carved maple bannisters ascended to the upper floor.

The place smelled of cloves and mint and, somehow, of what Oliver imagined dogs or horses must smell like—a musty old rug sitting on a floor grate. (He had never owned a dog and never seen a horse without a policeman on it, and never so close he could smell it.) Nobody had been through here in a long time, he thought. But everybody knew about Miss Belle Parkhurst and her place. And the chauffeur had been young. He wrinkled his nose; he did not like this place.

The dark wood door at the top of the stairs swung open silently. Nobody stood there waiting; it might have opened by itself. Oliver tried to speak, but his throat itched and closed. He coughed into his fist and shrugged his shoulders in a spasm. Then, eyes damp and hot with anger and fear and something more, he moved his lips and croaked, "I'm Oliver Jones. I'm here to get my momma."

The door remained unattended. He looked back into the parking garage, dark and quiet as a cave; nothing for him there. Then he ascended quickly to get it over with and passed through the door into the ill-reputed house of Miss Belle Parkhurst.

The city extends to the far horizon, divided into quarters by roads or canals or even train tracks, above or underground; and sometimes you know those divisions and know better than to cross them, and sometimes you don't. The city is broader than any man's life, and it is worth more than your life not to understand why you are where you are and must stay there.

The city encourages ignorance because it must eat.

The four quarters of the city are Snowside, Cokeside where few sane people go, Sleepside, and Sunside. Sunside is bright and rich and hazardous because that is where the swell folks live. Swell folks don't tolerate intruders. Not even the police go into Sunside without an escort. Toward the center of the city is uptown, and in the middle of uptown is where all four quarters meet at the Pillar of the Unknown Mayor. Outward is the downtown and scattered islands of suburbs, and no one knows where it ends.

The Joneses live in downtown Sleepside. The light there even at noon is not very bright, but neither is it burning harsh as in Cokeside where it can fry your skull. Sleepside is tolerable. There are many good people in Sleepside and Snowside, and though confused, the general run is not vicious. Oliver grew up there and carries it in his bones and meat. No doubt the Night Metro driver smelled his origins and knew here was a young man crossing a border going uptown. No doubt Oliver was still alive because Miss Belle Parkhurst had protected him. That meant Miss Parkhurst had protected Momma, and perhaps lured her, as well.

\* \* \*

The hallway was lighted by rows of candles held in gold eagle claws along each wall. At the end of the hall, Oliver stepped into a broad wood-paneled room set here and there with lush green ferns in brass spittoons. The Oriental carpet revealed a stylized Oriental garden in cream and black and red. Five empty black velvet-upholstered couches stood unoccupied, expectant, like a line of languorous women amongst the ferns. Along the walls, chairs covered by white sheets asserted their heavy wooden arms. Oliver stood, jaw open, not used to such luxury. He needed a long moment to take it all in.

Miss Belle Parkhurst was obviously a very rich woman, and not your ordinary whore. From what he had seen so far, she had power as well as money, power over cars and maybe over men and women. Maybe over Momma. "Momma?"

A tall, tenuous white-haired man in a cream-colored suit walked across the room, paying Oliver scant attention. He said nothing. Oliver watched him sit on a sheet-covered chair. He did not disturb the sheets, but sat through them. He leaned his head back reflectively, elevating a cigarette holder without a cigarette. He blew out clear air, or perhaps nothing at all, and then smiled at something just to Oliver's right. Oliver turned. They were alone. When he looked back, the man in the cream-colored suit was gone.

Oliver's arms tingled. He was in for more than he had bargained for, and he had bargained for a lot.

"This way," said a woman's deep voice, operatic, dignified, easy and friendly at once. He could not see her, but he squinted at the doorway, and she stepped between two fluted green onyx columns. He did not know at first that she was addressing him; there might be other gentlemen, or girls, equally as tenuous as the man in the cream-colored suit. But this small, imposing woman with upheld hands, dressed in gold and peach silk that clung to her smooth and silent, was watching only him with her large dark eyes. She smiled richly and warmly, but Oliver thought there was a hidden flaw in that smile, in her assurance. She was ill at ease from the instant their eyes met, though she might have been at ease before then, *thinking* of meeting him. She had had all things planned until that moment.

If he unnerved her slightly, this woman positively terrified him. She was beautiful and smooth-skinned, and he could smell the sweet roses and camellias and magnolia blossoms surrounding her like a crowd of familiar friends.

"This way," she repeated, gesturing through the doors.

"I'm looking for my momma. I'm supposed to meet Miss Belle Parkhurst."

"I'm Belle Parkhurst. You're Oliver Jones . . . aren't you?"

He nodded, face solemn, eyes wide. He nodded again and swallowed.

"I sent your momma on her way home. She'll be fine."

He looked back at the hallway. "She'll be on the Night Metro," he said.

"I sent her back in my car. Nothing will happen to her."

Oliver believed her. There was a long, silent moment. He realized he was twisting and wringing his hands before his crotch and he stopped this, embarrassed.

"Your momma's fine. Don't worry about her."

"All right," he said, drawing his shoulders up. "You wanted to talk to me?"

"Yes," she said. "And more."

His nostrils flared and he jerked his eyes hard right, his torso and then his hips and legs twisting that way as he broke into a scrambling rabbit-run for the hallway. The golden eagle claws on each side dropped their candles as he passed and reached out to hook him with their talons. The vast house around him seemed suddenly alert, and he knew even before one claw grabbed his collar that he did not have a chance.

He dangled helpless from the armpits of his jacket at the very end of the hall. In the far door appeared the whore, angry, fingers dripping small beads of fire onto the wooden floor. The floor smoked and sizzled.

"I've let your momma go," Belle Parkhurst said, voice deeper than a grave, face terrible and smoothly beautiful and very old, very experienced. "That was my agreement. You leave, and you break that agreement, and that means I take your sister, or I take back your momma."

She cocked an elegant, painted eyebrow at him and leaned her head to one side in query. He nodded as best he could with his chin jammed against the teeth of his jacket's zipper.

"Good. There's food waiting. I'd enjoy your company."

The dining room was small, no larger than his bedroom at home, occupied by two chairs and an intimate round table covered in white linen. A gold eagle claw candelabrum cast a warm light over the table top. Miss Parkhurst preceded Oliver, her long dress rustling softly at her heels. Other things rustled in the room as well; the floor might have been ankle-deep in windblown leaves by the sound, but it was spotless, a rich round red and cream Oriental rug centered beneath the table; and beneath that, smooth old oak flooring. Oliver looked up from his sneaker-clad feet. Miss Parkhurst waited expectantly a step back from her chair.

"Your momma teach you no manners?" she asked softly.

He approached the table reluctantly. There were empty gold plates and tableware on the linen now that had not been there before. Napkins seemed to drop from thin fog and folded themselves on the plates. Oliver stopped, his nostrils flaring.

"Don't you mind that," Miss Parkhurst said. "I live alone here. Good help is hard to find."

Oliver stepped behind the chair and lifted it by its maple headpiece, pulling it out for her. She sat and he helped her move closer to the table. Not once did he touch her; his skin crawled at the thought.

"The food here is very good," Miss Parkhurst said as he sat across from her.

"I'm not hungry," Oliver said.

She smiled warmly at him. It was a powerful thing, her smile. "I won't bite," she said. "Except supper. *That* I'll bite."

Oliver smelled wonderful spices and sweet vinegar. A napkin had been draped across his lap, and before him was a salad on a fine china plate. He was very hungry and he enjoyed salads, seeing fresh greens so seldom in Sleepside.

"That's it," Miss Parkhurst said soothingly, smiling as he ate. She lifted her fork in turn and speared a fold of olive-oiled butter lettuce, bringing it to her red lips.

The rest of the dinner proceeded in like fashion, but with no further conversation. She watched him frankly, appraising, and he avoided her eyes.

Down a corridor with tall windows set in an east wall, dawn gray and pink around their faint silhouettes on the west wall, Miss Parkhurst led Oliver to his room. "It's the quietest place in the mansion," she said.

"You're keeping me here," he said. "You're never going to let me go?"

"Please allow me to indulge myself. I'm not just alone. I'm lonely. Here, you can have anything you want . . . almost . . ."

A door at the corridor's far end opened by itself. Within, a fire burned brightly within a small fireplace, and a wide bed waited with covers turned down. Exquisitely detailed murals of forests and fields covered the walls; the ceiling was rich deep blue, flecked with gold and silver and jeweled stars. Books filled a case in one corner, and in another corner stood the most beautiful ebony grand piano he had ever seen. Miss Parkhurst did not approach the door too closely. There were no candles; within this room, all lamps were electric.

"This is your room. I won't come in," she said. "And after tonight, you don't ever come out after dark. We'll talk and see each other during the day, but never at night. The door isn't locked. I'll have to trust you."

"I can go anytime I want?"

She smiled. Even though she meant her smile to be nothing more than enigmatic, it shook him. She was deadly beautiful, the kind of woman his brothers dreamed about. Her smile said she might eat him alive, all of him that counted. Oliver could imagine his mother's reaction to Miss Belle Parkhurst.

He entered the room and swung the door shut, trembling. There were a dozen things he wanted to say; angry, frustrated, pleading things. He leaned against the door, swallowing them all back, keeping his hand from going to the gold and crystal knob.

Behind the door, her skirts rustled as she retired along the corridor. After a moment, he pushed off from the door and walked with an exaggerated swagger to the bookcase, mumbling. Miss Parkhurst would never have taken Oliver's sister Yolanda; that wasn't what she wanted. She wanted young boy flesh, he thought. She wanted to burn him down to his sneakers, smiling like that.

The books on the shelves were books he had heard about but had never found in the Sleepside library, books he wanted to read, that the librarians said only people from Sunside and the suburbs cared to read. His fingers lingered on the tops of their spines, tugging gently.

He decided to sleep instead. If she was going to pester him

during the day, he didn't have much time. She'd be a late riser, he thought; a night person.

Then he realized: whatever she did at night, she had not done this night. This night had been set aside for him.

He shivered again, thinking of the food and napkins and the eagle claws. Was this room haunted, too? Would things keep watch over him?

Oliver lay back on the bed, still clothed. His mind clouded with thoughts of living sheets feeling up his bare skin. Tired, almost dead out.

The dreams that came were sweet and pleasant and she did not walk in them. This really was his time.

At eleven o'clock by the brass and gold and crystal clock on the bookcase, Oliver kicked his legs out, rubbed his face into the pillows and started up, back arched, smelling bacon and eggs and coffee. A covered tray waited on a polished brass cart beside the bed. A vase of roses on one corner of the cart scented the room. A folded piece of fine ivory paper leaned against the vase. Oliver sat on the edge of the bed and read the note, once again written in golden ink in a delicate hand.

*I'm waiting for you in the gymnasium. Meet me after you've eaten. Got something to give to you.*

He had no idea where the gymnasium was. When he had finished breakfast, he put on a plush robe, opened the heavy door to his room—both relieved and irritated that it did not open by itself—and looked down the corridor. A golden arc clung to the base of each tall window. It was at least noon, Sunside time. She had given him plenty of time to rest.

A pair of new black jeans and a white silk shirt waited for him on the bed, which had been carefully made in the time it had taken him to glance down the hall. Cautiously, but less frightened now, he removed the robe, put on these clothes and the deerskin moccasins by the foot of the bed, and stood in the doorway, leaning as casually as he could manage against the frame.

A silk handkerchief hung in the air several yards away. It fluttered like a pigeon's ghost to attract his attention, then drifted slowly along the hall. He followed.

The house seemed to go on forever, empty and magnificent. Each public room had its own decor, filled with antique furniture, potted palms, plush couches and chairs, and love seats. Several times he thought he saw wisps of dinner jackets, top hats, eager, strained faces, in foyers, corridors, on staircases as he followed the handkerchief. The house smelled of perfume and dust, faint cigars, spilled wine, and old sweat.

He had climbed three flights of stairs before he stood at the tall ivory-white double door of the gymnasium. The handkerchief vanished with a flip. The doors opened.

Miss Parkhurst stood at the opposite end of a wide black-tile dance floor, before a band riser covered with music stands and instruments. Oliver inspected the low half-circle stage with narrowed eyes. Would she demand he dance with her, while all the instruments played by themselves?

"Good morning," she said. She wore a green dress the color of fresh wet grass, high at the neck and down to her calves. Beneath the dress she wore white boots and white gloves, and a white feather curled around her black hair.

"Good morning," he replied softly, politely.

"Did you sleep well? Eat hearty?"

Oliver nodded, fear and shyness returning. What could she possibly want to give him? Herself? His face grew hot.

"It's a shame this house is empty during the day," she said. *And at night?* he thought. "I could fill this room with

62

exercise equipment,'' she continued. "Weight benches, even a track around the outside.'' She smiled. The smile seemed less ferocious now, even wistful; younger.

He rubbed a fold of his shirt between two fingers. "I enjoyed the food, and your house is real fine, but I'd like to go home,'' he said.

She half turned and walked slowly from the stand. "You could have this house and all my wealth. I'd like you to have it.''

"Why? I haven't done anything for you.''

"Or to me, either,'' she said, facing him again. "You know how I've made all this money?''

"Yes, ma'am,'' he said after a moment's pause. "I'm not a fool.''

"You've heard about me. That I'm a whore.''

"Yes, ma'am. Mrs. Diamond Freeland says you are.''

"And what is a whore?''

"You let men do it to you for money,'' Oliver said, feeling bolder, but with his face hot all the same.

Miss Parkhurst nodded. "I've got part of them all here with me,'' she said. "My bookkeeping. I know every name, every face. They keep me company now that business is slow.''

"All of them?'' Oliver asked.

Miss Parkhurst's faint smile was part pride, part sadness, her eyes distant and moist. "They gave me all the things I have here.''

"I don't think it would be worth it,'' Oliver said.

"I'd be dead if I wasn't a whore,'' Miss Parkhurst said, eyes suddenly sharp on him, flashing anger. "I'd have starved to death.'' She relaxed her clenched hands. "We got plenty of time to talk about my life, so let's hold it here for a while. I got something you need, if you're going to inherit this place.''

"I don't want it, ma'am,'' Oliver said.

"If you don't take it, somebody who doesn't need it and deserves it a lot less will. I want you to have it. Please, be kind to me this once."

"Why me?" Oliver asked. He simply wanted out; this was completely off the planned track of his life. He was less afraid of Miss Parkhurst now, though her anger raised hairs on his neck; he felt he could be bolder and perhaps even demanding. There was a weakness in her: he was her weakness, and he wasn't above taking some advantage of that, considering how desperate his situation might be.

"You're kind," she said. "You care. And you've never had a woman, not all the way."

Oliver's face warmed again. "Please let me go," he said quietly, hoping it didn't sound as if he was pleading.

Miss Parkhurst folded her arms. "I can't," she said.

While Oliver spent his first day in Miss Parkhurst's mansion, across the city, beyond the borders of Sunside, Denver and Reggie Jones had returned home to find the apartment blanketed in gloom. Reggie, tall and gangly, long of neck and short of head, with a prominent nose, stood with back slumped in the front hall, mouth open in surprise. "He just took off and left you all here?" Reggie asked. Denver returned from the kitchen, shorter and stockier than his brother, dressed in black vinyl jacket and pants.

Yolanda's face was puffy from constant crying. She now enjoyed the tears she spilled, and had scheduled them at two-hour intervals, to her momma's sorrowful irritation. She herded the two babies into their momma's bedroom and closed a rickety gate behind them, then brushed her hands on the breast of her ragged blouse.

"You don't *get* it," she said, facing them and dropping her arms dramatically. "That whore took Momma, and Oliver traded himself for her."

"That whore," said Reggie, "is a rich old witch."

"Rich old bitch witch," Denver said, pleased with himself.

"That whore is opportunity knocking," Reggie continued, chewing reflectively. "I hear she lives alone."

"That's why she took Oliver," Yolanda said. The babies cooed and chirped behind the gate.

"Why him and not one of us?" Reggie asked.

Momma gently pushed the babies aside, swung open the gate, and marched down the hall, dressed in her best wool skirt and print blouse, wrapped in her overcoat against the gathering dark and cold outside. "Where you going?" Yolanda asked her as she brushed past.

"Time to talk to the police," she said, glowering at Reggie. Denver backed into the bedroom he shared with his brother, out of her way. He shook his head condescendingly, grinning: Momma at it again.

"Them dogheads?" Reggie said. "They got no say in Sunside."

Momma turned at the front door and glared at them. "How are you going to help your brother? He's the best of you all, you know, and you just stand here, flatfooted and jawboning yourselves."

"Momma's upset," Denver informed his brother solemnly.

"She should be," Reggie said sympathetically. "She was held prisoner by that witch bitch whore. We should go get Oliver and bring him home. We could pretend we was customers."

"She don't have customers anymore," Denver said. "She's too old. She's worn out." He glanced at his crotch and leaned his head to one side, glaring for emphasis. His glare faded into an amiable grin.

"How do you know?" Reggie asked.

"That's what I hear."

Momma snorted and pulled back the bars and bolts on the front door. Reggie calmly walked up behind her and stopped her. "Police don't do anybody any good, Momma," he said. "We'll go. We'll bring Oliver back."

Denver's face slowly fell at the thought. "We got to plan it out," he said. "We got to be careful."

"We'll be careful," Reggie said. "For Momma's sake."

With his hand blocking her exit, Momma snorted again, then let her shoulders droop and her face sag. She looked more and more like an old woman now, though she was only in her late thirties.

Yolanda stood aside to let her pass into the living room. "Poor Momma," she said, eyes welling up.

"What you going to do for your brother?" Reggie asked his sister pointedly as he in turn walked by her. She craned her neck and stuck out her chin resentfully. "Go trade places with him, work in *her* house?" he taunted.

"She's rich," Denver said to himself, cupping his chin in his hand. "We could make a whole lot of money, saving our brother."

"We start thinking about it now," Reggie mandated, falling into the chair that used to be their father's, leaning his head back against the lace covers Momma had made.

Momma, face ashen, stood by the couch staring at a family portrait hung on the wall in a cheap wooden frame. "He did it for me. I was so stupid, getting off there, letting her help me. Should of known," she murmured, clutching her wrist. Her face ashen, her ankle wobbled under her and she pirouetted, hands spread out like a dancer, and collapsed facedown on the couch.

The gift, the thing that Oliver needed to inherit Miss Parkhurst's mansion, was a small gold box with three buttons, like a garage door opener. She finally presented it to him in the dining room as they finished dinner.

Miss Parkhurst was nice to talk to, something Oliver had not expected, but which he should have. Whores did more than lie with a man to keep him coming back and spending his money; that should have been obvious. The day had not been the agony he expected. He had even stopped asking her to let him go. Oliver thought it would be best to bide his time, and when something distracted her, make his escape. Until then, she was not treating him badly or expecting anything he could not freely give.

"It'll be dark soon," she said as the plates cleared themselves away. He was even getting used to the ghostly service. "I have to go soon, and you got to be in your room. Take this with you, and keep it there." She lifted a tray cover to reveal a white silk bag. Unstringing the bag, she removed the golden opener and shyly presented it to him. "This was given to me a long time ago. I don't need it now. But if you want to run this place, you got to have it. You can't lose it, or let anyone take it from you."

Oliver's hands went to the opener involuntarily. It seemed very desirable, as if there were something of Miss Parkhurst in it: warm, powerful, a little frightening. It fit his hand perfectly, familiar to his skin; he might have owned it forever.

He tightened his lips and returned it to her. "I'm sorry," he said. "It's not for me."

"You remember what I told you," she said. "If you don't take it, somebody else will, and it won't do anybody any good then. I want it to do some good now, when I'm done with it."

"Who gave it to you?" Oliver asked.

"A pimp, a long time ago. When I was a girl."

Oliver's eyes betrayed no judgment or disgust. She took a deep breath.

"He made you do it . . . ?" Oliver asked.

"No. I was young, but already a whore. I had an old, kind pimp, at least he seemed old to me, I wasn't much more than a baby. He died, he was killed, so this new pimp came, and he was powerful. He had the magic. But he couldn't tame me. So he says . . ."

Miss Parkhurst raised her hands to her face. "He cut me up. I was almost dead. He says, 'You shame me, whore. You do this to me, make me lose control, you're the only one ever did this to me. So I curse you. You'll be the greatest whore ever was.' He gave me the opener then, and he put my face and body back together so I'd be pretty. Then he left town, and I was in charge. I've been here ever since, but all the girls have gone, it's been so long, died or left or I told them to go. I wanted this place closed, but I couldn't close it all at once."

Oliver nodded slowly, eyes wide.

"He gave me most of his magic, too. I didn't have any choice. One thing he didn't give me was a way out. Except . . ." This time, she was the one with the pleading expression.

Oliver raised an eyebrow.

"What I need has to be freely given. Now take this." She stood and thrust the opener into his hands. "Use it to find your way all around the house. But don't leave your room after dark."

She swept out of the dining room, leaving a scent of musk and flowers and something bittersweet. Oliver put the opener in his pocket and walked back to his room, finding his way without hesitation, without thought. He shut the door and went to the bookcase, sad and troubled and exultant all at once.

She had told him her secret. He could leave now if he wanted. She had given him the power to leave.

Sipping from a glass of sherry on the nightstand beside the bed, reading from a book of composers' lives, he decided to wait until morning.

Yet after a few hours, nothing could keep his mind away from Miss Parkhurst's prohibition—not the piano, the books, or the snacks delivered almost before he thought about them, appearing on the tray when he wasn't watching. Oliver sat with hands folded in the plush chair, blinking at the room's dark corners. He thought he had Miss Parkhurst pegged. She was an old woman tired of her life, a beautifully preserved old woman to be sure, very strong . . . But she was sweet on him, keeping him like some unused gigolo. Still, he couldn't help but admire her, and he couldn't help but want to be home, near Momma and Yolanda and the babies, keeping his brothers out of trouble—not that they appreciated his efforts.

The longer he sat, the angrier and more anxious he became. He felt sure something was wrong at home. Pacing around the room did nothing to calm him. He examined the opener time and again in the firelight, brow wrinkled, wondering what powers it gave him. She had said he could go anywhere in the house and know his way, just as he had found his room without her help.

He moaned, shaking his fists at the air. "She can't keep me here! She just *can't*!"

At midnight, he couldn't control himself any longer. He stood before the door. "Let me out, dammit!" he cried, and the door opened with a sad whisper. He ran down the corridor, scattering moonlight on the floor like dust, tears shining on his cheeks.

Through the sitting rooms, the long halls of empty bedrooms—now with their doors closed, shades of sound sifting from behind—through the vast deserted kitchen, with its rows of polished copper kettles and huge black coal cookstoves, through a courtyard surrounded by five stories of the mansion on all sides and open to the golden-starred night sky, past a tiled fountain guarded by three huge white porcelain lions, ears and empty eyes following him as he ran by, Oliver searched for Miss Parkhurst, to tell her he must leave.

For a moment, he caught his breath in an upstairs gallery. He saw faint lights under doors, heard more suggestive sounds. No time to pause, even with his heart pounding and his lungs burning. If he waited in one place long enough, he thought the ghosts might become real and make him join their revelry. This was Miss Parkhurst's past, hoary and indecent, more than he could bear contemplating. How could anyone have lived this kind of life, even if they were cursed?

Yet the temptation to stop, to listen, to give in and join in was almost stronger than he could resist. He kept losing track of what he was doing, what his ultimate goal was.

"Where are you?" he shouted, throwing open double doors to a game room, empty but for more startled ghosts, more of Miss Parkhurst's eternity of bookkeeping. Pale forms rose from the billiard tables, translucent breasts shining with an inner light, their pale lovers rolling slowly to one side, fat bellies prominent, ghost eyes black and startled. "Miss Parkhurst!"

Oliver brushed through hundreds of girls, no more substantial than curtains of raindrops. His new clothes became wet with their tears. *She* had presided over this eternity of sad lust. *She* had orchestrated the debaucheries, catered to what he felt inside him: the whims and deepest desires unspoken.

Thin antique laughter followed him.

He slid on a splash of sour-smelling champagne and came up abruptly against a heavy wooden door, a room he did not know. The golden opener told him nothing about what waited beyond.

"Open!" he shouted, but he was ignored. The door was

not locked, but it resisted his entry as if it weighed tons. He pushed with both hands and then laid his shoulder on the paneling, bracing his sneakers against the thick wool pile of a champagne-soaked runner. The door swung inward with a deep iron and wood grumble, and Oliver stumbled past, saving himself at the last minute from falling on his face. Legs sprawled, down on both hands, he looked up from the wooden floor and saw where he was.

The room was narrow, but stretched on for what might have been miles, lined on one side with an endless row of plain double beds, and on the other with an endless row of free-standing cheval mirrors. An old man, the oldest he had ever seen, naked, white as talcum, rose stiffly from the bed, mumbling. Beneath him, red and warm as a pile of glowing coals, Miss Parkhurst lay with legs spread, incense of musk and sweat thick about her. She raised her head and shoulders, eyes fixed on Oliver's, and pulled a black peignoir over her nakedness. In the gloom of the room's extremities, other men, old and young, stood by their beds, smoking cigarettes or cigars or drinking champagne or whisky, all observing Oliver. Some grinned in speculation.

Miss Parkhurst's face wrinkled in agony like an old apple and she threw back her head to scream. The old man on the bed grabbed clumsily for a robe and his clothes.

Her shriek echoed from the ceiling and the walls, driving Oliver back through the door, down the halls and stairways. The wind of his flight chilled him to the bone in his tear-soaked clothing. Somehow he made his way through the sudden darkness and emptiness, and shut himself in his room, where the fire still burned warm and cheery yellow. Shivering uncontrollably, Oliver removed the wet new clothes and called for his own in a high-pitched, frantic voice. But the invisible servants did not deliver what he requested.

He fell into the bed and pulled the covers tight about him, eyes closed. He prayed that she would not come after him, not come into his room with her peignoir slipping aside, revealing her furnace body; he prayed her smell would not follow him the rest of his life.

The door to his room did not open. Outside, all was quiet. In time, as dawn fired the roofs and then the walls and finally the streets of Sunside, Oliver slept.


"You came out of your room last night," Miss Parkhurst said over the late breakfast. Oliver stopped chewing for a moment, glanced at her through bloodshot eyes, then shrugged.

"Did you see what you expected?"

Oliver didn't answer. Miss Parkhurst sighed like a young girl.

"It's my life. This is the way I've lived for a long time."

"None of my business," Oliver said, breaking a roll in half and buttering it.

"Do I disgust you?"

Again no reply. Miss Parkhurst stood in the middle of his silence and walked to the dining-room door. She looked over her shoulder at him, eyes moist. "You're not afraid of me now," she said. "You think you know what I am."

Oliver saw that his silence and uncaring attitude hurt her, and relished for a moment this power. When she remained standing in the doorway, he looked up with a purposefully harsh expression—copied from Reggie, sarcastic and angry at once—and saw tears flowing steadily down her cheeks. She seemed younger than ever now, not dangerous, just very sad. His expression faded. She turned away and closed the door behind her.

Oliver slammed half the roll into his plate of eggs and pushed his chair back from the table. "I'm not even full-grown!'' he shouted at the door. "I'm not even a man! What do you want from me?'' He stood up and kicked the chair away with his heel, then stuffed his hands in his pockets and paced around the small room. He felt bottled up, and yet she had said he could go anytime he wished.

Go *where*? Home?

He stared at the goldenware and the plates heaped with excellent food. Nothing like this at home. Home was a place he sometimes thought he'd have to fight to get away from; he couldn't protect Momma forever from the rest of the family, he couldn't be a breadwinner for five extra mouths for the rest of his life . . .

And if he stayed here, knowing what Miss Parkhurst did each night? Could he eat breakfast each morning, knowing how the food was earned, and all his clothes and books and the piano, too? He really would be a gigolo then.

*Sunside*. He was here, maybe he could live here, find work, get away from Sleepside for good.

The mere thought gave him a twinge. He sat down and buried his face in his hands, rubbing his eyes with the tips of his fingers, pulling at his lids to make a face, staring at himself reflected in the golden carafe, big-nosed, eyes monstrously bleared. He had to talk to Momma. Even talking to Yolanda might help.

But Miss Parkhurst was nowhere to be found. Oliver searched the mansion until dusk, then ate alone in the small dining room. He retired to his room as dark closed in, spreading through the halls like ink through water. To banish the night, and all that might be happening in it, Oliver played the piano loudly.

When he finally stumbled to his bed, he saw a single yellow rose on the pillow, delicate and sweet. He placed it by the lamp on the nightstand and pulled the covers over himself, clothes and all.

In the early hours of morning, he dreamed that Miss Parkhurst had fled the mansion, leaving it for him to tend to. The ghosts and old men crowded around, asking why he was so righteous. "She never had a Momma like you," said one decrepit dude dressed in black velvet nightrobes. "She's lived times you can't imagine. Now you just blew her right out of this house. Where will she go?"

Oliver came awake long enough to remember the dream, and then returned to a light, difficult sleep.


Mrs. Diamond Freeland scowled at Yolanda's hand-wringing and mumbling. "You can't help your momma acting that way," she said.

"I'm no doctor," Yolanda complained.

"No doctor's going to help her," Mrs. Freeland said, eyeing the door to Momma's bedroom.

Denver and Reggie lounged uneasily in the parlor.

"You two louts going to look for your brother?"

"We don't have to look for him," Denver said. "We know where he is. We got a plan to get him back."

"Then why don't you do it?" Mrs. Freeland asked.

"When the time's right," Reggie said decisively.

"Your Momma's pining for Oliver," Mrs. Freeland told them, not for the first time. "It's churning her insides thinking he's with that witch and what she might be doing to him."

Reggie tried unsuccessfully to hide a grin.

"What's funny?" Mrs. Freeland asked sternly.

"Nothing. Maybe our little brother needs some of what she's got."

Mrs. Freeland glared at them. "Yolanda," she said, rolling her eyes to the ceiling in disgust. "The babies. They dry?"

"No, ma'am," Yolanda said. She backed away from Mrs. Freeland's severe look. "I'll change them."

"Then you take them into your momma."

"Yes, ma'am."

The breakfast went as if nothing had happened. Miss Parkhurst sat across from him, eating and smiling. Oliver tried to be more polite, working his way around to asking a favor. When the breakfast was over, the time seemed right.

"I'd like to see how Momma's doing," he said.

Miss Parkhurst considered for a moment. "There'll be a TV in your room this evening," she said, folding her napkin and placing it beside her plate. "You can use it to see how everybody is."

That seemed fair enough. Until then, however, he'd be spending the entire day with Miss Parkhurst; it was time, he decided, to be civil. Then he might actually test his freedom.

"You say I can go," Oliver said, trying to sound friendly.

Miss Parkhurst nodded. "Anytime. I won't keep you."

"If I go, can I come back?"

She smiled ever so slightly. There was the young girl in that smile again, and she seemed very vulnerable. "The opener takes you anywhere across town."

"Nobody messes with me?"

"Nobody touches anyone I protect," Miss Parkhurst said.

Oliver absorbed that thoughtfully, steepling his hands below his chin. "You're pretty good to me," he said. "Even when I cross you, you don't hurt me. Why?"

"You're my last chance," Miss Parkhurst said, dark eyes on him. "I've lived a long time, and nobody like you's come along. I don't think there'll be another for even longer. I can't wait that long. I've lived this way so many years, I don't know another, but I don't want any more of it."

Oliver couldn't think of a better way to put his next question. "Do you like being a whore?"

Miss Parkhurst's face hardened. "It has its moments," she said stiffly.

Oliver screwed up his courage enough to say what was on his mind, but not to look at her while doing it. "You enjoy lying down with any man who has the money?"

"It's work. It's something I'm good at."

"Even ugly men?"

"Ugly men need their pleasures, too."

"Bad men? Letting them touch you when they've hurt people, maybe killed people?"

"What kind of work have you done?" she asked.

"Clerked a grocery store. Taught music."

"Did you wait on bad men in the grocery store?"

"If I did," Oliver said swiftly, "I didn't know about it."

"Neither did I," Miss Parkhurst said. Then, more quietly, "Most of the time."

"All those girls you've made whore for you . . ."

"You have some things to learn," she interrupted. "It's not the work that's so awful. It's what you have to be to do it. The way people expect you to be when you do it. Should be, in a good world, a whore's like a doctor or a saint, she doesn't mind getting her hands dirty any more than they do. She gives pleasure and smiles. But in the city, people won't let it happen that way. Here, a whore's always got some empty place inside her, a place you've filled with self-respect, maybe. A whore's got respect, but not for herself. She loses that whenever anybody looks at her. She can be worth a million dollars on the outside, but inside, she knows. That's what makes her a whore. That's the curse. It's beat into you sometimes, everybody taking advantage, like you're dirt. Pretty soon you think you're dirt, too, and who cares what happens to dirt? Pretty soon you're just sliding along, trying to keep from getting hurt or maybe dead, but who cares?''

"You're rich," Oliver said.

"Can't buy everything," Miss Parkhurst commented dryly.

"You've got magic."

"I've got magic because I'm here, and to stay here, I have to be a whore.''

"Why can't you leave?"

She sighed, her fingers working nervously along the edge of the tablecloth.

"What stops you from just leaving?"

"If you're going to own this place," she said, and he thought at first she was avoiding his question, "you've got to know all about it. All about me. We're the same, almost, this place and I. A whore's no more than what's in her purse, every pimp knows that. You know how many times I've been married?''

Oliver shook his head.

"Seventeen times. Sometimes they left me, once or twice they stayed. Never any good. But then, maybe I didn't deserve any better. Those who left me, they came back when they were old, asking me to save them from Darkside. I couldn't. But I kept them here anyway. Come on.''

She stood and Oliver followed her down the halls, down the stairs, below the garage level, deep beneath the mansion's clutter-filled basement. The air was ageless, deep-earth cool, and smelled of old city rain. A few eternal clear light bulbs cast feeble yellow crescents in the dismal murk. They walked on boards over an old muddy patch, Miss Parkhurst lifting her skirts a few inches to clear the mire. Oliver saw her slim ankles and swallowed back the tightness in his throat.

Ahead, laid out in a row on moss-patched concrete biers, were fifteen black iron cylinders, each seven feet long and slightly flattened on top. They looked like big blockbuster bombs in storage. The first was wedged into a dark corner. Miss Parkhurst stood by its foot, running her hand along its rust-streaked surface.

"Two didn't come back. Maybe they were the best of the lot," she said. "I was no judge. I couldn't know. You judge men by what's inside you, and if you're hollow, they get lost in there, you can't know what you're seeing."

Oliver stepped closer to the last cylinder and saw a clear glass plate mounted at the head. Reluctant but fascinated, he wiped the dusty glass with two fingers and peered past a single cornered bubble. The coffin was filled with clear liquid. Afloat within, a face the color of green olives in a martini looked back at him, blind eyes murky, lips set in a loose line. The liquid and death had smoothed the face's wrinkles, but Oliver could tell nonetheless, this dude had been old, old.

"They all die," she said. "All but me. I keep them all, every john, every husband, no forgetting, no letting them go. We've always got this tie between us. That's the curse."

Oliver pulled back from the coffin, holding his breath, heart thumping with eager horror. Which was worse, this, or old men in the night? Old dead lusts laid to rest or lively ghosts? Wrapped in gloom at the far end of the line of bottle-coffins, Miss Parkhurst seemed for a moment to glow with the same furnace power he had felt when he first saw her.

"I miss some of these guys," she said, her voice so soft the power just vanished, a thing in his mind. "We had some good times together."

Oliver tried to imagine what Miss Parkhurst had lived through, the good times and otherwise. "You have any children?" he asked, his voice as thin as the buzz of a fly in a bottle. He jumped back as one of the coffins resonated with his shaky words.

Miss Parkhurst's shoulders shivered as well. "Lots," she said tightly. "All dead before they were born."

At first his shock was conventional, orchestrated by his Sundays in church. Then the colossal organic waste of effort came down on him like a pile of stones. All that motion, all that wanting, and nothing good from it, just these iron bottles and vivid lists of ghosts.

"What good is a whore's baby?" Miss Parkhurst asked. "Especially if the mother's going to stay a whore."

"Was your mother...?" It didn't seem right to use the word in connection with anyone's mother.

"She was, and her mother before her. I have no daddies, or lots of daddies."

Oliver remembered the old man chastising him in his dream. Before he could even sort out his words, wishing to give her some solace, some sign he wasn't completely unsympathetic, he said, "It can't be all bad, being a whore."

"Maybe not," she said. Miss Parkhurst hardly made a blot in the larger shadows. She might just fly away to dust if he turned his head.

"You said being a whore is being empty inside. Not everybody who's empty inside is a whore."

"Oh?" she replied, light as a cobweb. He was being pushed into an uncharacteristic posture, but Oliver was damned if he'd give in just yet, however much a fool he made of himself. His mixed feelings were betraying him.

"You've *lived*," he said. "You got memories nobody else has. You could write books. They'd make movies about you."

Her smile was a dull lamp in the shadows. "I've had important people visit me," she said. "Powerful men, even mayors. I had something they needed. Sometimes they opened up and talked about how hard it was not being little boys anymore. Sometimes, when we were relaxing, they'd cry on

79

my shoulder, just like I was their momma. But then they'd go away and try to forget about me. If they remembered at all, they were scared of me, because of what I knew about them. Now, they know I'm getting weak,'' she said. ''I don't give a damn about books or movies. I won't tell what I know, and besides, lots of those men are dead. If they aren't, they're waiting for me to die, so they can sleep easy.''

''What do you mean, getting weak?''

''I got two days, maybe three, then I die a whore. My time is up. The curse is almost finished.''

Oliver gaped. When he had first seen her, she had seemed as powerful as a diesel locomotive, as if she might live forever.

''And if I take over?''

''You get the mansion, the money.''

''How much power?''

She didn't answer.

''You can't give me any power, can you?''

''No,'' faint as the breeze from her eyelashes.

''The opener won't be any good.''

''No.''

''You lied to me.''

''I'll leave you all that's left.''

''That's not why you made me come here. You took Momma—''

''She stole from me.''

''My momma never stole anything!'' Oliver shouted. The iron coffins buzzed.

''She took something after I had given her all my hospitality.''

''What could she take from you? She was no thief.''

''She took a sheet of music.''

Oliver's face screwed up in sudden pain. He looked away, fists clenched. They had almost no money for his music. More often than not since his father died, he made up music, having no new scores to play. "Why'd you bring me here?" he croaked.

"I don't mind dying. But I don't want to die a whore."

Oliver turned back, angry again, this time for his momma as well as himself. He approached the insubstantial shadow. Miss Parkhurst shimmered like a curtain. "What do you want from me?"

"I need someone who loves me. Loves me for no reason."

For an instant, he saw standing before him a scrawny girl in a red shimmy, eyes wide. "How could that help you? Can that make you something else?"

"Just love," she said. "Just letting me forget all these" —she pointed to the coffins—"and all those," pointing up.

Oliver's body lost its charge of anger and accusation with an exhaled breath. "I can't love you," he said. "I don't even know what love is." Was this true? Upstairs, she had burned in his mind, and he *had* wanted her, though it upset him to remember how much. What *could* he feel for her? "Let's go back now. I have to look in on Momma."

Miss Parkhurst emerged from the shadows and walked past him silently, not even her skirts rustling. She gestured with a finger for him to follow.

She left him at the door to his room, saying, "I'll wait in the main parlor." Oliver saw a small television set on the nightstand by his bed and rushed to turn it on. The screen filled with static and unresolved images. He saw fragments of faces, patches of color and texture passing so quickly he couldn't make them out. The entire city might be on the screen at once, but he could not see any of it clearly. He twisted the channel knob and got more static. Then he saw the label past channel ⑬ on the dial: HOME, in small golden letters. He twisted the knob to that position and the screen cleared.

Momma lay in bed, legs drawn tightly up, hair mussed.

She didn't look good. Her hand, stretched out across the bed, trembled. Her breathing was hard and rough. In the background, Oliver heard Yolanda fussing with the babies, finally screaming at her older brothers in frustration.

*Why don't you help with the babies?* his sister demanded in a tinny, distant voice.

*Momma told you,* Denver replied.

*She did not. She told us all. You could help.*

Reggie laughed. *We got to make plans.*

Oliver pulled back from the TV. Momma was sick, and for all his brothers and sister and the babies could do, she might die. He could guess why she was sick, too; with worry for him. He had to go to her and tell her he was all right. A phone call wouldn't be enough.

Again, however, he was reluctant to leave the mansion and Miss Parkhurst. Something beyond her waning magic was at work here; he wanted to listen to her and to experience more of that fascinated horror. He wanted to watch her again, absorb her smooth, ancient beauty. In a way, she needed him as much as Momma did. Miss Parkhurst outraged everything in him that was lawful and orderly, but he finally had to admit, as he thought of going back to Momma, that he enjoyed the outrage.

He clutched the gold opener and ran from his room to the parlor. She waited for him there in a red velvet chair, hands gripping two lions at the end of the armrests. The lions' wooden faces grinned beneath her caresses. "I got to go," he said. "Momma's sick for missing me."

She nodded. "I'm not holding you," she said.

He stared at her. "I wish I could help you," he said.

She smiled hopefully, pitifully. "Then promise you'll come back."

Oliver wavered. How long would Momma need him?

What if he gave his promise and returned and Miss Parkhurst was already dead?

"I promise."

"Don't be too long," she said.

"Won't," he mumbled.


The limousine waited for him in the garage, white and beautiful, languid and sleek and fast all at once. No chauffeur waited for him this time. The door opened by itself and he climbed in; the door closed behind him, and he leaned back stiffly on the leather seats, gold opener in hand. "Take me home," he said. The glass partition and the windows all around darkened to an opaque smoky gold. He felt a sensation of smooth motion. *What would it be like to have this kind of power all the time?*

But the power wasn't hers to give.

Oliver arrived before the apartment building in a blizzard of swirling snow. Snow packed up over the curbs and coated the sidewalks a foot deep; Sleepside was heavy with winter. Oliver stepped from the limousine and climbed the icy steps, the cold hardly touching him even in his light clothing. He was surrounded by Miss Parkhurst's magic.

Denver was frying a pan of navy beans in the kitchen when Oliver burst through the door, the locks flinging themselves open before them. Oliver paused in the entrance to the kitchen. Denver stared at him, face slack, too surprised to speak.

"Where's Momma?"

Yolanda heard his voice in the living room and screamed.

Reggie met him in the hallway, arms open wide, smiling broadly. "Goddamn, little brother! You got away?"

"Where's Momma?"

"She's in her room. She's feeling low."

"She's sick," Oliver said, pushing past his brother. Yolanda stood before Momma's door as if to keep Oliver out. She sucked her lower lip between her teeth. She looked scared.

"Let me by, Yolanda," Oliver said. He almost pointed the opener at her, and then pulled back, fearful of what might happen.

"You made Momma si-ick," Yolanda squeaked, but she stepped aside. Oliver pushed through the door to Momma's room. She sat up in bed, face drawn and thin, but her eyes danced with joy. "My boy!" She sighed. "My beautiful boy."

Oliver sat beside her and they hugged fiercely. "Please don't leave me again," Momma said, voice muffled by his shoulder. Oliver set the opener on her flimsy nightstand and cried against her neck.

The day after Oliver's return, Denver stood lank-legged by the window, hands in frayed pants pockets, staring at the snow with heavy-lidded eyes. "It's too cold to go anywhere now," he mused.

Reggie sat in their father's chair, face screwed in thought. "I listened to what he told Momma," he said. "That whore sent our little brother back here in a limo. A big white limo. See it out there?"

Denver peered down at the street. A white limousine waited at the curb, not even dusted by snow. A tiny vanishing curl of white rose from its tailpipe. "It's still there," he said.

"Did you see what he had when he came in?" Reggie asked. Denver shook his head. "A gold box. *She* must have given that to him. I bet whoever has that gold box can visit Miss Belle Parkhurst. Want to bet?"

Denver grinned and shook his head again.

"Wouldn't be too cold if we had that limo, would it?" Reggie asked.

\* \* \*

Oliver brought his momma chicken soup and a half-rotten, carefully trimmed orange. He plumped her pillow for her, shushing her, telling her not to talk until she had eaten. She smiled weakly, beatific, and let him minister to her. When she had eaten, she lay back and closed her eyes, tears pooling in their hollows before slipping down her cheeks. "I was so afraid for you," she said. "I didn't know what she would do. She seemed so nice at first. I didn't see her. Just her voice, inviting me in over the security buzzer, letting me sit and rest my feet. I knew where I was... was it bad of me, to stay there, knowing?"

"You were tired, Momma," Oliver said. "Besides, Miss Parkhurst isn't that bad."

Momma looked at him dubiously. "I saw her piano. There was a shelf next to it with the most beautiful sheet music you ever saw, even big books of it. I looked at some. Oh, Oliver, I've never taken anything in my life..." She cried freely now, sapping what little strength the lunch had given her.

"Don't you worry, Momma. She used you. She *wanted* me to come." As an afterthought, he added, not sure why he lied, "Or Yolanda."

Momma absorbed that while her eyes examined his face in tiny, caressing glances. "You won't go back," she said, "will you?"

Oliver looked down at the sheets folded under her arms. "I promised. She'll die if I don't," he said.

"That woman is a liar," Momma stated unequivocally. "If she wants you, she'll do anything to get you."

"I don't think she's lying, Momma."

She looked away from him, a feverish anger flushing her cheeks. "Why did you promise her?"

"She's not that bad, Momma," he said again. He had thought that coming home would clear his mind, but Miss Parkhurst's face, her plea, stayed with him as if she were only a room away. The mansion seemed just a fading dream, unimportant; but Belle Parkhurst stuck. "She needs help. She wants to change."

Momma puffed out her cheeks and blew through her lips like a horse. She had often done that to his father, never before to him. "She'll always be a whore," she said.

Oliver's eyes narrowed. He saw a spitefulness and bitterness in Momma he hadn't noticed before. Not that spite was unwarranted; Miss Parkhurst had treated Momma roughly. Yet...

Denver stood in the doorway. "Reggie and I got to talk to Momma," he said. "About you." He jerked his thumb back over his shoulder. "Alone." Reggie stood grinning behind his brother. Oliver took the tray of dishes and sidled past them, going into the kitchen.

In the kitchen, he washed the last few days' plates methodically, letting the lukewarm water slide over his hands, eyes focused on the faucet's dull gleam. He had almost lost track of time when he heard the front door slam. Jerking his head up, he wiped the last plate and put it away, then went to Momma's room. She looked back at him guiltily. Something was wrong. He searched the room with his eyes, but nothing was out of place. Nothing that was normally present...

The opener.

His brothers had taken the gold opener.

"Momma!" he said.

"They're going to pay her a visit," she said, the bitterness plain now. "They don't like their momma mistreated."

It was getting dark and the snow was thick. He had hoped to return this evening. If Miss Parkhurst hadn't lied, she would be very weak by now, perhaps dead tomorrow. His lungs seemed to shrink within him, and he had a hard time taking a breath.

"I've got to go," he said. "She might *kill* them, Momma!'' But that wasn't what worried him. He put on his heavy coat, then his father's old cracked rubber boots with the snow tread soles. Yolanda came out of the room she shared with the babies. She didn't ask any questions, just watched him dress for the cold, her eyes dull.

"They got that gold box," she said as he flipped the last metal clasp on the boots. "Probably worth a lot."

Oliver hesitated in the hallway, then grabbed Yolanda's shoulders and shook her vigorously. "You take care of Momma, you hear?"

She shut her jaw with a clack and shoved free. Oliver was out the door before she could speak.

Day's last light filled the sky with a deep peachy glow tinged with cold gray. Snow fell golden above the buildings and smudgy brown within their shadow. The wind swirled around him mournfully, sending gust-fingers through his coat searching for any warmth that might be stolen. For a nauseating moment, all his resolve was sucked away by a vacuous pit of misery. The streets were empty; he briefly wondered what night this was, and then remembered it was the twenty-third of December, but too cold for whatever stray shoppers Sleepside might send out. *Why go? To save two worthless idiots?* Not that so much, although that would have been enough, since their loss would hurt Momma, and they *were* his brothers; not that so much as his promise. And something else.

He was afraid for Belle Parkhurst.

He buttoned his coat collar and leaned into the wind. He hadn't put on a hat. The heat flew from his scalp, and in a few moments he felt drained and exhausted. But he made it to the subway entrance and staggered down the steps, into the warmer heart of the city, where it was always sixty-four degrees.

Locked behind her thick glass and metal booth, wrinkled eyes weary with night's wisdom, the fluorescent-lighted token seller took his money and dropped cat's head tokens into the steel tray with separate, distinct *chinks*. Oliver glanced at her face and saw the whore's printed there instead; this middle-aged woman did not spread her legs for money, but had sold her youth and life away sitting in this cavern. Whose emptiness was more profound?

"Be careful," she warned vacantly through the speaker grill. "Night Metro any minute now."

He dropped a token into the turnstile and pushed through, then stood shivering on the platform, waiting for the Sunside train. It seemed to take forever to arrive, and when it did, he was not particularly relieved. The driver's pit-eyes winked green, bull's head turning as the train slid to a halt beside the platform. The doors opened with an oiled groan, and Oliver stepped aboard, into the hard, cold, and unforgiving glare of the train's interior.

At first, Oliver thought the car was empty. He did not sit down, however. The hair on his neck and arm bristled. Hand gripping a stainless steel handle, he leaned into the train's acceleration and took a deep, half-hiccup breath.

He first consciously noticed the other passengers as their faces gleamed in silhouette against the passing dim lights of ghost stations. They sat almost invisible, crowding the car; they stood beside him, less substantial than a breath of air. They watched him intently, bearing no ill will for the moment, perhaps not yet aware that he was alive and they were not. They carried no overt signs of their wounds, but how they had come to be here was obvious to his animal instincts.

This train carried holiday suicides: men, women, teenagers, even a few children, delicate as expensive crystal in a shop window. Maybe the bull's head driver collected them, culling them out and caging them as they stumbled randomly aboard his train. Maybe he controlled them.

Oliver tried to sink away in his coat. He felt guilty, being alive and healthy, enveloped in strong emotions; they were so flimsy, with so little hold on this reality.

He muttered a prayer, stopping as they all turned toward him, showing glassy disapproval at this reverse blasphemy. Silently, he prayed again, but even that seemed to irritate his fellow passengers, and they squeaked among themselves in voices that only a dog or a bat might hear.

The stations passed one by one, mosaic symbols and names flashing in pools of light. When the Sunside station approached and the train slowed, Oliver moved quickly to the door. It opened with oily grace. He stepped onto the platform, turned, and bumped up against the tall, dark uniform of the bull's head driver. The air around him stank of grease and electricity and something sweeter, perhaps blood. He stood a bad foot and a half taller than Oliver, and in one outstretched, black-nailed, leathery hand he held his long silver shears, points spread wide, briefly suggesting Belle Parkhurst's horizontal position among the old men.

"You're in the wrong place, at the wrong time," the driver warned in a voice deeper than the train motors. "Down here, I can cut your cord." He closed the shears with a slick, singing whisper.

"I'm going to Miss Parkhurst's," Oliver said, voice quavering.

"Who?" the driver asked.

"I'm leaving now," Oliver said, backing away. The driver followed, slowly hunching over him. The shears sang open, angled toward his eyes. The crystal dead within the train passed through the open door and glided around them. Gluey waves of cold shivered the air.

"You're a bold little bastard," the driver said, voice managing to descend off any human scale and still be heard.

The white tile walls vibrated. ''All I have to do is cut your cord, right in front of your face''—he snicked the shears inches from Oliver's nose—''and you'll never find your way home.''

The driver backed him up against a cold barrier of suicides. Oliver's fear could not shut out curiosity. Was the bull's head real, or was there a man under the horns and hide and bone? The eyes in their sunken orbits glowed ice-blue. The scissors crossed before Oliver's face again, even closer; mere hairs away from his nose.

''You're mine,'' the driver whispered, and the scissors closed on something tough and invisible. Oliver's head exploded with pain. He flailed back through the dead, dragging the driver after him by the pinch of the shears on that something unseen and very important. Roaring, the driver applied both hands to the shears' grips. Oliver felt as if his head were being ripped away. Suddenly he kicked out with all his strength between the driver's black-uniformed legs. His foot hit flesh and bone as unyielding as rock and his agony doubled. But the shears hung for a moment in air before Oliver's face, and the driver slowly curled over.

Oliver grabbed the shears, opened them, released whatever cord he had between himself and his past, his home, and pushed through the dead. The scissors reflected elongated gleams over the astonished, watery faces of the suicides. Suddenly, seeing a chance to escape, they spread out along the platform, some up the station's stairs, some to both sides. Oliver ran through them up the steps and stood on the warm evening sidewalk of Sunside. All he sensed from the station's entrance was a sour breath of oil and blood and a faint chill of fading hands as the dead evaporated in the balmy night air.

A quiet crowd had gathered at the front entrance to Miss Parkhurst's mansion. They stood vigil, waiting for something, their faces shining with a greedy sweat.

He did not see the limousine. His brothers must have arrived by now; they were inside, then.

Catching his breath as he ran, he skirted the old brownstone and looked for the entrance to the underground garage. On the south side, he found the ramp and descended to slam his hands against the corrugated metal door. Echoes replied. "It's me!" he shouted. "Let me in!"

A middle-aged man regarded him dispassionately from the higher ground of the sidewalk. "What do you want in there, young man?" he asked.

Oliver glared back over his shoulder. "None of your business," he said.

"Maybe it is, if you want in," the man said. "There's a way any man can get into that house. It never turns gold away."

Oliver pulled back from the door a moment, stunned. The man shrugged and walked on.

He still grasped the driver's shears. They weren't gold, they were silver, but they had to be worth something. "Let me in!" he said. Then, upping the ante, he dug in his pocket and produced the remaining cat's head token. "I'll pay!"

The door grumbled up. The garage's lights were off, but in the soft yellow glow of the streetlights, he saw an eagle's claw thrust out from the brick wall just within the door's frame, supporting a golden cup. Token in one hand, shears in another, Oliver's eyes narrowed. To pay Belle's mansion now was no honorable deed; he dropped the token into the cup, but kept the shears as he ran into the darkness.

A faint crack of light showed beneath the stairwell door. Around the door, the bones of ancient city dwellers glowed in their compacted stone, teeth and knuckles bright as fireflies. Oliver tried the door; it was locked. Inserting the point of the shears between the door and catchplate, he pried until the lock was sprung.

The quiet parlor was illuminated only by a few guttering candles clutched in drooping gold eagle's claws. The air was thick with the blunt smells of long-extinguished cigars and cigarettes. Oliver stopped for a moment, closing his eyes and listening. There was a room he had never seen in the time he had spent in Belle Parkhurst's house. She had never even shown him the door, but he knew it had to exist, and that was where she would be, alive or dead. Where his brothers were, he couldn't tell; for the moment he didn't care. He doubted they were in any mortal danger. Belle's power was as weak as the scattered candles.

Oliver crept along the dark halls, holding the gleaming shears before him as a warning to whatever might try to stop him. He climbed two more flights of stairs, and on the third floor, found an uncarpeted hallway, walls bare, that he had not seen before. The dry floorboards creaked beneath him. The air was cool and still. He could smell a ghost of Belle's rose perfume. At the end of the hall was a plain panel door with a tarnished brass knob.

This door was also unlocked. He sucked in a breath for courage and opened it.

This was Belle's room, and she was indeed in it. She hung suspended above her plain iron-frame bed in a weave of glowing threads. For a moment, he drew back, thinking she was a spider, but it immediately became clear she was more like a spider's prey. The threads reached to all corners of the room, transparent, binding her tightly, but to him as insubstantial as the air.

Belle turned to face him, weak, eyes clouded, skin like paper towels. "Why'd you wait so long?" she asked.

From across the mansion, he heard the echoes of Reggie's delighted laughter.

Oliver stepped forward. Only the blades of the shears

plucked at the threads; he passed through unhindered. Arm straining at the silver instrument, he realized what the threads were; they were the cords binding Belle to the mansion, connecting her to all her customers. Belle had not one cord to her past, but thousands. Every place she had been touched, she was held by a strand. Thick twining ropes of the past shot from her lips and breasts and from between her legs; not even the toes of her feet were free.

Without thinking, Oliver lifted the driver's silver shears and began methodically snipping the cords. One by one, or in ropy clusters, he cut them away. With each meeting of the blades, they vanished. He did not ask himself which was her first cord, linking her to her childhood, to the few years she had lived before she became a whore; there was no time to waste worrying about such niceties.

"Your brothers are in my vault," she said. "They found my gold and jewels. I crawled here to get away."

"Don't talk," Oliver said between clenched teeth. The strands became tougher, more like wire the closer he came to her thin gray body. His arm muscles knotted and cold sweat soaked his clothes. She dropped inches closer to the bed.

"I never brought any men here," she said.

"Shh."

"This was my place, the only place I had."

There were hundreds of strands left now, instead of thousands. He worked for long minutes, watching her grow more and more pale, watching her one-time furnace heat dull to less than a single candle, her eyes lose their feverish glitter. For a horrified moment, he thought cutting the cords might actually weaken her; but he hacked and swung at the cords, regardless. They were even tougher now, more resilient.

Far off in the mansion, Denver and Reggie laughed together, and there was a heavy clinking sound. The floor shuddered.

Dozens of cords remained. He had been working at them for an eternity, and now each cord took a concentrated effort, all the strength left in his arms and hands. He thought he might faint or throw up. Belle's eyes had closed. Her breathing was undetectable.

Five strands left. He cut through one, then another. As he applied the shears to the third, a tall man appeared on the opposite side of her bed, dressed in pale gray with a wide-brimmed gray hat. His fingers were covered with gold rings. A gold eagle's claw pinned his white silk tie.

"I was her friend," the man said. "She came to me and she cheated me."

Oliver held back his shears, eyes stinging with rage. "Who are you?" he demanded, nearly doubled over by his exertion. He stared up at the gray man through beads of sweat on his eyebrows.

"That other old man, he hardly worked her at all. I put her to work right here, but she cheated me."

"You're her *pimp*," Oliver spat out the word.

The gray man grinned.

"Cut that cord, and she's nothing."

"She's nothing now. Your curse is over and she's dying."

"She shouldn't have messed with me," the pimp said. "I was a strong man, lots of connections. What do you want with an old drained-out whore, boy?"

Oliver didn't answer. He struggled to cut the third cord but it writhed like a snake between the shears.

"She would have been a whore even without me," the pimp said. "She was a whore from the day she was born."

"That's a lie," Oliver said.

"Why do you want to get at her? She give you a pox and you want to finish her off?"

Oliver's lips curled and he flung his head back, not looking as he brought the shears together with all his remaining strength, boosted by a killing anger. The third cord parted and the shears snapped, one blade singing across the room and sticking in the wall with a spray of plaster chips. The gray man vanished like a double-blown puff of cigarette smoke, leaving a scent of onions and stale beer.

Belle hung awkwardly by two cords now. Swinging the single blade like a knife, he parted them swiftly and fell over her, lying across her, feeling her cool body for the first time. She could not arouse lust now. She might be dead.

"Miss Parkhurst," he said. He examined her face, almost as white as the bed sheets, high cheekbones pressing through waxy flesh. "I don't want anything from you," Oliver said. "I just want you to be all right." He lowered his lips to hers, kissed her lightly, dripping sweat on her closed eyes.

Far away, Denver and Reggie cackled with glee.

The house grew quiet. All the ghosts, all accounts received, had fled, had been freed.

The single candle in the room guttered out, and they lay in the dark alone. Oliver fell against his will into an exhausted slumber.

Cool, rose-scented fingers lightly touched his forehead. He opened his eyes and saw a girl in a white nightgown leaning over him, barely his age. Her eyes were very big and her lips bowed into a smile beneath high, full cheekbones. "Where are we?" she asked. "How long we been here?"

Late morning sun filled the small, dusty room with warmth. He glanced around the bed, looking for Belle, and then turned back to the girl. She vaguely resembled the chauffeur who had brought him to the mansion that first night, though younger, her face more bland and simple.

"You don't remember?" he asked.

"Honey," the girl said sweetly, hands on hips, "I don't remember much of anything. Except that you kissed me. You want to kiss me again?"

Momma did not approve of the strange young woman he brought home, and wanted to know where Reggie and Denver were. Oliver did not have the heart to tell her. They lay cold as ice in a room filled with mounds of cat's head subway tokens, bound by the pimp's magic. They had dressed themselves in white, with broad white hats; dressed themselves as pimps. But the mansion was empty, stripped during that night of all its valuables by the greedy crowds.

They were pimps in a whorehouse without whores. As the young girl observed, with a tantalizing touch of wisdom beyond her apparent years, there was nothing much lower than that.

"Where'd you find that girl? She's hiding something, Oliver. You mark my words."

Oliver ignored his mother's misgivings, having enough of his own. The girl agreed she needed a different name now, and chose Lorelei, a name she said "Just sings right."

He saved money, lacking brothers to borrow and never repay, and soon rented a cheap studio on the sixth floor of the same building. The girl came to him sweetly in his bed, her mind no more full—for the most part—than that of any young girl. In his way, he loved her—and feared her, though less and less as days passed.

She played the piano almost as well as he, and they planned to give lessons. They had brought a trunk full of old sheet music and books with them from the mansion. The crowds had left them at least that much.

Momma did not visit for two weeks after they moved in. But visit she did, and eventually the girl won her over.

"She's got a good hand in the kitchen," Momma said. "You do right by her, now."

Yolanda made friends with the girl quickly and easily, and Oliver saw more substance in his younger sister than he had before. Lorelei helped Yolanda with the babies. She seemed a natural.

Sometimes, at night, he examined her while she slept, wondering if there still weren't stories, and perhaps skills, hidden behind her sweet, peaceful face. Had she forgotten everything?

In time, they were married.

And they lived—

Well, enough.

They lived.

# Webster

**D**ry.

It lingered in the air, a word of rustlings and whisperings. Vultures fanned her hair. Or—she ran her lean finger, covered in skin like pink parchment, up the page—dinosaur eggs, Roy Chapman Andrews in the middle of the Gobi, gray film flickering as fist-sized ovoids are lifted unhatched from their graves.

She folded the dictionary on her finger. It gripped her with a firm, friendly pressure.

Miss Abigail Coates did not enjoy her life. She took no joy in the bored pain of people in the streets. She felt imprisoned by light when the sun bounced from city walls and pavement and intruded into her small apartment. In this cosmos, her thin body gave no pleasure, caused no surprises, spurred no uncontrollable passions.

Miss Coates was fifty and, my God the needle in her throat when she thought of it, she had never borne a child; she had never even had a man.

Once, she had shared a lonely love with a boy five years younger than she. He could have blunted the needle pain in her throat; he had begged to be given the chance. *But no. I shall use my love as bait and let them who wish it pay the toll.*

"I am a pitiful woman," she said, drawing herself up from the overstuffed chair in her small apartment, standing straight and lean at five feet seven and three-quarters inches. *I weep inside, then read the dear Bible and the even more dear dictionary. They tell me weeping is a sin. Despair, of my few fell sins, is by far the lowest.*

She looked around the dry, comfortable room and shielded her eyes from the gloom of the place where she slept, as if blinded by shadow. The place wasn't a bedroom because in a *bedroom* you slept with a man or men and she had none. Her eyes moved up the door frame, nicked in one corner where clumsy movers had knocked her bed against the wood, twenty years ago; down to the worn carpet that rubbed the bottoms of her feet like raw canvas. To the chair behind her, coming unstuffed in the middle. To the wallpaper, chosen by someone else, stained with water along the cornice from some ancient rain. And finally she looked down at her feet, toes wriggling in loose frayed nylons, toenails thick and well-manicured; all parts of her body looked after but the core, the soul.

She went into the place where she slept and lay down. The bedsheets caressed her in an obligatory manner, wrinkles and folds in blankets rubbing her thighs, her breasts. The pillow accepted her peppery hair, and in the dark, she told herself to sleep.

The morning was better. Afternoon passed like a dull ache. In the twilight she wept as she fixed her small pale dinner of potatoes and veal. In the dark, she sat in her chair with the two books at her feet and stared at the flowers on the wall.

The morning was fine. The afternoon was hot and sticky and she took a walk, wearing sunglasses. She watched all the young people on this fine Saturday afternoon. *They hold hands and walk in parks and there, on that bench; she'll be in trouble if she keeps that up. Oh, to have the distant chance of being in trouble.* She went back to the apartment, always waiting, smooth sliding lock on the door always faithful and undisturbed. The evening passed slowly in the heat. By midnight a cool breeze fluttered the sun-browned curtains in the window, then blew them in like the flapping wings of ghost-birds. She read the dictionary, looking for comfort, and found instead words she didn't wish to be reminded of; medical words, biological words. They came at her unbidden from the pages and would not leave her alone. She didn't think them obscene; they seemed marvelous. The sound of them made her tremble and ache. Again, the evening ended in tears.

She had spent her evenings like this, with few variations, for the past five years.

"I need a lover," she told herself firmly as the yellow morning sunlight crept across the ironing board and her fanciest dress, burgundy in shadows, orange in the glare. But one found lovers in offices and she didn't work; in trains and she didn't travel; in distant countries and she never left town. "I need a little common sense, a little self-control, to make me stop thinking like a reckless teenager." But the truth was she did not lack self-control. It was her prime virtue.

Her name, Coates, was not in the dictionary. There was Coati, Coatimundi, coat of arms, coat of mail, and then Miss

Co-author, lover to a handsome author. They would collaborate, corroborate, celebrate. Celibate. She shut the book.

Miss Coates drew the curtains on the window and slowly stripped off her dress, tugging the zipper down the back with the practiced flourish of a crochet hook, rubbing the small of her back with her dry fingertips, chin held high, eyes closed to slits. Cool breezes came through the dark beyond the window and the heat in the apartment to fan her skin. Sweat lodged in the cleft between her breasts. She was proud of her breasts; they did not sag appreciably when she removed her bra. She squatted and marched her hands behind her to sit and then lie on the floor. Spreading her arms against the rough carpet, Miss Coates pressed her chin into her clavicle and peered at her breasts, now flat and boyish against the prominent ribş. Unspoiled goods. She cupped them in both hands. A thin crucifixion with legs straight and toes together.

Her head lay near the window. She looked up to see the curtains fluttering like her lungs. Mouth open. Tongue rubbing the backs of teeth. She moved her hands to her stomach and let them lie on flat warmth. *I am not so undesirable. No flab, few wrinkles. My thighs are not heavy, not dimpled with gross flesh.*

No more. She lifted her hands and rolled over to rise on one elbow. She looked at the dictionary, mouthing a word: *Lover.*

The dictionary and Bible sat small and tightly noncommittal in buckram and black leather.

"Help me," she asked the dictionary, gently pushing the Bible aside. "Book of all books, massive thing I can hardly lift, every thought lies in you, all human possibilities. Everything I can feel can be expressed through the words you hold. Lives exist in you, people and places I've never seen, things dead and things unborn. Haven of ghosts and the preternatural, home of tyrants and saints. Surely you can make a man for me. Small word, little work. You can even *tell* me how to make a man from you.'' She could almost see that; a man rising from the open book, spinning like a man-shaped bird cage filled with light.

The curtains puffed.

''Can't you?'' she asked. The dictionary remained silent. She crossed her legs in a lotus next to the thick book and waited for the dust of each word, the microscopic, homeopathic bits of ink, each charged with the shape of a letter, a word, to sift between the fibers of the paper and confer with each other.

Dry magic. The words smelled sweet in the cool midnight breeze. *Dead bits of ink, charged with thought, arise.*

*Veni*

Her tongue swelled with the dryness of the ink. She unfolded and lay flat on her stomach to let the rough carpet mold her skin with criss-crossword puzzle lines.

Miss Coates flopped the dictionary around to face her, then threw its cover and clumps of pages open to the middle. Her finger searched randomly on the page and found a word. She gasped. *Man*, it said, clear as could be next to her colorless nail. Man! She moved her finger and sucked in her breath.

''There *is* a man in you!'' she told the book, laughing. It was a joke, after all; she was not that far gone. Still grinning, she rubbed her finger against the inside of her cheek and pressed the dampness onto the word. ''Here,'' she said. ''A few of my cells.'' Oh, she was clever, she was brilliant! ''Clone them.'' Then she thought better of it and said, ''But don't make him look like me. Change him with your medical words, plastic surgery and eugenics and genotype.'' The page darkened where the tip of her finger had pressed. The ink did not blur. She shut the book and returned to her lotus. *As my trunk rises from the flower of my legs and the seat of my womb, so, man arise from the book of books.*

Would it thunder? Only silence. The dictionary trembled and the Bible looked somber in shadow. The yellow bulb in the shaded lamp sang faintly. The air grew heavy. *Don't falter,* she told herself. *Don't lose faith, don't drop the flower of your legs and the seat of your womb. A bit of blood? Or milk from unsucked breasts? Catalysts . . . Or, God forbid, something living, a fly between the pages, the heart of a bird, or—* She shuddered, almost ill with excitement, with a kind of belief, *the clear seed of a dead man.*

The book. It almost lifted its cover. It *breathed.*

"That was it," she whispered, awed. "It knows how."

It sucked warmth from the air. Frost clung to its brown binding. The cover flew back, just a sudden wind from the window sweeping through the room. The pages flapped, but two stuck together, struggling, bulging . . . splitting.

Rising, a figure, arms spread, twirling like an ice skater, soaking up dust and air and heat, tightening and coalescing.

*Handsome! Make him handsome and rugged and kind, and smart as I am, if not smarter. Make him like a father but not my father and like a son and a lover especially a lover, warm, and give him breath that melts my lips and softens my hair like steam from jungles. Concentrate there yes large and strong and full. He should like warm dry days and going to lakes and fishing, but actually he likes reading to me more than fishing, and he should like cold winter days and ice-skating with me he could if you will allow me to suggest he could be brown-haired with a shadow of red and his cheeks rough with fresh young beard I can watch grow and he should—*

His eyes! They flashed as he spun, molten beacons still indefinite. His nose became apparent and she approved. His hair danced and gleamed, dark brown with a hint of red. Arms, fingers, legs, crawled with words. An ant's nest of dry-ink "foot"'s and clustered at his base, tangling with "heel"'s and "ankle"'s. Then—the words became flesh and bone.

His breasts were firm and square and dark-nippled. The hair on his chest was dark and silky. He was still spinning. She cried out, staring at his groin.

Clothes? "Yes!" she said. "I have no clothes for men."

A suit, a pink shirt with cuff links and pearl decorations.

His eyes blinked and his mouth opened and closed. His head drooped and a moan flew out like a whirling weight loosed from a string.

"Stop!" she shouted. "Please stop, he's finished!"

The man stood on the dictionary, knees wobbly, threatening to topple. She jumped up from the floor to catch him, but he fell away from her and collapsed on the carpet beside the chair. The book lay kicked and sprawled by his feet, top pages wrinkled and torn.

Miss Coates stood over the man, hands fluttering at her breasts. He lay on his side, chest heaving, eyes closed. Her wide gaze darted from point to point on his body, lower lip held by tiny white upper teeth. After a few minutes, she was able to look away from him. She squinted more closely at the dictionary, frowned, then bent to riffle through the pages. Every page was blank.

"I am naked," she told herself, stretching out her hands, using the realization to shock herself to sensibility. She went into the place where she slept to put on some clothes. Away from the man, she wondered what she would call him. He probably did not have a name, not a Christian name at any rate. It seemed appropriate to call him by a name like everyone else, even if she had raised him from paper and ink, from a dictionary.

"Webster," she said, nodding sharply at the obvious. "I'll call him Webster."

She returned to the living room and looked at the man. He seemed to be resting peacefully. How could she move him to a more comfortable place? The couch was too small to hold his ungainly body; he was very tall, well over six feet. She measured him with the tape from her sewing kit. Six feet two inches. His eyes were still shut; what color were they? She squatted beside him, face flushed, thinking thoughts she warned herself she must not think, not yet.

She was in her best dress, wrapped in smooth dark burgundy, against which her pale skin showed to best advantage. It was one o'clock in the morning, however, and she was exhausted. "You seem comfortable enough for now," she told the man, who did not move. "I'll leave you on the floor."

Abigail Coates went into her bedroom to sleep. Tired as she was, she could not just close her eyes and drift off. She felt like shouting for joy and tears dampened the pillow and moistened her pepper hair.

In the darkness, *he* breathed. Dreaming, did he cause the words to flow through her drowsing thoughts? Or was it simply his breath filling the house with the odor of printer's ink?

In the night, *he* moved. Shifting an arm, a leg, sending atoms of words up like dust. His eyes flickered open, then closed. Then his mouth. He moaned and was still again.

Abigail Coates's neck hair prickled with the first rays of morning and she awoke with a tiny shriek, little more than a high-pitched gasp. She rolled from her stomach onto her back and pulled up the sheet and bedspread.

Webster stood in the doorway, smiling. She could barely see him in the dawn light. Her eyelids were gummy with sleep. "Good morning, Regina," he said.

Regina Abigail Coates. Everyone had called her Abbie, when there had been friends to call her anything. No one had ever called her Regina.

"Regina," Webster repeated. "It's a name to remind one of queens and Canadian coins."

"Good morning," she said feebly. "How are you? How...do you feel?"

A ghost of a smile. He nodded slowly. "As well as could be expected." He walked into her room, stopping at the foot of her bed. "I'm rather well-dressed. Too well-dressed. It's uncomfortable." Her heart was a little piston in her throat, hardly lubricated by the phlegm that threatened to choke her.

He moved to the side of the bed. Her side.

"You brought me out. Why?"

She stared up at his bright green eyes, like drops of water raised from the depths of an ocean trench. His hand touched her shoulder, lingered on the strap of her nightgown. One finger slipped under the strap, tugging it up a quarter of an inch. She felt the pressure of the cloth beneath her breast.

"Why?"

His breath sprinkled words over her face and hair. "And why...do I feel so obliged to..."

He pulled down the blind and closed the drapes and there was the sound of cloth dropped onto a chair. In the darkness, a knee pressed the edge of her bed. A finger touched her neck and lips descended to cover hers and part them. A tongue explored.

In the early morning hours, Regina Abigail Coates gave a tiny, squeezed-in scream.


Webster sat in the overstuffed chair and watched her leave. She shut the door and leaned against the wall, not knowing what to think or feel. "Of course," she whispered to herself, as if there were no wind or strength left in her. "Of course a man made of words doesn't like the sun." But why should that be so obvious? He was a man like any other in all ways but that one. . . .

She walked down the hallway, past the doors of neighbors with whom she had only a nodding acquaintance, and descended the stairs to the first floor. The street was filled with cars passing back and forth endlessly. Flattening nonexistent wrinkles from her dress, she stepped into the sunlight and faced the world, the new Regina Coates, debutante.

"I *know* what all you other women know," she said softly, with a bitter edge of triumph. "All of you!" She looked up and noticed the sky, perhaps for the first time in twenty years; it was rich with clouds, scattered across a bright blue sheet, demanding of her, *Breathe deeply.* She was part of the world now, the real world.

Webster still sat in the chair when she returned with two bags of groceries. He was reading her Bible. Her face grew hot and she put down the bags and removed it quickly from his hands. She could not face his querying stare, so she lay the book on a table, out of his reach, and said, "You don't want to read that."

"Why?" he asked. She didn't answer, picking up the bags again by their doubled and folded paper corners, taking them one in each hand into the kitchen and opening the old refrigerator to stock away the perishables.

"When you're gone," Webster said, "I feel as if I fade into the room."

She glanced up at the small mirror over the sink. Her shoulders twitched and a shudder ran up her back. *I am very far gone now.*

She fixed lunch but he refused to eat. Still, he sat across from her at the small table, face placid. The afternoon newspaper arrived and he held his hand out with a pleading expression; she gave it to him with an uncertain smile. He rubbed his fingers over the pages, turning them slowly, seeming to absorb more than read. She ate her small trimmed sandwich and drank her glass of grapefruit juice. Glancing at him from all sides, surreptitiously, she straightened up the tiny kitchen.

What was there to say to a man between morning and night? She had expected that a man made of words would be full of conversation, but Webster had very little experience, and so while the words existed in him, they had yet to be connected. Or so she surmised. Still, his very presence gratified her. He made her as real as she had made him.

He refused dinner, even declining to share a glass of wine with her after (she had only one glass). "I expect there should be some awkwardness in the early days," she said. "Don't you? Some quiet times when we can just sit and be with each other. Like today."

Webster stood by the window, finger touching his lips, and nodded. He agreed with most things she said.

"Let's go to bed," she suggested.

In the dark, when her solitude had again been sundered and her brow was sprinkled with warm salty drops of exertion, he lay next to her, and—

He *moved*.

He *breathed*.

But he did not sleep.

Regina lay with her back to him, eyes wide, staring at the flowers on the ancient wallpaper and a wide trapezoid of streetlight glare transfixing a small table and its vase. She felt ten years—no, twenty!—sliding away from her, and yet she couldn't tell him how she felt, didn't dare turn and talk. The air was full of him. Full of words not her own, unorganized, potential. She breathed in a million random thoughts, deep or slight, complex or simple, eloquent or crude. Webster was becoming a generator. Kept in the apartment, his substance was reacting with itself; shut away from experience, he was making up his own patterns and organizations, subtle as smoke.

Even lying still, waiting for the slight movement of air through the window to cool him, he worked inside and his breath filled the air with his potential.

But Regina was tired and deliciously filled, and that satisfaction at least was hers. She luxuriated in it and slept.

In the morning, she lay alone in the bed. She flung off the covers and padded into the living room, pulling down her rucked-up nightgown, shivering against the morning chill. He stood by the window again, naked, not caring if people on the streets looked up and saw.

She stood beside him and gently enclosed his upper arm with her fingers, leaning her cheek against his shoulder, a motion that came so naturally she surprised herself with her own grace. "What do you want?" she asked.

"No," he said tightly. "The question is, what do *you* want?"

"I'll get some breakfast. You *must* be hungry by now."

"No."

"I'll get some food," she continued obstinately, letting go of his arm. "Do you want some milk?"

"No."

"I don't want you to get sick."

"I don't get sick. I don't get hungry. You haven't answered my question."

"I love you," she said, with much less grace.

"You don't love me. You need me."

"Isn't that the same?"

"Not at all."

"Shall we get out today?" she asked airily, backing away, realizing she was doing a poor imitation of some actress in the movies, her voice light, tripping.

"I can't. I don't get sick, I don't get hungry. I don't go places."

"You're being obtuse," she said petulantly, hating that tone, tears of frustration in her eyes. *How must I behave? Is he mine, or am I his?*

"Obtuse, acute, equilateral, isosceles, vector, derivative, sequesential, psych-integrative, mersauvin powers..." He shook his head, grinning sadly. "That's the future of mathematics for the next century."

"Did you think about those last night?" she asked. She cared nothing for mathematics; what could a man made of words know about numbers?

"Words mix in blood, my blood is made of words.... I can't stop thinking, even at night. Words are numbers, too. Signs and portents, measures and relations, variables and qualifiers."

"You're flesh," she said. "I gave you substance."

"You gave me existence, but no substance."

She laughed harshly, caught herself, forced herself to be demure again. Taking his hand, she led him back to the chair. She kissed him on the cheek, a chaste gesture considering their state of undress, and said she would stay with him all day today, to help him orientate. "But tomorrow we have to buy you some more clothes."

"Clothes," he said softly, then smiled as if all was well. She leaned her head forward and smiled back, a fire radiating from her stomach through her legs and arms. With a soft step and a skip she danced on the carpet, hair swinging. Webster watched her, still smiling.

"And while you're out," he said, "bring back another dictionary."

"Of course. We can't use *that* one anymore, can we? The same kind?"

"Doesn't matter," he said, shaking his head.

The uncertainty of Webster's introverted afternoon hours became a dull, sugarcoated ache for Regina Coates. She tried to disregard her fears—that he found her a disappointment, inadequate; that he was weakening, fading—and reasoned that if she was his *mistress,* she could make him do or be whatever she wished. Unless she did not know what to wish. Could a man's behavior be wished for, or must it simply be experienced?

At night the words again poured into her, and she grinned in the dark, lying beside the warmth of the shadow that smelled of herself and printer's ink, wondering if they should be taking precautions. She was a late fader in the biological department and there was a certain risk. . . .

She grinned, thinking about it. All she could imagine was a doctor holding up a damp bloody thing in his hands and saying, "Miss Coates, you're the proud mother of an eight-pound . . . dictionary."

"Abridged?" she asked wickedly.

She shopped carefully, picking for him the best clothes she could afford, in a wide variety of styles, dipping into her savings to pay the bill. For herself she chose a new dress that showed her slim waist to advantage and hid her thin thighs. She looked girlish in it, summery. That was what she wanted. She purchased the dictionary and looked through gift shops for something else to give him. "Something witty and interesting for him to do." She settled on a game of Scrabble.

Webster was delighted with the dictionary. He regarded the game dubiously, but played it with her a few times. "An appetizer," he called it.

"Are you going to eat the book?" she asked, half in jest.

"No," he said.

She wondered why they didn't argue. She wondered why

they didn't behave like a normal couple, ignoring her self-derisive inner voice crying out, *Normal?*

*My God*, she said to herself after two weeks, staring at the hard edge of the small table in the kitchen. *Creating men from dictionaries, making love until the bed is damp—at* my *age! He still smells like ink, not flesh. He doesn't sweat and he refuses to go outside. Nobody sees him but me. Me. Who am* I *to judge whether he's really there?*

*What would happen to Webster if I were to take a gun and put a hole in his stomach, above the navel? A man with a navel, not born of woman, is an abomination indeed.*

If he spoke to her simply and without emotion just once more, or twice, she thought she would try that experiment and see.

She bought a gun, furtive as a mouse but a respectable citizen, for protection, a small gray pistol, and hid it in her drawer.

She thought better of it a few hours after, shuddered in disgust, and removed the bullets, flinging them out of the apartment's rear window into the dead garden in the narrow courtyard below.

On the last day, when she went shopping, she carried the empty gun with her so he wouldn't find it—although he showed no interest in snooping, which would at least have been a sign of caring. The bulge in her purse made her nervous.

She did not return until dinnertime. *The apartment is not my own now. It oppresses me. He oppresses me.* She walked quietly through the front door, saw the living room was empty, and heard a small sound from behind the closed bedroom door. The light flop of something stiff hitting the floor.

"Webster?" Silence. She knocked lightly on the door. "Are you ready to talk?"

No reply.

*He makes me mad when he doesn't answer like that. If I scare him, make him react to me in some way.* She took out the pistol, fumbling it, pressing its grip into her palm. It felt formidable in her hand.

The door was locked. Outraged that she should be closed out of her own bedroom, she carried the revolver into the kitchen and found a hairpin in a drawer, the same she had used months before when the door had locked accidentally. She knelt before the doorknob and fumbled, teeth clenched, lips tight.

With a small cry, she forced the door open.

Webster sat with legs crossed on the floor beside the bed. Before him lay the dictionary, opened almost to the back. "Not now," he said, tracing a finger along the rows of words. Her mouth dropped open. "What are you looking at?" she asked, tightening her fingers on the pistol.

She stepped closer, looked down, and saw that he was examining the "W" section.

"I don't know," he said. He found the word he was looking for, reached into his mouth with one finger and scraped his inner cheek. Smeared the wetness on the page.

"No," she said. Then, "Why. . . ?"

There were tears on his cheeks. The man of dry ink was crying. Somehow that made her furious. "I'm not even a human being," he said. She hated him, hated this weakness; she had never liked weak men. He adjusted his lotus position and gripped the edges of the dictionary with both hands. "Why can't you find a human being for yourself?" he asked, looking up at her. "I'm nothing but a dream."

She held the pistol firmly to her side. "What are you doing?"

"Need," he said. "That's all I am. Your hunger and your need. Do you know what I'm good for, what I can do? No.

You'd be afraid if you did. You keep me here like some commodity.''

"I wanted you to go out with me," she said tightly.

"What has the world done to you that you'd want to create *me*?"

"You're going to make a woman from that thing, aren't you?" she asked. "Nothing worthwhile has ever happened to me without it going away the moment I . . ."

"Need," he said, raising his hands over the book. "You cannot love unless you need, Miss Regina Abigail Coates. You cannot love the real. The here. You must change the thing you love to please yourself, and damn it should it echo what hides within. Within *you*."

"You *thing*," she breathed, lips curled back. Webster looked at her and at the barrel of the gun she now pointed at him and laughed.

"You don't need that," he told her. "You don't need something real to kill a dream. All you need is a little sunlight."

She lowered the gun, eyebrows lifted, and smiled around her gritted teeth. She pointed the index finger of her left hand and her face went lax. Listlessly, she whispered, "Bang."

The smell of printer's ink became briefly more intense, then faded on the warm breeze passing through the apartment. She kicked the dictionary shut.

How lonely it was going to be, in the dark with only her own sweat.

# A Martian Ricorso

**M**artian night. The cold and the dark and the stars are so intense they make music, like a faint tinkle of ice xylophones. Maybe it's my air tank hose scraping; maybe it's my imagination. Maybe it's real.

Standing on the edge of Swift Plateau, I'm afraid to move or breathe deeply, as I whisper into the helmet recorder, lest I disturb something holy: God's sharp scrutiny of Edom Crater. I've gone outside, away from the lander and my crewmates, to order my thoughts about what has happened.

The Martians came just twelve hours ago, like a tide of five-foot-high laboratory rats running and leaping on their thick, powerful legs. To us, it seemed as if they were storming the lander, intent on knocking it over. But it seems now we were merely in their way.

We didn't just sit here and let them swamp us. We didn't hurt or kill any of them—Cobb beat at them with a roll of foil and I used the parasol of the damaged directenna to shoo them off. First contact, and we must have looked like clowns in an old silent comedy. The glider wings came perilously close to being severely damaged. We foiled and doped what few tears had been made before nightfall. They should suffice, if the polymer sylar adhesive is as good as advertised.

But our luck this expedition held true to form. The stretching frame's pliers broke during the repairs. We can't afford another swarm, even if they're just curious.

Cobb and Link have had bitter arguments about self-defense. I've managed to stay neutral so far, but my sympathies at the moment lie with Cobb. Still, my desire to stay alive won't stop me from feeling horribly guilty if we *do* have to kill a few Martians.

We've had quite a series of revelations the last few days. Schiaparelli was right. And Percival Lowell, the eccentric genius of my own home state. He was not as errant an observer as we've all thought this past century.

I have an hour before I have to return to the lander and join my mates in sleep. I can last here in the cold that long. Loneliness may weigh on me sooner, however. I don't know why I came out here; perhaps just to clear my head, we've all been in such a constrained, tightly controlled, oh-so-disguised panic. I need to know what I think of the whole situation, without benefit of comrades.

The plateau wall and the floor of Edom are so barren. With the exception, all around me, of the prints of thousands of feet . . . Empty and lifeless.

Tomorrow morning we'll brace the crumpled starboard sled

pads and rig an emergency automatic release for the RATO units on the glider. Her wings are already partially spread for a fabric inspection—accomplished just before the Winter Troops attacked—and we've finished transferring fuel from the lander to the orbit booster. When the glider gets us up above the third jet stream, by careful tacking we hope to be in just the right position to launch our little capsule up and out. A few minutes burn and we can dock with the orbiter if Willy is willing to pick us up.

If we don't make it, these records will be all there is to explain, on some future date, why we never made it back. I'll feed the helmet memory into the lander telterm, stacked with flight telemetry and other data in computer-annotated garble, and instruct the computer to store it all on hard-copy glass disks.

The dust storm that sand-scrubbed our directenna and forced me to this expedient subsided two days ago. We have not reported our most recent discovery to mission control; we are still organizing our thoughts. After all, it's a momentous occasion. We don't want to make any slips and upset the folks back on Earth.

Here's the situation on communications. We can no longer communicate directly with Earth. We are left with the capsule radio, which Willy can pick up and boost for rebroadcast whenever the conditions are good enough. At the moment, conditions are terrible. The solar storm that dogged our Icarus heels on the way out, forcing us deep inside Willy's capacious hull, is still active. The effect on the Martian atmosphere has been most surprising.

There's a communicator on the glider body as well, but that's strictly short-range and good for little more than telemetry. So we have very garbled transmissions going out, reasonably clear coming back, and about twenty minutes of complete blackout when Willy is out of line of sight, behind or below Mars.

We may be able to hit Willy with the surveyor's laser, adapted for signal transmission. For the moment we're going to save that for the truly important communications, like time of launch and approximate altitude, calculated from the fuel we have left after the transfer piping exploded . . . was it three days ago? When the night got colder than the engineers thought possible and exceeded the specs on the insulation.

I'm going back in now. It's too much out here. Too dark. No moons visible.

Now at the keyboard. Down to meaningful mono-logue.

Mission Commander Linker, First Pilot Cobb, and myself, Mission Specialist Mercer, have finished ninety percent of the local survey work and compared it with Willy's detailed map-ping. What we've found is fascinating.

At one time there were lines on Mars, stripes like canals. Until a century ago, any good telescope on Earth, on a good night, could have revealed them to a sharp-eyed observer. As the decades went by, it was not the increased skill of astrono-mers and the quality of instruments that erased these lines, but the end of the final century of the *Anno Fecundis*. Is my Latin proper? I have no dictionary to consult.

With the end of the Fertile Year, a thousand centuries long, came the first bleak sandy winds and the lowering of the Martian jet streams. They picked up sand and scoured.

The structures must have resembled fairy palaces before they were swept down. I once saw a marketplace full of empty vinegar jugs in the Philippines, made from melted Coca Cola bottles. They used glass so thin you could break them with a thumbnail tap in the right place—but they easily held twenty or thirty gallons of liquid. These colonies must have looked like grape-clusters of thousands of thin glass vinegar bottles, dark as emeralds, mounted on spiderweb stilts and fed with water pumped through veins as big as Roman aqueducts. We surveyed one field and found the fragments buried in red sand across a strip thirty miles wide. From a mile or so up, the edge of the structure can still be seen, if you know where to look.

Neither of the two previous expeditions found them.

They're *ours*.

Linker believes these ribbons once stretched clear around the planet. Before the sandstorm, Willy's infrared mapping proved him correct. We could trace belts of ruins in almost all the places Lowell had mapped—even the civic centers some of his followers said he saw. Aqueducts laced the planet like the ribs on a basketball, meeting at ocean-sized black pools covered by glassy membranes. The pools were filled with a thin purple liquid, a kind of resin, warming in the sun, undergoing photo-synthesis. The resin was pumped at high pressure through tissue and glass tubes, nourishing the plantlike colonies inhabiting the bottles.

They probably lacked any sort of intelligence. But their architectural feats put all of ours to shame, nonetheless.

Sandstorms and the rapidly drying weather of the last century are still bringing down the delicate structures. Ninety-five percent or more have fallen already, and the rest are too rickety to safely investigate. They are still magnificent. Standing on the edge of a plain of broken bottles and shattered pylons stretching to the horizon, we can't help but feel very young and very small.

A week ago, we discovered they've left spores buried deep in the red-orange sand, tougher than coconuts and about the size of medicine balls.

Six days ago, we learned that Mars provides children for

all his seasons. Digging for ice lenses that Willy had located, we came across a cache of leathery eggshells in a cavern shored up with a translucent organic cement. We didn't have time to investigate thoroughly. We managed to take a few samples of the cement—scrupulously avoiding disturbing the eggs—and vacated before our tanks ran empty. While cutting out the samples, we noticed that the walls had been patterned with hexagonal carvings, whether as a structural aid or decoration we couldn't tell.

Yesterday, that is, about twenty-six hours ago, we saw what we believe must be the hatchlings: the Winter Troops, five or six of them, walking along the edge of the plateau, not much more than white specks from where we sat in the lander.

We took the sand sled five kilometers from the landing to investigate the cache again, and to see what Willy's mapping revealed as the last standing fragments of an aqueduct bridge in our vicinity. We didn't locate our original cache. Collapsed caverns filled with leathery egg skins pocked the landscape. More than sandstorms had been at the ruins. The bridges rested on the seeds of their own destruction—packs of kangaroo-rat Winter Troops crawled over the structure like ants on a carcass, breaking off bits, eating or just cavorting like sand fleas.

Linker named them. He snapped pictures enthusiastically. As a trained exobiologist, he was in a heat of excitement and speculation. His current theory is that the Winter Troops are on a binge of destruction, programmed into their genes and irrevocable. We retreated on the sled, unsure whether we might be swamped as well.

Linker babbled—pardon me, expounded—all the way back to the lander. "It's like Giambattista Vico resurrected from the historian's boneyard!" We barely listened; Linker was way over our heads. "Out with the old, in with the new! Vico's historical *ricorso* exemplified."

Cobb and I were much less enthusiastic. "Indiscriminate buggers," he grumbled. "How long before they find us?"

I had no immediate reaction. As in every situation in my life, I decided to sit on my emotions and wait things out.

Cobb was prescient. Unluckily for us, our lander and glider rise above the ground like a stray shard of an aqueduct-bridge. At that stage of their young lives, the Winter Troops couldn't help but swarm over everything.

An hour ago, I braved the hash and our own confusion and sent out descriptions of our find. So far, we've received no reply to our requests for first contact instructions. The likelihood was so small nobody planned for it.

The message was probably garbled.

But enough pessimism. Where does this leave us, so far, in our speculations?

Gentlemen, we sit on the cusp between cycles. We witness the end of the green and russet Mars of humanity's youth, ribbed with fairy bridges and restrained seas, and come upon a grimmer, more practical world, buttoning down for the long winter.

We haven't studied the white Martians in any detail, so there's no way of knowing whether or not they're intelligent. They may be the new masters of Mars. How do we meet them—passively, as Linker seems to think we should, or as Cobb believes: defending ourselves against creatures who may or may not belong to our fraternal order of Thinkers?

What can we expect if we *don't* defend ourselves?

Let your theologians and exobiologists speculate on *that*. Are we to be the first to commit the sin of an interplanetary Cain? Or are the Martians?

It will take us nine or ten hours tomorrow to brace the lander pads. Our glider sits with sylar wings half flexed, crinkling and snapping in the rising wind, silver against the low sienna hills of the Swift Plateau.

Sunlight strikes the top of the plateau. Pink sky to the east; fairy bridges, fairy landscape! Pink and dreamlike. Ice-crystal clouds obscure a faded curtain of aurora. The sky overhead is black as obsidian. Between the pink sunrise and the obsidian is a band of hematite, a dark rainbow like carnival glass, possibly caused by crystalline powder from the aqueduct-bridges elevated into the jet streams. From our vantage on the plateau, we can see dust devils crossing Edom's eastern rim and the tortured mounds and chasms of the Moab-Marduk range, rising like the pillars of some ancient temple.

Since writing the above, I've napped for an hour or so. Willy relayed a new chart. He's found construction near the western rim of Edom Crater—recent construction, not there a few days ago when the area was last surveyed. Hexagonal formations—walls and what could be roads. From his altitude, they must rival the Great Wall of China. How could such monumental works be erected in just days? Were they missed on the previous passes? Not likely.

So there we have it. The colonies that erected the aqueduct-bridges were not the only architects on Mars. The Winter Troops are demonstrating their skills. But are they intelligent, or just following some instinctual imperative? Or *both?*

Both men are sleeping again now. They've been working hard, as have I, and their sleep is sound. The telterm clicking doesn't wake them. I can't sleep much—no more than a hour at a stretch before I awake in a sweat. My body is running on supercharge and I'm not ready to resort to tranquilizers. So here I sit, endlessly observing.

Linker is the largest of us. Though I worked with him for three years before this mission, and we have spent over eight months in close quarters, I hardly know the man. He's not a quiet man, and he's always willing to express his opinions, but he still surprises me. He has a way of raising his eyebrows when he listens, opening his dark eyes wide and wrinkling his forehead, that reminds me of a dog cocking its ears. But it would have to be a devilishly bright dog. Perhaps I haven't plumbed Linker's depths because I'd go in over my head if I tried. He's certainly more dedicated than either Cobb or I. He's been in the USN for twenty-one years, fifteen of them in space, specializing in planetary geology and half a dozen other disciplines.

Cobb, on the other hand, can be read like a book. He tends toward bulk, more in appearance than mass; he weighs only a little more than I do. He's shorter and works with a frown; it seems to take twice his normal concentration to finish some tasks. I do him no injustice by saying that; he gets the work done, and well, but it costs him more than it would Linker. The extra effort sometimes takes the edge off his nonessential reasoning. He's not light on his mental feet, particularly in a situation like this. Doggedness and quick reflexes brought him to his prominence in the Mars lander program; I respect him none the less for that, but . . . He tends to the technical, loving machines more than men, I've often thought, and from my more liberal arts background, I've resented that.

Linker and I once had him close to tears on the outward voyage. We conversed on five or six subjects at once, switching topics every three or four minutes. It was a cruel game and neither of us are proud of it, but I for one can peg part of the blame on the mission designers. Three is too small a community for a three-year mission in space. Hell. Space has been billed as making children out of us all, eh? A two-edged sword.

I have (as certain passages above might indicate) been thinking about the Bible lately. My old childhood background has been stimulated by the danger and moral dilemmas—hair of the dog that bit me. The maps of Mars, with their Biblical names, have contributed to my thoughts. We're not far from

Eden as gliders go. We sit in fabled Moab, above the Moab-Marduk range, Marduk being one of the chief "baals" in the Old Testament. Edom Crater—Edom means red, an appropriate name for a Martian crater. I have red hair. Call me Esau!

Mesogaea—Middle Earth. Other hair, other dogs.

Back on the recorder again. Time weighs heavily on me. I've retreated to the equipment bay to weather a bit of grumpiness between Linker and Cobb. Actually, it was an out and out argument. Linker, still the pacifist, expressed his horror of committing murder against another species. His scruples are oddly selective—he fought in Mexico in the nineties. Neither has been restrained by rank; this could lead to really ugly confrontations, unless danger straightens us all out and makes brothers of us.

Three comrades, good and true, tolerant of different opinions.

Oh, God, here they come again! I'm looking out the equipment bay port, looking east. They must number five or six thousand, lining a distant hill like Indians. That many attacking... Cobb can have his way, and it won't matter, we'll still have had the course. If they rip a section of wing sylar larger than we can stretch by hand, we're stuck.

That was close. Cobb fired bursts of the surveyor's laser over their heads. Enough dust had been raised by their movement and by the wind to make a fine display. They moved back slowly and then vanished behind the hill. The laser is powerful enough to burn them should the necessity arise.

Linker has as much as said he'd rather die than extend the sin of Cain. I'm less worried about that sin than I am about lifting off. We have yet to brace the sled pad. Linker's out below the starboard hatch now, rigging the sling that will keep one section of the slider body level when the RATOs fire.

More dust to the east now. Night is coming slowly. After the sun sets, it'll be too cold to work outside for long. If the Winter Troops are water-based, how do they survive the night? Antifreeze in their blood, like Arctic fish? Can they keep up their activity in temperatures between fifty and one hundred below? Or will we be out of danger until sunrise, with the Martians warm in their blankets, and we in our trundle-bed, nightmaring?

I've helped Linker rig the sling. We've all worked on the sled pad. Cobb has mounted the laser on a camera tripod— clever warrior. Linker advised him to beware the fraying power cable. Cobb looked at him with a sad sort of resentment and went about his work. Other than the few bickerings and person- ality games of the trip out, we managed to keep respect for one another until the last few days. Now we're slipping. At one time, I had the fantasy we'd all finish the mission lifetime friends, visiting each other years after, comparing pictures of our grandchildren and complaining about the quality of young officers after our retirement. What a dream.

Steam rises from the hoarfrost accumulated during the night. It vanishes like a tramp after dinner.

Should we wish to send a message to Willy now, we shall have to unship the laser and remount it. The hash has increased and Willy says our signal is deteriorating.

More ice falls during the night. Linker kept track of them. My insomnia has communicated itself to him—ideal for standing long watches. Ice falls are more frequent here than on Earth—the leavings of comets and the asteroids come through this thin atmosphere more easily. A small chunk came to within sixty meters of our site, leaving an impres- sive crater.

\*　　\*　　\*

Another break. Willy has relayed a message from Control. They managed to pick up and reconstruct our request for instructions on first contact. They must have thought we were joking. Here's part of the transmission:

"We think you're not content with finding giant vegetables on Mars. Dr. Wender advised on Martians . . . (hash) . . . some clear indications of their ability to fire large cylindrical bodies into space. Beware tripod machines. Second opinion from Frank: Not all green Martians are Tharks. He wants sample from Dejah Thoris—can you arrange for egg?"

I put on a pressure suit and went for a walk after the disappointment of the transmission. Linker suited up after me and followed for a while. I armed myself with a piece of aluminum from the salvaged pad. He carried nothing.

Swift Plateau is about four hundred kilometers across. At its northern perimeter, an aqueduct had once hoisted itself a kilometer or so and vaulted across the flats, covering fifteen kilometers of upland before dropping over the south rim into the Moab-Marduk Range. Our landing site is a kilometer from the closest stretch of fragments. Linker followed me to the edge of the field of green and blue grass, keeping quiet, looking behind apprehensively as if he expected something to pop up between us and the lander.

I had a notebook in my satchel and paused to sketch some of the piers the Winter Troops hadn't yet brought down. None of them were over four meters tall.

"I'm afraid of them," Linker said over the suit radio. I stopped my sketching to look at him.

"So?" I inquired with a touch of irritation. "We're all afraid of them."

"I'm not afraid because they'll hurt me. It's because of what they might bring out in me, if I give them half a chance. I don't want to hate them."

"Not even Cobb *hates* them," I said.

"Oh, yes he does," Linker said, nodding his head within the bulky helmet. "But he's afraid for his life. I fear for my self-respect."

I shook my helmet to show I didn't understand.

"Because I can't understand them. They're irrational. They don't seem to *see* us. They run around us, fulfilling some mission . . . they don't care whether we live or die. Yet I have to respect them—they're *alien*. The first intelligent creatures we've ever met."

"If they're intelligent," I reminded him.

"Come on, Mercer, they must be. They build."

"So did these," I said, waving a gloved hand at the field of shattered green bottles.

"I'm trying to make myself clear," he said, exasperated. "When I was in Mexico, I didn't understand the nationalists. Or the communists. Both sides were willing to kill their own people or allow them to starve if it won some small objective. It was sick. I even hated the ones we were supporting."

"The Martians aren't humans," I said. "We can't expect to understand their motives."

"Comes back double, then, don't you see? I want to understand, to know why—"

He suddenly switched his radio off, raised his hands in frustration, and turned to walk back to the lander.

Our automatic interrupts clicked on and Cobb spoke to us. "That's it, friends. We're blanketed by hash. I can't get through to Willy. We'll have to punch through with the laser."

"I'm on my way back," Linker said. "I'll help you set it up."

In a few minutes, I was alone on the field of ruins. I sat on a weather-pocked boulder and took out my sketchbook again. I mapped the directions from which we had been approached and attacked and compared them with the site of the eggs we had found. What I was looking for, with such ridiculously slim evidence, was a clear pattern of migration—say, from the hatcheries in a line with the sunrise. Nothing came of it.

Disgusted at my desperation, I was lost in a fog of something approaching misery when I glanced up . . . And jumped to my feet so fast I leaped a good three feet into the air, twisting my ankle as I came down. Two white Martians stared at me with their wide, blank gray eyes, eyelashes as long and expressive as a camel's. The fingers on their hands—each had three arms, but only two legs—shivered like mouse-whiskers, not nervous but seeking information. We had been too involved fending them off before to take note of their features. Now, at a loss what to do, I had all the time in the world.

Three long webbed toes, leather and dead-looking like sticks, met an odd two-jointed ankle which even now I can't reproduce on paper. Their thighs were knotted with muscles and covered with red and white stippled fur. They could hop or run like frightened deer—that much I knew from experience. Their hips were thickly furred. They defied my few semesters of training in biology by having trilateral symmetry between hips and neck, and bilateral below the hips. Three arms met at ingenious triangular shoulders, rising to short necks and mouselike faces. Their ears were mounted atop their heads and could fan out like unfolded directennas, or hide away if rough activity threatened them.

The Martians were fast when they wanted to be, and I had no idea what else they could eat besides the ruins, so I made no false moves.

One whickered like a horse, its voice reedy and distant in the thin atmosphere. The noise must have been impressively loud to reach my small, helmeted ears. It looked behind itself, twisting its head one-eighty to look as its behind-arm scratched a tuft of hair on its right shoulder. The back fur rippled appreciatively. Parrotlike, the head returned to calmly stare at me.

After half an hour, I sat down again on the boulder. I could still see the lander and the linear glint of the glider wings, but there was no sign of Cobb or Linker. Nobody was searching for me.

My suit was getting cold. Slowly, I checked my battery pack gauge and saw it was showing a low charge. Cautiously, in distinct stages, I stood and brushed my pressure suit. The Martian to my right jerked, fingers trembling, and I held my pose, apprehensive. With a swift motion, it pulled a green, fibrous piece of aqueduct-bridge girder from its stiff rump fur with its behind-arm and held it out to me. The piece was about thirty centimeters long, chewed all around. I straightened, extended one hand and accepted the gift.

Without further ado, the Martians twisted around and leaped across the plateau, running and leaping simultaneously.

Clutching my gift, I returned to the lander. My feet and fingers were numb when I arrived.

The tripod lay on the ground, legs spraddled. The ladder was nowhere to be seen. I had a moment's panic, thinking the lander had been attacked—but since I had kept it in sight, that didn't seem likely. I climbed into the lander's primary lock.

Inside, Linker clutched the laser in both hands, one finger resting lightly, nervously, on the unsheathed and delicate scandium-garnet rod. Cobb sat on the opposite side of the cabin, barely two meters from Linker, fuming.

"What in hell is going on?" I asked, puffing on my fingers and stamping my feet.

"Listen, Thoreau," Cobb said bitterly, "while you were out communing with nature, Gandhi here decided to make sure we can't harm any of the sweet little creatures."

I turned to Linker, focusing on his uncertain finger and the garnet. "What are you doing?"

"I'm not sure, Dan," he answered calmly, face blank. "I have a firm conviction, that's all I know. I have to be firm. Otherwise I'll be just like you and Cobb."

"I have a conviction, too," Cobb said. "I'm convinced you're nuts."

"You're seriously thinking about breaking that garnet?" I asked.

"Damned serious."

"We can fight them off with other things if we have to," I reasoned. "The assay charges, the core sample gun—"

"Don't give Cobb any more ideas," Linker said.

"But we can't talk to Willy if you break that garnet."

"Cobb saw two of the Winter Troops. He was going to take a potshot at them with this." Linker lifted the laser, face still blank.

I blinked for a few seconds, feeling myself flush with anger. "Jesus. Cobb, is that true?"

"I was sighting on them, in case there were more—"

"Were you going to shoot?"

"It was convenient. They might have been a vanguard."

"That's not very rational," I observed.

"I'm not sure I'm being rational, either," Linker said, fully aware how fragmented we were now, the sadness we all felt coming to the surface. His eyes were doglike, searching my face for understanding.

"I'll do anything necessary to make sure we all survive," Cobb said. "If that means killing a few Martians, then I'll do it. If it means disobeying the mission commander, then I'll do that, too."

"He refused to put the laser down, even when I gave him a direct order. That's mutiny."

"This isn't getting us anywhere," Cobb said.

"I won't vouch for your sanity," I said to Linker. "Not if you break that garnet. And I won't vouch for Cobb's, either. Taking potshots at possibly intelligent aliens." I remembered the stick. Damn it, they *were* intelligent! They had to be, advancing on a stranger and giving him a gift. . . . "I don't know what sort of speculative first-contact training we should have had, but in spirit if not in letter, Linker has to be closer to the ideal than you.

"We should be testing the brace on the pad and leveling the field in front of the glider. When we get out of here, we can argue philosophy all the way home. And to get home, we *need the laser*."

Linker nodded. "We'll just agree not to use it for anything but communication."

I looked at Cobb, finally making my decision, and wondering whether I was crazy, too. "I think Linker's right."

"Okay," Cobb said softly. "But there's going to be a hell of a row after we debrief."

"That's an understatement," I said.

This record, even if it survives, will probably be kept in the administration files for fifty or sixty years—or longer—to "protect the feelings of the families." But who can gainsay the judgment of the folks who put us here? Not I, humble Thoreau on Mars, as Cobb described me.

I did not reveal the gift to my crewmates until the laser had been remounted in the lander. I simply laid it on the table, wrapped in an airtight transparent specimen bag, while we rested and sipped hot chocolate. Linker was the first to pick it up, glancing at me, puzzled.

"We have enough of these, don't we?" he asked.

"It's been chewed on," I pointed out, reaching to run my

finger along the stick's surface. I told them about the two Martians. Cobb looked decidedly uncomfortable then.

"Did they chew on it in your presence?" Linker asked.

"No."

"Maybe they were offering food," Cobb said. "A peace offering?" His expression was sad, as if all the energy and anger had been drained and nothing much was left but regret.

"It's more than food," Linker said. "It's like stick-writing. . . . Ogham. The Irish and Britons used something similar centuries ago. Notches on the side of a stone or stick—a kind of alphabet. But this is much more complex. Here—there's an oval—"

"Unless it's a tooth mark," I said.

"Whether it's a tooth mark or not, it isn't random. There are five long marks beside it, and one mark about half the length of the others. That's about equal to one Deimotic month—five and a half days." My respect for Linker increased. He raised his eyebrows, looking for comfirmation, and started to hand the stick to me, then stopped and swung it around to Cobb. Mission commander reintegrating a disgruntled crew-member. A mist of tears came to my eyes.

"I don't think they've reached a high level of technology yet," Linker said.

Cobb looked up from the gift and grinned. "Technology?"

"They built the walls and structures Willy saw. I don't think any of us can argue that they're not intent on changing their environment. Unless we make asses out of ourselves and say their work is no more significant than a beaver dam, it's obvious they're advancing rapidly. They might use notched sticks for relaying information."

"So what's this?" I asked, pointing to the gift.

"Maybe it's a subpoena," Linker said.

*　　*　　*

While I've been recording the above, Cobb has gone outside to see how long it will take to clear the glider path. The field was chosen to be free of boulders—but anything bigger than a fist could skew us around dangerously. The sleds have been deployed. I've finished tamping the braces on the pad.

The glider and capsule check out. In an hour we'll laser a message to Willy and give our estimate on launch and rendezvous.

Willy tells us that most of Mesogaea and Memnonia are covered with walls. Meridiani Sinus, according to his telescope observations, has been crisscrossed with roads or trails. The white Martians are using the sand-filled black old resin reservoirs for some unknown purpose.

Edom Crater is as densely packed as a city. All this in less than two days. There must be millions of hatchlings at work.

I'll break again and supervise the glider power-up.

Linker and Cobb are dead.

Jesus, that hurts to write.

We had just tested the RATO automatic timers when a horde of Winter Troops marched across the plateau, about ninety deep and a good four kilometers abreast. I'm certain they weren't out to get us. It was one of those migrational sweeps, a screwball mass survey of geography, and incidentally a leveling of all the aqueduct-bridges from the last cycle.

They gave us our chance. We didn't reply.

Linker had finished clearing the path. They caught him a half kilometer from the lander. I think they just trampled him to death. They were moving much faster than a man can run. I imagine his face, eyebrows rising in query, maybe he even tried to smile or greet them, lifting a hand . . .

I can't get that out of my head. I have to concentrate.

Cobb knew exactly what to do. I think he didn't mount the laser solidly, leaving a few brackets loose enough so he could unship it and bring it down, ready for hand use at a minute's notice. He took it outside the ship with just helmet and oxygen on—it's about five or six degrees outside, daylight—and fired on the Winter Troops just before they reached the glider. There are dead and dying or blinded Martians all along the edge of the path.

They paid their casualties no heed. They did not bother with us, just pushed around and through, touching nothing, staying away from the area he was sweeping—the edge of the path.

They can climb like monkeys. They dropped over the rim of the plateau.

They didn't touch Cobb. The frayed cord on the laser killed him when he stepped on it coming back in.

Where was I? Inside the glider, monitoring the power-up. I couldn't hear a thing. It was all over by the time I got outside.

The laser is gone, but we've already sent our data to Willy. I have the return message. That's all I need for the moment. The glider and capsule are powered and ready.

I'll launch it by myself. I can do that.

When Willy's position is right. The timer is going. Everything will be automatic.

I'll make it to orbit.

Two hours. Less. I can't bring them in. I could, but what use? There are no facilities for dead astronauts aboard the orbiter. What hurts is I'll have a better margin with them gone, more fuel. I did not want it that way, I never thought of that, I swear to God.

The glider wings are crackling in the wind. The wind is coming at a perfect angle, thin but fast, about one hundred kilometers an hour. Enough to feel if I were outside.

I trust in an awful lot now that Linker and Cobb are gone.

Maybe it'll be over soon and I can stop this writing and stop feeling this pain.

Waiting. Just the right instant for launch. Timers, everything, on auto. I sit helpless and wait. My last instructions: three buttons and an instruction to the remotes to expand the wings to takeoff width and increase tension. Like a square-rigger. They check okay, flat now, waiting for the best gust and RATO fire. Then they'll drop into the proper configuration, dragonfly wings, for high atmosphere.

I spent some time learning Martian anatomy as I cleared the path of the few Cobb had let through. There are still a couple out there.

I killed one. It was in the Martian equivalent of pain. Pain/Cain. I hit it over the head with a rock pick. It died just like we do.

Linker died innocent.

I think I'm going to be sick.

Here it comes. RATOs on.

I'm in the first jet stream. Second wing mode—fore and aft foils have been jettisoned. I'm riding directly into the black wind. I can see stars, can see Mars red and brown and gray below.

Third wing mode. All wings jettisoned. Falling, my stomach says. Main engines on capsule are firing and I'm through the glider framework. I can see the glare and feel the punch and the wings are far down to port, twirling like a child's toy.

In low, uncertain orbit.

Willy's coming.

Last orbit before going home. Willy looked awfully good. I climbed inside of him through the transfer tunnel and requested a long drink of miserable orbiter water. "Hey, Willy Ley," I said, "you're the most beautiful thing I've ever seen." Of course, all he did was take care of me. No accusations.

He's the only friend I have now.

I spoke to mission control. That was not easy. An hour ago. I'm sitting by the telescope, having pushed Willy's sensors out of the way, doing my own surveying and surmising.

So far, the Winter Troops—I *assume* they're responsible—have zoned and partially built up Mare Tyrennhum, Hesperia, and Mare Cimmerium. They've done something I can't decipher or really describe in Aethiopis. By now I'm sure they've got to the old expedition landers in Syrtis Major and Minor. I don't know what they'll do with them. Maybe add them to the road-building material.

Maybe *understand* them.

I have no idea what they're like, no idea at all. I can't. We can't. They move too fast, grow along instinctive lines, perhaps. Instinct for culture and technology. They may not be intelligent in the way we define intelligence, not as individuals, anyway. But they do *move*.

Perhaps they're just resurrecting what their ancestors left them fifty, a hundred thousand years ago, before the long, warm, wet Spring of Mars drove them underground and brought up the sprouts of aqueduct-bridges.

At any rate, I've been in orbit for a week and a half. They've gone from cradle to sky in that time.

I've seen their balloons.

And I've seen the distant fires of their rockets, icy blue and sharp like hydroxy torches. They seem to be testing. In a few days, they'll have it.

Beware, Control. These brave lads will go far.

# Dead Run

**T**here aren't many hitchhikers on the road to Hell.

I noticed this dude from four miles away. He stood where the road is straight and level, crossing what looks like desert except it has all these little empty towns and motels and shacks. I had been on the road for about six hours and the folks in the cattle trailers behind me had been quiet for the last three—resigned, I guess—so my nerves had settled a bit and I decided to see what the dude was up to. Maybe he was one of the employees. That would be interesting, I thought.

Truth to tell, once the wailing settled down, I got pretty bored.

The dude was on the right-hand side of the road, thumb out. I piano-keyed down the gears and the air brakes hissed and squealed at the tap of my foot. The semi slowed and the big diesel made that gut-deep dinosaur-belch of shuddered-downness. I leaned across the cab as everything came to a halt and swung the door open.

"Where you heading?" I asked.

He laughed and shook his head, then spit on the soft shoulder. "I don't know," he said. "Hell, maybe." He was thin and tanned with long greasy black hair and bluejeans and a vest. His straw hat was dirty and full of holes, but the feathers around the crown were bright and new-looking, pheasant if I was any judge. A worn gold chain hung out of his vest going into his watch pocket. He wore old Frye boots with the toes turned up and soles thinner than my spare's retread. He looked an awful lot like I had when I hitchhiked out of Fresno, broke and unemployed, looking for work.

"Can I take you there?" I asked.

"Sho'." He climbed in and eased the door shut behind him, took out a kerchief and mopped his forehead, then blew his long nose and stared at me with bloodshot sleepless eyes. "What you hauling?" he asked.

"Souls," I said. "Whole shitload of them."

"What kind?" He was young, not more than twenty-five. He wanted to sound nonchalant but I could hear the nerves.

"Usual kind," I said. "Human. Got some Hare Krishnas this time. Don't look too close anymore."

I coaxed the truck along, wondering if the engine was as bad as it sounded. When we were up to speed—eighty, eighty-five, no smokies on *this* road—he asked, "How long you been hauling?"

"Two years."

"Good pay?"

"It'll do."

"Benefits?"

"Union like everyone else."

"I heard about that," he said. "In that little dump about two miles back."

"People live there?" I asked. I didn't think anything lived along the road.

"Yeah. Real down folks. They said Teamster bosses get carried in limousines when they go."

"Don't really matter how you get there, I suppose. The trip's short and forever is a long time."

"Getting there's all the fun?" he asked, trying for a grin. I gave him a shallow one.

"What're you doing out here?" I asked a few minutes later. "You aren't dead, are you?" I'd never heard of dead folks running loose or looking quite as vital as he did but I couldn't imagine anyone else being on the road. Dead folks—and drivers.

"No," he said. He was quiet for a bit. Then, slow, as if it embarrassed him, "I came to find my woman."

"Yeah?" Not much surprised me but that was a new twist. "There ain't no returning, you know."

"Sherill's her name, spelled like sheriff but with two L's."

"Got a cigarette?" I asked. I didn't smoke but I could use them later. He handed me the last three in a crush-proof pack, not just one but all, and didn't say anything.

"Haven't heard of her," I said. "But then, I don't get to converse with everybody I haul. And there are lots of trucks, lots of drivers."

"I know," he said. "But I heard about them benefits."

He had a crazy kind of sad look in his eye when he glanced at me and that made me angry. I tightened my jaw and stared straight ahead.

"You know," he said, "back in that town they tell some crazy stories. About how they use old trains for China and

**147**

India, and in Russia there's a tramline. In Mexico it's old buses
along roads, always at night—''

"Listen. I don't use all the benefits," I said. "I know
some do but I don't.''

"Sure, I got you," he said, nodding that exaggerated
goddamn youngfolks' nod, his whole neck and shoulders moving along, it's all right everything's cool.

"How you gonna find her?" I asked.

"I don't know. Do the road, ask the drivers.''

"How'd you get in?''

He didn't answer for a moment. "I'm coming here when I
die. That's pretty sure. It's not so hard for folks like me to get
in beforehand. And . . . my daddy was a driver. He told me the
route. By the way, my name's Bill.''

"Mine's John," I said.

"Glad to meet you.''

We didn't say much after that for a while. He stared out
the right window and I watched the desert and faraway shacks
go by. Soon the mountains came looming up—space seems
compressed on the road, especially once past the desert—and I
sped up for the approach. There was some noise from the back.

"What'll you do when you get off work?" Bill asked.

"Go home and sleep.''

"Nobody knows?''

"Just the union.''

"That's the way it was with Daddy, until just before the
end. Look, I didn't mean to make you mad or nothing. I'd just
heard about the perks, and I thought . . .'' He swallowed, his
Adam's apple bobbing. "Thought you might be able to help. I
don't know how I'll ever find Sherill. Maybe back in the
annex . . .''

"Nobody in their right minds goes into the yards by

choice," I said. "And you'd have to look over everybody that's died in the last four months. They're way backed up."

Bill took that like a blow across the face and I was sorry I'd said it. "She's only been gone a week," he said.

"Well," I said.

"My mom died two years ago, just before Daddy."

"The High Road," I said.

"What?"

"IIope they both got the High Road."

"Mom, maybe. Yeah. She did. But not Daddy. He knew." Bill hawked and spit out the window. "Sherill, she's here—but she don't belong."

I couldn't help but grin.

"No, man, I mean it, I belong but not her. She was in this car wreck couple of months back. Got pretty badly messed up. I'd dealed her dope at first and then fell in love with her and by the time she landed in the hospital she was, you know, hooked on about four different things."

My arms stiffened on the wheel.

"I tried to tell her when I visited that it wouldn't be good for her to get anything, no more dope, but she begged me. What could I do? I loved her." He wasn't looking out the window now. He was looking down at his worn boots and nodding. "She begged me, man. So I brought her stuff. I mean she took it all when they weren't looking. She just took it *all*. They pumped her out but her insides were just gone. I didn't hear about her being dead until two days ago and that really burned me. I was the only one who loved her and they didn't even tell me. I had to go up to her room and find her bed empty. Jesus. I hung out at Daddy's union hall. Someone talked to someone else and I found her name on a list. The Low Road."

I hadn't known it was that easy to find out; but then, I'd never traveled in dopers' territory. Dope can loosen a lot of lips.

"I don't use any of those perks," I said, just to make it clear I couldn't help him. "Folks in back got enough trouble without me. I think the union went too far there."

"Bet they felt you'd get lonely, need company," Bill said quietly, looking at me. "It don't hurt the folks back there. Maybe give them another chance to, you know, think things over. Give 'em relief for a couple of hours, a break from the mash—"

"Listen, a couple of hours don't mean nothing in relation to eternity. I'm not so sure I won't be joining them someday, and if that's the way it is I want it smooth, nobody pulling me out of a trailer and putting me back in."

"Yeah," he said. "Got you, man. I know where that's at. But she might be back there right now, and all you'd have to—"

"Bad enough I'm driving this rig in the first place." I wanted to change the subject.

"Yeah. How'd that happen?"

"Couple of accidents. Hot-rodding with an old fart in a Triumph. Nearly ran over some joggers on a country road. My premiums went up to where I couldn't afford payments and finally they took my truck away."

"You coulda gone without insurance."

"Not me," I said. "Anyway, some bad word got out. No companies would hire me. I went to the union to see if they could help. They told me I was a dead-ender, either get out of trucking or . . ." I shrugged. "This. I couldn't leave trucking. It's bad out there, getting work. Lots of unemployed. Couldn't see myself pushing a hack in some big city."

"No, man," Bill said, giving me that whole-body nod again. He cackled sympathetically.

"They gave me an advance, enough for a down payment on my rig." The truck was grinding a bit but maintaining. Over the mountains, through a really impressive pass like from an old engraving, and down in a rugged rocky valley, was the City. I'd deliver my cargo, get my slip, and take the rig (with Bill) back to Baker. Park it in the yard next to my cottage after letting him out someplace sane.

Get some sleep.

Start over again next Monday, two loads a week.

"I don't think I'd better go on," Bill said. "I'll hitch with some other rig, ask around."

"Well, I'd feel better if you rode with me back out of here. Want my advice?" Bad habit. "Go home—"

"No," Bill said. "Thanks anyway. I can't go home. Not without Sherill. She don't belong here." He took a deep breath. "I'll try to work up a trade. I stay, she goes to the High Road. That's the way the game runs down here, isn't it?"

I didn't tell him otherwise. I couldn't be sure he wasn't right. He'd made it this far. At the top of the pass I pulled the rig over and let him out. He waved at me, I waved back, and we went our separate ways.

Poor rotten doping sonofabitch. I'd screwed up my life half a dozen different ways—three wives, liquor, three years at Tehachapi—but I'd never done dope. I felt self-righteous just listening to the dude. I was glad to be rid of him, truth be told.

The City looks a lot like a county full of big white cathedrals. Casting against type. High wall around the perimeter, stretching as far as my eye can see. No horizon but a vanishing point, the wall looking like an endless highway turned on its side. As I geared the truck down for the decline, the noise in the trailers got irritating again. They could smell what was coming, I guess, like pigs stepping up to the man with the knife.

I pulled into the disembarkation terminal and backed the first trailer up to the holding pen. Employees let down the gates and used some weird kind of prod to herd them. These people were past mortal.

Employees unhooked the first trailer and I backed in the second.

I got down out of the cab and an employee came up to me, a big fellow with red eyes and brand new coveralls. "Good ones this load?" he asked. His breath was like the end of a cabbage, bean and garlic dinner.

I shook my head and held a cigarette out for a light. He pressed his fingernail against the tip. The tip flared and settled down to a steady glow. He looked at it with pure lust.

"Listen," I said. "You had anyone named Sherill through here?"

"Who's asking?" he grumbled, still eyeing the cigarette. He started to do a slow dance.

"Just curious. I heard you guys knew all the names."

"So?" He stopped. He had to walk around, otherwise his shoes melted the asphalt and got stuck. He came back and stood, lifting one foot, twisting a bit, then putting it down and lifting the other.

"So," I said, with as much sense.

"Like Cherry with an L?

"No. Sherill, like sheriff but with two L's."

"Couple of Cheryls. No Sherills," he said. "Now . . ."

I handed him the cigarette. They loved the things. "Thanks," I said. I pulled another out of the pack and gave it to him. He popped both of them into his mouth and chewed, bliss pushing over his seamed face. Tobacco smoke came out his nose and he swallowed. "Nothing to it," he said, and walked on.

The road back is shorter than the road in. Don't ask how. I'd have thought it was the other way around but barriers are what's important not distance. Maybe we all get our chances so the road to Hell is long. But once we're there, there's no returning. You have to save on the budget somewhere.

I took the empties back to Baker. Didn't see Bill. Eight hours later I was in bed, beer in hand, paycheck on the bureau, my eyes wide open.

Shit, I thought. Now my conscience was working. I could have sworn I was past that. But then I didn't use the perks. I wouldn't drive without insurance.

I wasn't really cut out for the life.

There are no normal days and nights on the road to Hell. No matter how long you drive, it's always the same time when you arrive as when you left, but it's not necessarily the same time from trip to trip.

The next trip it was cool dusk and the road didn't pass through desert and small, empty towns. Instead, it crossed a bleak flatland of skeletal trees, all the same uniform gray as if cut from paper. When I pulled over to catch a nap—never sleeping more than two hours at a stretch—the shouts of the damned in the trailers bothered me even more than usual. Silly things they said, like:

"You can take us back, mister! You really can!"

"Can he?"

"Shit no, mofuck pig."

"You can let us out! We can't hurt you!"

That was true enough. Drivers were alive and the dead could never hurt the living. But I'd heard what happened when you let them out. There were about ninety of them in back and in any load there was always one would make you want to use your perks.

I scratched my itches in the narrow bunk, looking at the Sierra Club calendar hanging just below the fan. The Devil's

Postpile. The load became quieter as the voices gave up, one after the other. There was one last shout—some obscenity—then silence.

It was then I decided I'd let them out and see if Sherill was there, or if anyone knew her. They mingled in the annex, got their last socializing before the City. Someone might know. Then if I saw Bill again—

What? What could I do to help him? He had screwed Sherill up royally, but then she'd had a hand in it too, and that was what Hell was all about. Poor stupid sons of bitches.

I swung out of the cab, tucking in my shirt and pulling my straw hat down on my crown. "Hey!" I said, walking alongside the trailers. Faces peered at me from the two inches between each white slat. "I'm going to let you out. Just for a while. I need some information."

"Ask!" someone screamed. "Just ask, goddammit!"

"You know you can't run away. You can't hurt me. You're all dead. Understand?"

"We know," said another voice, quieter.

"Maybe we can help."

"I'm going to open the gates one trailer at a time." I went to the rear trailer first, took out my keys and undid the Yale padlock. Then I swung the gates open, standing back a little like there was some kind of infected wound about to drain.

They were all naked but they weren't dirty. I'd seen them in the annex yards and at the City; I knew they weren't like concentration camp prisoners. The dead can't really be unhealthy. Each just had some sort of air about him telling why he was in Hell; nothing specific but subliminal.

Like three black dudes in the rear trailer, first to step out. Why they were going to Hell was all over their faces. They weren't in the least sorry for the lives they'd led. They wanted to keep on doing what had brought them here in the first place—scavenging, hurting, hurting *me* in particular.

"Stupid ass mofuck," one of them said, staring at me beneath thin, expressive eyebrows. He nodded and swung his fists, trying to pound the slats from the outside, but the blows hardly made them vibrate.

An old woman crawled down, hair white and neatly coifed. I couldn't be certain what she had done but she made me uneasy. She might have been the worst in the load. And lots of others, young, old, mostly old. Quiet for the most part.

They looked me over, some defiant, most just bewildered.

"I need to know if there's anyone here named Sherill," I said, "who happens to know a fellow named Bill."

"That's my name," said a woman hidden in the crowd.

"Let me see her." I waved my hand at them. The black dudes came forward. A funny look got in their eyes and they backed away. The others parted and a young woman walked out. "How do you spell your name?" I asked.

She got a panicked expression. She spelled it, hesitating, hoping she'd make the grade. I felt horrible already. She was a Cheryl.

"Not who I'm looking for," I said.

"Don't be hasty," she said, real soft. She wasn't trying hard to be seductive but she was succeeding. She was very pretty with medium-sized breasts, hips like a teenager's, legs not terrific but nice. Her black hair was clipped short and her eyes were almost Oriental. I figured maybe she was Lebanese or some other kind of Middle Eastern.

I tried to ignore her. "You can walk around a bit," I told them. "I'm letting out the first trailer now." I opened the side gates on that one and the people came down. They didn't smell, didn't look hungry, they just all looked pale. I wondered if the

155

torment had begun already, but if so, I decided, it wasn't the physical kind.

One thing I'd learned in my two years was that all the Sunday school and horror movie crap about Hell was dead wrong.

"Woman named Sherill," I repeated. No one stepped forward. Then I felt someone close to me and I turned. It was the Cheryl woman. She smiled. "I'd like to sit up front for a while," she said.

"So would we all, sister," said the white-haired old woman. The black dudes stood off separate, talking low.

I swallowed, looking at her. Other drivers said they were real insubstantial except at one activity. That was the perk. And it was said the hottest ones always ended up in Hell.

"No," I said. I motioned for them to get back into the trailers. Whatever she was on the Low Road for, it wouldn't affect her performance in the sack, that was obvious.

It had been a dumb idea all around. They went back and I returned to the cab, lighting up a cigarette and thinking what had made me do it.

I shook my head and started her up. Thinking on a dead run was no good. "No," I said, "goddamn," I said, "good."

Cheryl's face stayed with me.

Cheryl's body stayed with me longer than the face.

Something always comes up in life to lure a man onto the Low Road, not driving but riding in the back. We all have some weakness. I wondered what reason God had to give us each that little flaw, like a chip in crystal, you press the chip hard enough everything splits up crazy.

At least now I knew one thing. My flaw wasn't sex, not this way. What most struck me about Cheryl was wonder. She was so pretty; how'd she end up on the Low Road?

For that matter, what had Bill's Sherill done?

I returned hauling empties and found myself this time outside a small town called Shoshone. I pulled my truck into the cafe parking lot. The weather was cold and I left the engine running. It was about eleven in the morning and the cafe was half full. I took a seat at the counter next to an old man with maybe four teeth in his head, attacking French toast with downright solemn dignity. I ordered eggs and hashbrowns and juice, ate quickly, and went back to my truck.

Bill stood next to the cab. Next to him was an enormous young woman with a face like a bulldog. She was wrapped in a filthy piece of plaid fabric that might have been snatched from a trash dump somewhere. "Hey," Bill said. "Remember me?"

"Sure."

"I saw you pulling up. I thought you'd like to know . . . This is Sherill. I got her out of there." The woman stared at me with all the expression of a brick. "It's all screwy. Like a power failure or something. We just walked out on the road and nobody stopped us."

Sherill could have hid any number of weirdnesses beneath her formidable looks and gone unnoticed by ordinary folks. But I didn't have any trouble picking out the biggest thing wrong with her: she was dead. Bill had brought her out of Hell. I looked around to make sure I was in the World. I was. He wasn't lying. Something serious had happened on the Low Road.

"Trouble?" I asked.

"Lots." He grinned at me. "Pan-demon-ium." His grin broadened.

"That can't happen," I said. Sherill trembled, hearing my voice.

"He's a *driver*, Bill," she said. "He's the one takes us there. We should git out of here." She had that soul-branded air and the look of a pig that's just escaped slaughter, seeing the butcher again. She took a few steps backward. Gluttony, I thought. Gluttony and buried lust and a real ugly way of seeing life, inner eye pulled all out of shape by her bulk.

Bill hadn't had much to do with her ending up on the Low Road.

"Tell me more," I said.

"There's folks running all over down there, holing up in them towns, devils chasing them—"

"Employees," I corrected.

"Yeah. Every which way."

Sherill tugged on his arm. "We got to go, Bill."

"We got to go," he echoed. "Hey, man, thanks. I found her!" He nodded his whole-body nod and they were off down the street, Sherill's plaid wrap dragging in the dirt.

I drove back to Baker, wondering if the trouble was responsible for my being rerouted through Shoshone. I parked in front of my little house and sat inside with a beer while it got dark, checking my calendar for the next day's run and feeling very cold. I can take so much supernatural in its place, but now things were spilling over, smudging the clean-drawn line between my work and the World. Next day I was scheduled to be at the annex and take another load.

Nobody called that evening. If there was trouble on the Low Road, surely the union would let me know, I thought.

I drove to the annex early in the morning. The crossover from the World to the Low Road was normal; I followed the route and the sky muddied from blue to solder-color and I was on the first leg to the annex. I backed the rear trailer up to the yard's gate and unhitched it, then placed the forward trailer at a ramp, all the while keeping my ears tuned to pick up interesting conversation.

The employees who work the annex look human. I took my invoice from a red-faced old guy with eyes like billiard balls and looked at him like I was in the know but could use some updating. He spit smoking saliva on the pavement, returned my look slantwise and said nothing. Maybe it was all settled. I hitched up both full trailers and pulled out.

I didn't even mention Sherill and Bill. Like in most jobs keeping one's mouth shut is good policy. That and don't volunteer.

It was the desert again this time, only now the towns and tumbledown houses looked bomb-blasted, like something big had come through flushing out game with a howitzer.

Eyes on the road. Push that rig.

Four hours in, I came to a roadblock. Nobody on it, no employees, just big carved-lava barricades cutting across all lanes and beyond them a yellow smoke which, the driver's unwritten instructions advised, meant absolutely no entry.

I got out. The load was making noises. I suddenly hated them. Nothing beautiful there—just naked Hell-bounders shouting and screaming and threatening like it wasn't already over for them. They'd had their chance and crapped out and now they were still bullshitting the World.

Least they could do was go with dignity and spare me their misery.

That's probably what the engineers on the trains to Auschwitz thought. Yeah, yeah, except I was the fellow who might be hauling those engineers to their just deserts.

Crap, I just couldn't be one way or the other about the whole thing. I could feel mad and guilty and I could think Jesus, probably I'll be complaining just as much when my time comes. Jesus H. Twentieth Century Man Christ.

I stood by the truck, waiting for instructions or some indication what I was supposed to do. The load became quieter after a while but I heard noises off the road, screams mostly and far away.

"There isn't anything," I said to myself, lighting up one of Bill's cigarettes even though I don't smoke and dragging deep, "*anything* worth this shit." I vowed I would quit after this run.

I heard something come up behind the trailers and I edged closer to the cab steps. High wisps of smoke obscured things at first but a dark shape three or four yards high plunged through and stood with one hand on the top slats of the rear trailer. It was covered with naked people, crawling all over, biting and scratching and shouting obscenities. It made little grunting noises, fell to its knees, then stood again and lurched off the road. Some of the people hanging on saw me and shouted for me to come help.

"Help us get this sonofabitch down!"

"Hey, you! We've almost got 'im!"

"He's a driver—"

"Fuck 'im, then."

I'd never seen an employee so big before, nor in so much trouble. The load began to wail like banshees. I threw down my cigarette and ran after it.

Workers will tell you. Camaraderie extends even to those on the job you don't like. If they're in trouble it's part of the mystique to help out. Besides, the unwritten instructions were very clear on such things and I've never knowingly broken a job rule—not since getting my rig back—and couldn't see starting now.

Through the smoke and across great ridges of lava, I ran until I spotted the employee about ten yards ahead. It had shaken off the naked people and was standing with one in each hand. Its shoulders smoked and scales stood out at all angles. They'd really done a job on the bastard. Ten or twelve of the dead were picking themselves off the lava, unscraped, unbruised. They saw me.

The employee saw me.

Everyone came at me. I turned and ran for the truck, stumbling, falling, bruising and scraping myself everywhere. My hair stood on end. People grabbed me, pleading for me to haul them out, old, young, all fawning and screeching like whipped dogs.

Then the employee swung me up out of reach. Its hand was cold and hard like iron tongs kept in a freezer. It grunted and ran toward my truck, opening the door wide and throwing me roughly inside. It made clear with huge, wild gestures that I'd better turn around and go back, that waiting was no good and there was no way through.

I started the engine and turned the rig around. I rolled up my window and hoped the dead weren't substantial enough to scratch paint or tear up slats.

All rules were off now. What about the ones in my load? All the while I was doing these things my head was full of questions, like how could souls fight back and wasn't there some inflexible order in Hell that kept such things from happening? That was what had been implied when I hired on. Safest job around.

I headed back down the road. My load screamed like no load I'd ever had before. I was afraid they might get loose but they didn't. I got near the annex and they were quiet again, too quiet for me to hear over the diesel.

The yards were deserted. The long, white-painted cement platforms and whitewashed wood-slat loading ramps were unattended. No souls in the pens.

The sky was an indefinite gray. An out-of-focus yellow sun gleamed faintly off the stark white employee's lounge. I stopped the truck and swung down to investigate.

There was no wind, only silence. The air was frosty without being particularly cold. What I wanted to do most was

unload and get out of there, go back to Baker or Barstow or
Shoshone.

I hoped that was still possible. Maybe all exits had been
closed. Maybe the overseers had closed them to keep any more
souls from getting out.

I tried the gate latches and found I could open them. I did
so and returned to the truck, swinging the rear trailer around
until it was flush with the ramp. Nobody made a sound. "Go on
back," I said. "Go on back. You've got more time here. Don't
ask me how."

"Hello, John." That was behind me. I turned and saw an
older man without any clothes on. I didn't recognize him at
first. His eyes finally clued me in.

"Mr. Martin?" My high school history teacher. I hadn't
seen him in maybe twenty years. He didn't look much older,
but then I'd never seen him naked. He was dead, but he wasn't
like the others. He didn't have that look that told me why he
was here.

"This is not the sort of job I'd expect one of my students
to take," Martin said. He laughed the smooth laugh he was
famous for, the laugh that seemed to take everything he said in
class and put it in perspective.

"You're not the first person I'd expect to find here," I
responded.

"The cat's away, John. The mice are in charge now. I'm
going to try to leave."

"How long you been here?" I asked.

"I died a month ago, I think," Martin said, never one to
mince words.

"You can't leave," I said. Doing my job even with Mr.
Martin. I felt the ice creep up my throat.

"Team player," Martin said. "Still the screwball team
player, even when the team doesn't give a damn what you do."

I wanted to explain but he walked away toward the annex and the road out. Looking back over his shoulder, he said, "Get smart, John. Things aren't what they seem. Never have been."

"Look!" I shouted after him. "I'm going to quit, honest, but this load is my responsibility." I thought I saw him shake his head as he rounded the corner of the annex.

The dead in my load had pried loose some of the ramp slats and were jumping off the rear trailer. Those in the forward trailer were screaming and carrying on, shaking the whole rig.

Responsibility, shit, I thought. As the dead followed after Mr. Martin, I unhitched both trailers. Then I got in the cab and swung away from the annex, onto the incoming road. "I'm going to quit," I said. "Sure as anything, I'm going to quit."

The road out seemed awfully long. I didn't see any of the dead, surprisingly, but then maybe they'd been shunted away. I was taking a route I'd never been on before and I had no way of knowing if it would put me where I wanted to be. But I hung in there for two hours, running the truck dead-out on the flats.

The air was getting grayer like somebody turning down the contrast on a TV set. I switched on the high-beams but they didn't help. By now I was shaking in the cab and saying to myself, Nobody deserves this. Nobody deserves going to Hell no matter what they did. I was scared. It was getting colder.

Three hours and I saw the annex and yards ahead of me again. The road had looped back. I swore and slowed the rig to a crawl. The loading docks had been set on fire. Dead were wandering around with no idea what to do or where to go. I sped up and drove over the few that were on the road. They'd come up and the truck's bumper would hit them and I wouldn't feel a thing, like they weren't there. I'd see them in the rearview mirror, getting up after being knocked over. Just knocked over. Then I was away from the loading docks and there was no doubt about it this time.

I was heading straight for Hell.

The disembarkation terminal was on fire, too. But beyond it the City was bright and white and untouched. For the first time I drove past the terminal and took the road into the City.

It was either that or stay on the flats with everything screwy. Inside, I thought maybe they'd have things under control.

The truck roared through the gate between two white pillars maybe seventy or eighty feet thick and as tall as the Washington Monument. I didn't see anybody, employees or the dead. Once I was through the pillars—and it came as a shock—

There was no City, no walls, just the road winding along and countryside in all directions, even behind.

The countryside was covered with shacks, houses, little clusters and big clusters. Everything was tight-packed, people working together on one hill, people sitting on their porches, walking along paths, turning to stare at me as the rig barreled on through. No employees—no monsters. No flames. No bloody lakes or rivers.

This must be the outside part, I thought. Deeper inside it would get worse.

I kept on driving. The dog part of me was saying let's go look for authority and ask some questions and get out. But the monkey was saying let's just go look and find out what's going on, what Hell is all about.

Another hour of driving through that calm, crowded land-scape and the truck ran out of fuel. I coasted to the side and stepped down from the cab, very nervous.

Again I lit up a cigarette and leaned against the fender, shaking a little. But the shaking was running down and a tight kind of calm was replacing it.

The landscape was still condensed, crowded, but nobody looked tortured. No screaming, no eternal agony. Trees and shrubs and grass hills and thousands and thousands of little houses.

It took about ten minutes for the inhabitants to get around to investigating me. Two men came over to my truck and nodded cordially. Both were middle-aged and healthy-looking. They didn't look dead. I nodded back.

"We were betting whether you're one of the drivers or not," said the first, a black-haired fellow. He wore a simple handwoven shirt and pants. "I think you are. That so?"

"I am."

"You're lost, then."

I agreed. "Maybe you can tell me where I am?"

"Hell," said the second man, younger by a few years and just wearing shorts. The way he said it was just like you might say you came from Los Angeles or Long Beach. Nothing big, nothing dramatic.

"We've heard rumors there's been problems outside," a woman said, coming up to join us. She was about sixty and skinny. She looked like she should be twitchy and nervous but she acted rock-steady. They were all rock-steady.

"There's some kind of strike," I said. "I don't know what it is, but I'm looking for an employee to tell me."

"They don't usually come this far in," the first man said. "We run things here. Or rather, nobody tells us what to do."

"You're alive?" the woman asked, a curious hunger in her voice. Others came around to join us, a whole crowd. They didn't try to touch. They stood their ground and stared and talked.

"Look," said an old black fellow. "You ever read about the Ancient Mariner?"

I said I had in school.

"Had to tell everybody what he did," the black fellow said. The woman beside him nodded slowly. "We're all Ancient Mariners here. But there's nobody to tell it to. Would you like to know?'' The way he asked was pitiful. ''We're sorry. We just want everybody to know how sorry we are.''

''I can't take you back,'' I said. ''I don't know how to get there myself.''

''We can't go back,'' the woman said. ''That's not our place.''

More people were coming and I was nervous again. I stood my ground trying to seem calm and the dead gathered around me, eager.

''I never thought of anybody but myself,'' one said. Another interrupted with, ''Man, I fucked my whole life away, I hated everybody and everything. I was burned out—''

''I thought I was the greatest. I could pass judgment on everybody—''

''I was the stupidest goddamn woman you ever saw. I was a sow, a pig. I farrowed kids and let them run wild, without no guidance. I was stupid and cruel, too. I used to hurt things—''

''Never cared for anyone. Nobody ever cared for me. I was left to rot in the middle of a city and I wasn't good enough not to rot.''

''Everything I did was a lie after I was about twelve years old—''

''Listen to me, mister, because it hurts, it hurts so bad—''

I backed up against my truck. They were lining up now, organized, not like any mob. I had a crazy thought they were behaving better than any people on Earth, but these were the damned.

I didn't hear or see anybody famous. An ex-cop told me about what he did to people in jails. A Jesus-freak told me that knowing Jesus in your heart wasn't enough. ''Because I should have made it, man, I should have made it.''

''A time came and I was just broken by it all, broke myself

really. Just kept stepping on myself and making all the wrong decisions—''

They confessed to me, and I began to cry. Their faces were so clear and so pure, yet here they were, confessing, and except maybe for specific things—like the fellow who had killed Ukrainians after the Second World War in Russian camps—they didn't sound any worse than the crazy sons of bitches I called friends who spent their lives in trucks or bars or whorehouses.

They were all recent. I got the impression the deeper into Hell you went, the older the damned became, which made sense; Hell just got bigger, each crop of damned got bigger, with more room on the outer circles.

"We wasted it," someone said. "You know what my greatest sin was? I was dull. Dull and cruel. I never saw beauty. I saw only dirt. I loved the dirt and the clean just passed me by."

Pretty soon my tears were uncontrollable. I kneeled down beside the truck, hiding my head, but they kept on coming and confessing. Hundreds must have passed, talking quietly, gesturing with their hands.

Then they stopped. Someone had come and told them to back away, that they were too much for me. I took my face out of my hands and a very young-seeming fellow stood looking down on me. "You all right?" he asked.

I nodded, but my insides were like broken glass. With every confession I had seen myself, and with every tale of sin I had felt an answering echo.

"Someday, I'm going to be here. Someone's going to drive me in a cattle car to Hell," I mumbled. The young fellow helped me to my feet and cleared a way around my truck.

"Yeah, but not now," he said. "You don't belong here yet." He opened the door to my cab and I got back inside.

"I don't have any fuel," I said.

He smiled that sad smile they all had and stood on the step, up close to my ear. "You'll be taken out of here soon anyway. One of the employees is bound to get around to you." He seemed a lot more sophisticated than the others. I looked at him maybe a little queerly, like there was some explaining in order.

"Yeah, I know all that stuff," he said. "I was a driver once. Then I got promoted. What are they all doing back there?" He gestured up the road. "They're really messing things up now, ain't they?"

"I don't know," I said, wiping my eyes and cheeks with my sleeve.

"You go back, and you tell them that all this revolt on the outer circles, it's what I expected. Tell them Charlie's here and that I warned them. Word's getting around. There's bound to be discontent."

"Word?"

"About who's in charge. Just tell them Charlie knows and I warned them. I know something else, and you shouldn't tell anybody about this . . ." He whispered an incredible fact into my ear then, something that shook me deeper than what I had already been through.

I closed my eyes. Some shadow passed over. The young fellow and everybody else seemed to recede. I felt rather than saw my truck being picked up like a toy.

Then I suppose I was asleep for a time.

In the cab in the parking lot of a truck stop in Bakersfield, I jerked awake, pulled my cap out of my eyes and looked around. It was about noon. There was a union hall in Bakersfield. I checked and my truck was full of diesel, so I started her up and drove to the union hall.

I knocked on the door of the office. I went in and recognized the fat old dude who had given me the job in the first place. I was tired and I smelled bad but I wanted to get it all done with now.

He recognized me but didn't know my name until I told him. "I can't work the run anymore," I said. The shakes were on me again. "I'm not the one for it. I don't feel right driving them when I know I'm going to be there myself, like as not."

"Okay," he said, slow and careful, sizing me up with a knowing eye. "But you're out. You're busted then. No more driving, no more work for us, no more work for any union we support. It'll be lonely."

"I'll take that kind of lonely any day," I said.

"Okay." That was that. I headed for the door and stopped with my hand on the knob.

"One more thing," I said. "I met Charlie. He says to tell you word's getting around about who's in charge, and that's why there's so much trouble in the outer circles."

The old dude's knowing eye went sort of glassy. "You're the fellow got into the City?"

I nodded.

He got up from his seat real fast, jowls quivering and belly doing a silly dance beneath his work blues. He flicked one hand at me, come 'ere. "Don't go. Just you wait a minute. Outside in the office."

I waited and heard him talking on the phone. He came out smiling and put his hand on my shoulder. "Listen, John, I'm not sure we should let you quit. I didn't know you were the one who'd gone inside. Word is, you stuck around and tried to help when everybody else ran. The company appreciates that. You've been with us a long time, reliable driver, maybe we should give you some incentive to stay. I'm sending you to Vegas to talk with a company man . . . ."

The way he said it, I knew there wasn't much choice and I

better not fight it. You work union long enough and you know when you keep your mouth shut and go along.

They put me up in a motel and fed me and by late morning I was on my way to Vegas, arriving about two in the afternoon. I was in a black union car with a silent driver and air conditioning and some *Newsweek*s to keep me company.

The limo dropped me off in front of a four-floor office building, glass and stucco, with lots of divorce lawyers and a dentist and small companies with anonymous names. White plastic letters on a ribbed felt background in a glass case. There was no name on the office number I had been told to go to, but I went up and knocked anyway.

I don't know what I expected. A district supervisor opened the door and asked me a few questions and I said what I'd said before. I was adamant. He looked worried. "Look," he said. "It won't be good for you now if you quit."

I asked him what he meant by that but he just looked unhappy and said he was going to send me to somebody higher up.

That was in Denver, nearer my God to thee. The same black car took me there and Saturday morning, bright and early, I stood in front of a very large corporate building with no sign out front and a bank on the bottom floor. I went past the bank and up to the very top.

A secretary met me, pretty but her hair done up very tight and her jaw grimly square. She didn't like me. She let me into the next office, though.

I swear I'd seen the fellow before, but maybe it was just a passing resemblance. He wore a narrow tie and a tasteful but conservative gray suit. His shirt was pastel blue and there was a big Rembrandt Bible on his desk, sitting on the glass top next to an alabaster pen holder. He shook my hand firmly and perched on the edge of the desk.

"First, let me congratulate you on your bravery. We've had some reports from the ... uh ... field, and we're hearing nothing but good about you." He smiled like that fellow on TV who's always asking the audience to give him some help. Then his face got sincere and serious. I honestly believe he was sincere; he was also well trained in dealing with not-very-bright people. "I hear you have a report for me. From Charles Frick."

"He said his name was Charlie." I told him the story. "What I'm curious about, what did he mean, this thing about who's in charge?"

"Charlie was in Organization until last year. He died in a car accident. I'm shocked to hear he got the Low Road." He didn't look shocked. "Maybe I'm shocked but not surprised. To tell the truth, he was a bit of a troublemaker." He smiled brightly again and his eyes got large and there was a little too much animation in his face. He had on these MacArthur wire-rimmed glasses too big for his eyes.

"What did he mean?"

"John, I'm proud of all our drivers. You don't know how proud we all are of you folks down there doing the dirty work."

"What did Charlie mean?"

"The abortionists and pornographers, the hustlers and muggers and murderers. Atheists and heathens and idol-worshippers. Surely there must be some satisfaction in keeping the land clean. Sort of a giant sanitation squad, you people keep the scum away from the good folks. The plain good folks. Now we know that driving's maybe the hardest job we have in the company, and that not everyone can stay on the Low Road indefinitely. Still, we'd like you to stay on. Not as a driver— unless you really wish to continue. For the satisfaction of a tough job. No, if you want to move up—and you've earned it by now, surely—we have a place for you here. A place where you'll be comfortable and—"

171

"I've already said I want out. You're acting like I'm hot stuff and I'm just shit. You know that, I know that. What is going on?"

His face hardened on me. "It isn't easy up here, either, buster." The "buster" bit tickled me. I laughed and got up from the chair. I'd been in enough offices and this fancy one just made me queasy. When I stood, he held up his hand and pursed his lips as he nodded. "Sorry. There's incentive, there's certainly a reason why you should want to work here. If you're so convinced you're on your way to the Low Road, you can work it off here, you know."

"How can you say that?"

Bright smile. "Charlie told you something. He told you about who's in charge here."

Now I could smell something terribly wrong, like with the union boss. I mumbled, "He said that's why there's trouble."

"It comes every now and then. We put it down gentle. I tell you where we really need good people, compassionate people. We need them to help with the choosing."

"Choosing?"

"Surely you don't think the Boss does all the choosing directly?"

I couldn't think of a thing to say.

"Listen, the Boss . . . let me tell you. A long time ago, the Boss decided to create a new kind of worker, one with more decision-making ability. Some of the supervisors disagreed, especially when the Boss said the workers would be around for a long, long time—that they'd be indestructible. Sort of like nuclear fuel, you know. Human souls. The waste builds up after a time, those who turn out bad, turn out to be chronically unemployable. They don't go along with the scheme, or get out of line. Can't get along with their fellow workers. You know the type. What do you do with them? Can't just let them go away—they're indestructible, and that ain't no joke, so—''

''Chronically unemployable?''

''You're a union man. Think of what it must feel like to be out of work . . . *forever*. Damned. Nobody will hire you.''

I knew the feeling, both the way he meant it and the way it had happened to me.

''The Boss feels the project half succeeded, so He doesn't dump it completely. But He doesn't want to be bothered with all the pluses and minuses, the bookkeeping.''

''*You're* in charge,'' I said, my blood cooling.

And I knew where I had seen him before.

On television.

God's right-hand man.

And human. Flesh-and-blood.

*We* ran Hell.

He nodded. ''Now, that's not the sort of thing we'd like to get around.''

''You're in charge, and you let the drivers take their perks on the loads, you let—'' I stopped, instinct telling me I would soon be on a rugged trail with no turnaround.

''I'll tell you the truth, John. I have only been in charge here for a year, and my predecessor let things get out of hand. He wasn't a religious man, John, and he thought this was a job like any other, where you could compromise now and then. I know that isn't so. There's no compromise here, and we'll straighten out those inequities and bad decisions very soon. You'll help us, I hope. You may know more about the problems than we do.''

''How do you . . . how do you qualify for a job like this?'' I asked. ''And who offered it to you?''

''Not the Boss, if that's what you're getting at, John. It's been kind of traditional. You may have heard about me. I'm the one, when there was all this talk about after-death experiences and everyone was seeing bright light and beauty, I'm the one who wondered why no one was seeing the other side. I found people who had almost died and had seen Hell, and I turned their lives around. The management in the company decided a fellow with my ability could do good work here. And so I'm here. And I'll tell you, it isn't easy. I sometimes wish we had a little more help from the Boss, a little more guidance, but we don't, and somebody has to do it. Somebody has to clean out the stables, John." Again the smile.

I put on my mask. "Of course," I said. I hoped a gradual increase in piety would pass his sharp-eyed muster.

"And you can see how this all makes you much more valuable to the organization."

I let light dawn slowly.

"We'd hate to lose you now, John. Not when there's security, so much security, working for us. I mean, here we learn the real ins and outs of salvation."

I let him talk at me until he looked at his watch, and all the time I nodded and considered and tried to think of the best ploy. Then I eased myself into a turnabout. I did some confessing until his discomfort was stretched too far—I was keeping him from an important appointment—and made my concluding statement.

"I just wouldn't feel right up here," I said. "I've driven all my life. I'd just want to keep on, working where I'm best suited."

"Keep your present job?" he said, tapping his shoe on the side of the desk.

"Lord, yes," I said, grateful as could be.

Then I asked him for his autograph. He smiled real big and gave it to me, God's right-hand man, who had prayed with presidents.

\*  \*  \*

The next time out, I thought about the incredible thing that Charlie Frick had told me. Halfway to Hell, on the part of the run that he had once driven, I pulled the truck onto the gravel shoulder and walked back, hands in pockets, squinting at the faces. Young and old. Mostly old, or in their teens or twenties. Some were clearly bad news . . . But I was looking more closely this time, trying to discriminate. And sure enough, I saw a few that didn't seem to belong.

The dead hung by the slats, sticking their arms through, beseeching. I ignored as much of that as I could. "You," I said, pointing to a pale, thin fellow with a listless expression. "Why are you here?"

They wouldn't lie to me. I'd learned that inside the City. The dead don't lie.

"I kill people," the man said in a high whisper. "I kill children."

That confirmed my theory. I had *known* there was something wrong with him. I pointed to an old woman, plump and white-haired, lacking any of the signs. "You. Why are you going to Hell?"

She shook her head. "I don't know," she said. "Because I'm bad, I suppose."

"What did you do that was bad?"

"I don't know!" she said, flinging her hands up. "I really don't know. I was a librarian. When all those horrible people tried to take books out of my library, I fought them. I tried to reason with them . . . They wanted to remove Salinger and Twain and Baum . . ."

I picked out another young man. "What about you?"

"I didn't think it was possible," he said. "I didn't believe that God hated me, too."

"What did you do?" These people *didn't need to confess*.

"I loved God. I loved Jesus. But, dear Lord, I couldn't help it. I'm gay. I never had a choice. God wouldn't send me here just for being gay, would he?"

I spoke to a few more, until I was sure I had found all I had in this load. "You, you, you and you, out," I said, swinging open the rear gate. I closed the gate after them and led them away from the truck. Then I told them what Charlie Frick had told me, what he had learned on the road and in the big offices.

"Nobody's really sure where it goes," I said. "But it doesn't go to Hell, and it doesn't go back to Earth."

"Where, then?" the old woman asked plaintively. The hope in her eyes made me want to cry, because I just wasn't sure.

"Maybe it's the High Road," I said. "At least it's a chance. You light out across this stretch, go back of that hill, and I think there's some sort of trail. It's not easy to find, but if you look carefully, it's there. Follow it."

The young man who was gay took my hand. I felt like pulling away, because I've never been fond of homos. But he held on and he said, "Thank you. You must be taking a big risk."

"Yes, thank you," the librarian said. "Why are you doing it?"

I had hoped they wouldn't ask. "When I was a kid, one of my Sunday schoolteachers told me about Jesus going down to Hell during the three days before he rose up again. She told me Jesus went to Hell to bring out those who didn't belong. I'm certainly no Jesus, I'm not even much of a Christian, but that's what I'm doing. She called it Harrowing Hell." I shook my head. "Never mind. Just go," I said. I watched them walk across the gray flats and around the hill, then I got back into my truck and took the rest into the annex. Nobody noticed. I suppose the records just aren't that important to the employees.

None of the folks I've let loose have ever come back.

I'm staying on the road. I'm talking to people here and there, being cautious. When it looks like things are getting chancy, I'll take my rig back down to the City. And then I'm not sure what I'll do.

I don't want to let everybody loose. But I want to know who's ending up on the Low Road who shouldn't be. People unpopular with God's right-hand man.

My message is simple.

The crazy folks are running the asylum. We've corrupted Hell.

If I get caught, I'll be riding in back. And if you're reading this, chances are you'll be there, too.

Until then, I'm doing my bit. How about you?

# Schrödinger's Plague

*Interdepartmental Memo—Werner Dietrich to Carl Kranz*
Carl: I'm not sure what we should do about the Lambert journal. We know so little about the whole affair—but there's no doubt in my mind we should hand it over to the police. Incredible as the entries are, they directly relate to the murders and suicides, and they even touch on the destruction of the lab. Just reading them in your office isn't enough: I'll need copies of the journal. And how long did it circulate in the system before you noticed it?

*Kranz to Dietrich*
Werner: It must have been in the system since just before the events, so a month at least. Copies enclosed of the appropri-

ate entries. The rest, I think, is irrelevant and private. I'd like to return the journal to Richard's estate. The police would probably hold it. And—well, I have other reasons for wanting to keep it to ourselves. For the moment, anyway. Examine the papers carefully. As a physicist, tell me if there's anything in them you find completely unbelievable. If not, more thought should be applied to the whole problem.

P.S. I'm verifying the loss from Bernard's lab now. Lots of hush-hush over there. It's definite Bernard was working on a government CBW contract, apparently in defiance of the university's guidelines. ?—How did Goa get access to the materials? Tight security over there.

Enc.: five pages.

*The Journal*
## April 15, 1981

Today has been a puzzler. Marty convened an informal meeting of the Hydroxyl Radicals for lunch—on him. In attendance, the physics contingent: Martin Goa himself, Frederik Newman, and the new member, Kaye (pr: *Kie*) Parkes; the biologists, Oscar Bernard and yours truly; and the sociologist, Thomas Fauch. We met outside the lounge, and Marty took us to the auxiliary physics building to give us a brief tour of an experiment. Nothing spectacular. Then back to the lounge for lunch. Why he should waste our time thus is beyond me. Call it intuition, but something is up. Bernard is a bit upset for reason or reasons unknown.

## May 14, 1981

Radicals convened again today, at lunch. Some of the most absurd shit I've ever heard in my life. Marty at it again. The detail is important here.

"Gentlemen," Marty said in the private lounge, after we had eaten. "I have just destroyed an important experiment. And I have just resigned my position with the university. I'm to have all my papers and materials off campus by this date next month."

Pole-axed silence.

"I have my reasons. I'm going to establish something once and for all."

"What's that, Marty?" Frederik asked, looking irritated. None of us approve of theatrics.

"I'm putting mankind's money where our mouth is. Our veritable collective scientific mouth. Frederik, you can help me explain. You are all aware how good a physicist Frederik is. Better at grants, better at subtleties. Much better than I am. Frederik, what is the most generally accepted theory in physics today?"

"Special relativity," Frederik said without hesitating.

"And the next?"

"Quantum electrodynamics."

"Would you explain Schrödinger's cat to us?"

Frederik looked around the table, obviously a bit put-upon, then shrugged his shoulders. "The final state of a quantum event—an event on a microcosmic scale—appears to be defined by the making of an observation. That is, the event is indeterminate until it is measured. Then it assumes one of a variety of possible states. Schrödinger proposed linking quantum events to macrocosmic events. He suggested putting a cat in an enclosed box, and also a device which would detect the decay of a single radioactive nucleus. Let's say the nucleus has a fifty-fifty chance of decaying in an arbitrary length of time. If it does decay, it triggers the device, which drops a hammer on a vial of cyanide, releasing the gas into the box and killing the cat. The scientist conducting this experiment has no way of knowing whether the nucleus decayed or not without opening the box. Since the final state of the nucleus is not determined without first making a measurement, and the measurement in this case is the opening of the box to discover whether the cat is dead, Schrödinger suggested that the cat would find itself in an undetermined state, neither alive nor dead, but somewhere in between. Its fate is uncertain until a qualified observer opens the box.''

"And could you explain some of the implications of this thought experiment?'' Marty looked a bit like a cat himself—one who has swallowed a canary.

"Well,'' Frederik continued, "if we dismiss the cat as a qualified observer, there doesn't seem to be any way around the conclusion that the cat is neither alive nor dead until the box is opened.''

"Why not?'' Fauch, the sociologist, asked. "I mean, it seems obvious that only one state is possible.''

"Ah,'' Frederik said, warming to the subject, "but we have linked a quantum event to the macrocosm, and quantum events are tricky. We have amassed a great deal of experimental evidence to show that quantum states are not definite until they are observed, that in fact they fluctuate, interact, as if two or more universes—each containing a potential outcome—are meshed together, until the physicist causes the collapse into the final state by observing. Measuring.''

"Doesn't that give consciousness a godlike importance?'' Fauch asked.

"It does indeed,'' said Frederik. "Modern physics is on a heavy power trip.''

"It's all just theoretical, isn't it?'' I asked, slightly bored.

"Not at all,'' Frederik said. "Established experimentally.''

"Wouldn't a machine—or a cat—serve just as well to make the measurement?'' Oscar, my fellow biologist, asked.

"That depends on how conscious you regard a cat as being. A machine—no, because its state would not be certain until the physicist looked over the record it had made."

"Commonly," said Parkes, his youthful interest piqued, "we substitute Wigner's friend for the cat. Wigner was a physicist who suggested putting a man in the box. Wigner's friend would presumably be conscious enough to know whether he was alive or dead, and to properly interpret the fall of the hammer and the breaking of the vial to indicate that the nucleus has, in fact, decayed."

"Wonderful," Goa said. "And this neat little fable reflects the attitudes of those who work with one of the most accepted theories in modern science."

"Well, there are elaborations," Frederik said.

"Indeed, and I'm about to add another. What I'm about to say will probably be interpreted as a joke. It isn't. I'm not joking. I've been working with quantum mechanics for twenty years now, and I've always been uncertain—pardon the pun—whether I could accept the foundations of the very discipline which provided my livelihood. The dilemma has bothered me deeply. It's more than bothered me—it's caused sleepless nights, nervous distress, made me go to a psychiatrist. None of what Frederik calls 'elaborations' have provided any relief. So I've used my influence—and my contacts—to somewhat crooked advantage. I've begun an experiment. Not being happy with just a cat, or with Wigner's friend, I've involved all of you in the experiment, and myself, as well. Ultimately, many more people—conscious observers—will be involved."

Oscar smiled, trying to keep from laughing. "I do believe you've gone mad, Martin."

"Have I? Have I indeed, my *dear* Oscar? While I have been driven to distraction by intellectual considerations, why haven't you been driven to distraction by ethical ones?"

"What?" Oscar asked, frowning.

"You are, I believe, trying to locate a vial labeled DERVM-74."

"How did you—"

"Because I stole the vial while looking over your lab. And I cribbed a few of your notes. Now. You're among friends, Oscar. Tell us about DERVM-74. Tell them, or I will."

Oscar looked like a carp out of water for a few seconds. "That's classified," he said. "I refuse."

"DERVM-74," Marty said, "stands for Dangerous Experimental RhinoVirus, Mutation 74. Oscar does some moonlighting on contract for the government. This is one of his toys. Tell us about its nature, Oscar."

"You have the vial?"

"Not anymore," Marty said.

"You idiot! That virus is deadly. I was about to destroy it when the culture disappeared. It's of no use to anybody!"

"How does it work, Oscar?"

"It has a very long gestation period—about 330 days. Much too long for military uses. After that time, death is certain in ninety-eight percent of those who have contracted it. It can be spread by simple contact, by breathing the air around a contaminated subject." Oscar stood. "I must report this, Martin."

"Sit down." Marty pulled a broken glass tube out of his pocket, with a singed label still wrapped around it. He handed it to Oscar, who paled. "Here's my proof. You're much too late to stop the experiment."

"Is this all true?" Parkes asked.

"That's the vial," Oscar said.

"What in *hell* have you done?" I asked, loudly.

The other Radicals were as still as cold agar.

"I made a device which measures a quantum event, in this

case the decay of a particle of radioactive Americium. Over a small period of time, I exposed an instrument much like a Geiger counter to the possible effects of this decay. In that time, there was exactly a fifty-fifty chance that a nucleus in the particle would decay, triggering the Geiger counter. If the Geiger counter was triggered, it released the virus contained in this vial into a tightly sealed area. Immediately afterward, I entered the area, and an hour later, I gave all five of you a tour through the same area. The device was then destroyed, and everything in the chamber sterilized, including the vial. If the virus was not released, it was destroyed along with the experimental equipment. If it was released, then we have all been exposed.''

''Was it released?'' Fauch asked.

''I don't know. It's impossible to tell—yet.''

''Oscar,'' I said, ''it's been a month since Marty did all this. We're all influential people—giving talks, attending meetings, we all travel a fair amount. How many people have been exposed—potentially?''

''It's very contagious,'' Oscar said. ''Simple contact guarantees passage from one vector . . . to another.''

Fauch took out his calculator. ''If we exposed five people each day, and they went on to expose five more . . . Jesus Christ. By now, everyone on Earth could have it.''

''Why did you do this, Marty?'' Frederik asked.

''Because if the best mankind can do is come up with an infuriating theory like this to explain the universe, then we should be willing to live or die by our belief in the theory.''

''I don't get you,'' Frederik said.

''You know as well as I. Oscar, is there any way to detect contamination by the virus?''

''None. Marty, that virus was a mistake—useless to everybody. Even my notes were going to be destroyed.''

"Not useless to me. That's unimportant now, anyway. Frederik, what I'm saying is, according to theory, nothing has been determined yet. The nucleus may or may not have decayed, but that hasn't been decided. We may have better than a fifty-fifty chance—if we truly believe in the theory."

Parkes stood up and looked out the window. "You should have been more thorough, Marty. You should have researched this thing more completely."

"Why?"

"Because I'm a hypochondriac, you bastard. I have a very difficult time telling whether I'm sick or not."

"What does that have to do with anything?" Oscar asked.

Frederik leaned forward. "What Marty is implying is, since the quantum event hasn't been determined yet, the measurement that will flip it into one state or another is our sickness, or health, about three hundred days from now."

I picked up on the chain of reasoning. "And since Parkes is a hypochondriac, if he believes he's ill, that will flip the event into certainty. It will determine the decay, after the fact—" My head began to ache. "Even after the particle has been destroyed, and all other records?"

"If he truly believes he's ill," Marty said. "Or if any of us truly believes. Or if we actually become ill. I'm not sure there's any real difference, in this case."

"So you're going to jeopardize the entire world—" Fauch began, then he started to laugh. "This is a diabolical joke, Martin. You can stop it right here."

"He's not joking," Oscar said, holding up the vial. "That's my handwriting on the label."

"Isn't it a beautiful experiment?" Marty asked, grinning. "It determines so many things. It tells us whether our theory of quantum events is correct, it tells us the rôle of consciousness in determining the universe, and, in Parkes's case, it—"

"Stop it!" Oscar shouted. At that point, we had to restrain the biologist from attacking Marty, who danced away, laughing.

## May 17, 1981

Today all of us—except Marty—convened. Frederik and Parkes presented documentary evidence to support the validity of quantum theory, and, perversely enough, the validity of Marty's experiment. The evidence was impressive, but I'm not convinced. Still, it was a marathon session, and we now know more than we ever cared to know about the strange world of quantum physics.

The physicists—and Fauch, and Oscar, who is very quiet nowadays—are completely convinced that Marty's nucleus is— or was—in an undetermined state, and that all the causal chains leading to the potential release of the rhinovirus mutation are also in a state of flux. Whether the human race will live or die has not been decided yet.

And Parkes is equally convinced that, as soon as the gestation period passes, he will begin having symptoms, and he will feel—however irrationally—that he has contracted the disease. We cannot convince him otherwise.

In one way, we were very stupid. We had Oscar describe the symptoms—the early signs—of the disease to us. If we had thought things out more carefully, we would have withheld the information, at least from Parkes. But since Oscar knows, if he became convinced he had the disease, that would be enough to flip the state, Frederik believes. Or would it? We don't know yet how many of us will need to be convinced. Would Marty alone suffice? Is a consensus necessary? A two-thirds majority?

It all seemed—seems—totally preposterous to me. I've always been suspicious of physicists, and now I know why.

Then Frederik made a horrible proposal.

**May 23, 1981**

Frederik made the proposal again at today's meeting.

The others considered the proposal seriously. Seeing how serious they were, I tried to make objections but got nowhere. I am completely convinced that there is nothing we can do, that if the nucleus decayed, then we are doomed. In three hundred days, the first signs will appear—backache, headache, sweaty palms, piercing pains behind the eyes. If they don't, we won't. Even Frederik saw the ridiculous nature of his proposal, but he added, "The symptoms aren't that much different from flu, you know. And if just one of us becomes convinced . . ."

Indicating that the flipping of the state, because of human frailty, was almost certainly going to result in release of the virus. Had resulted.

His proposal—I write it down with great difficulty—is that we should all commit suicide, all six of us. Since we are the only ones who know about the experiment, we are the only ones, he feels, who can flip the state, make things certain. Parkes, he says, is particularly dangerous, but we are all potential hypochondriacs. With the strain of almost ten months waiting between now and the potential appearance of symptoms, we may all be near the breaking point.

**May 30, 1981**

I have refused to go along with them. Everyone has been extremely quiet, stayed away from each other. But I suspect Parkes and Frederik are doing something. Oscar is morose—he seems suicidal anyway, but is too much of a coward to go it alone. Fauch . . . I can't reach him.

—Ah, Christ. Frederik called. He said I can't hold out. They've killed Marty and destroyed the lab building to wipe out all traces of the experiment, so that no one will know it ever took place. The group is coming over to my apartment now. I just have time to put this in the university pick-up box. What can I do, run?

They're too close.


*Dietrich to Kranz*

Carl: I've read the journal, although I'm not sure I've assimilated it. What have you found out about Bernard?

*Kranz to Dietrich*

Werner: Oscar Bernard was indeed working on a rhinovirus mutation around the time of the incident. I haven't been able to find out much—lots of people in gray suits wandering through the corridors over there. But the rumor is that all his notes on certain projects are missing.

Do you believe it? I mean—do you believe the theory enough to agree with me, that word about the journal should end here? I feel both scared and silly.

*Dietrich to Kranz*

Carl: We have to find out the complete list of symptoms— besides headache, sweaty palms, backache, pains behind the eyes.

Yes. I'm a firm believer in the theory. And if Goa did what the journal says . . . you and I can flip the state.

Anyone who reads this can flip the state.

What in God's name are we going to do?

# Through Road
# No Whither

The long black Mercedes rumbled out of the fog on the road south from Dijon, moisture running in cold trickles across its windshield. Horst von Ranke carefully read the maps spread on his lap, eyeglasses perched low on his nose, while Waffen Schutzstaffel Oberleutnant Albert Fischer drove. "Thirty-five kilometers," Von Ranke said under his breath. "No more."

"We are lost," Fischer said. "We've already come thirty-six."

"Not quite that many. We should be there any minute now."

Fischer nodded and then shook his head. His high cheekbones and long, sharp nose only accentuated the black uniform with silver death's heads on the high, tight collar. Von Ranke wore a broad-striped gray suit; he was an undersecretary in the Propaganda Ministry. They might have been brothers, yet one had grown up in Czechoslovakia, the other in the Ruhr; one was the son of a brewer, the other of a coal-miner. They had met and become close friends in Paris, two years before, and were now sightseeing on a three-day pass in the countryside.

"Wait," Von Ranke said, peering through the drops on the side window. "Stop."

Fischer braked the car and looked in the direction of Von Ranke's long finger. Near the roadside, beyond a copse of young trees, was a low, thatch-rocfed house with dirty gray walls, almost hidden by the fog.

"Looks empty," Von Ranke said.

"It is occupied; look at the smoke," Fischer said. "Perhaps somebody can tell us where we are."

They pulled the car over and got out, Von Ranke leading the way across a mud path littered with wet straw. The hut looked even dirtier close-up. Smoke curled in a darker brown-gray twist from a hole in the peak of the thatch. Fischer nodded at his friend and they cautiously approached. Over the crude wooden door, letters wobbled unevenly in some alphabet neither knew, and between them they spoke nine languages. "Could that be Rom?" Fischer asked, frowning. "It does look familiar—like Slavic Rom."

"Gypsies? Romany don't live in huts like this, and besides, I thought they were rounded up long ago."

"That's what it looks like," Von Ranke repeated. "Still, maybe we can share some language, if only French."

He knocked on the door. After a long pause, he knocked again, and the door opened before his knuckles made the final rap. A woman too old to be alive stuck her long, wood-colored nose through the crack and peered at them with one good eye. The other was wrapped in a sunken caul of flesh. The hand that gripped the door edge was filthy, its nails long and black. Her toothless mouth cracked into a wrinkled, round-lipped grin. "Good evening," she said in perfect, even elegant, German. "What can I do for you?"

"We need to know if we are on the road to Dôle," Von Ranke said, controlling his revulsion.

"Then you're asking the wrong guide," the old woman said. Her hand withdrew and the door started to close. Fischer kicked out and pushed her back. The door swung open and began to lean on worn-out leather hinges.

"You do not treat us with the proper respect," he said. "What do you mean, 'the wrong guide'? What kind of guide are you?"

"So *strong*," the old woman crooned, wrapping her hands in front of her withered chest and backing away into the gloom. She wore colorless, ageless gray rags. Worn knit sleeves extended to her wrists.

"Answer me!" Fischer said, advancing despite the strong odor of urine and decay in the hut.

"The maps I know are not for this land," she sang, doddering before a cold and empty hearth.

"She's crazy," Von Ranke said. "Let the local authorities take care of her. Let's be off." But a wild look was in Fischer's eyes. So much filth, so much disarray, and impudence as well; these things made him angry.

"What maps do you know, crazy woman?" he demanded.

"Maps in time," the old woman said. She let her hands fall to her sides and lowered her head, as if, in admitting her specialty, she were suddenly humble.

"Then tell us where we are," Fischer sneered.

"Come," Von Ranke said, but he knew it was too late. There would be an end, but it would be on his friend's terms, and it might not be pleasant.

"On a through road no whither," the old woman said.

"What?" Fischer towered over her. She stared up as if at some prodigal son, her gums shining spittle.

"If you wish a reading, sit," she said, indicating a low table and three tattered cane and leather chairs. Fischer glanced at her, then at the table.

"Very well," he said, suddenly and falsely obsequious. Another game, Von Ranke realized. Cat and mouse.

Fischer pulled out a chair for his friend and sat across from the old woman. "Put your hands on the table, palms down, both of them, both of you," she said. They did so. She lay her ear to the table as if listening, eyes going to the beams of light coming through the thatch. "Arrogance," she said. Fischer did not react.

"A road going into fire and death," she said. "Your cities in flame, your women and children shriveling to black dolls in the heat of their burning homes. The camps are found and you stand accused of hideous crimes. Many are tried and hung. Your nation is disgraced, your cause abhorred." Now a peculiar light came into her eye. "Only psychotics will believe in you, the lowest of the low. Your nation will be divided between your enemies. All will be lost."

Fischer's smile did not waver. He pulled a coin from his pocket and threw it down before the woman, then pushed the chair back and stood. "Your maps are as crooked as your chin, you filthy old hag," he said. "Let's go."

"I've been suggesting that," Von Ranke said. Fischer made no move to leave. Von Ranke tugged on his arm but the SS Oberleutnant shrugged free of his friend's grip.

"Gypsies are few, now, hag," he said. "Soon to be fewer by one." Von Ranke managed to urge him just outside the door. The woman followed and shaded her eye against the misty light.

"I am no gypsy," she said. "You do not even recognize the words?" She pointed at the letters above the door.

Fischer squinted, and the light of recognition dawned in his eyes. "Yes," he said. "Yes, I do, now. A dead language."

"What are they?" Von Ranke asked, uneasy.

"Hebrew, I think," Fischer said. "She is a Jewess."

"No!" the woman cackled. "I am no Jew."

Von Ranke thought the woman looked younger now, or at least stronger, and his unease deepened.

"I do not care what you are," Fischer said quietly. "I only wish we were in my father's time." He took a step toward her. She did not retreat. Her face became almost youthfully bland, and her bad eye seemed to fill in. "Then, there would be no regulations, no rules—I could take this pistol"—he tapped his holster—"and apply it to your filthy Kike head, and perhaps kill the last Jew in Europe." He unstrapped the holster. The woman straightened in the dark hut, as if drawing strength from Fischer's abusive tongue. Von Ranke feared for his friend. Rashness could get them in trouble.

"This is not our fathers' time," he reminded Fischer.

Fischer paused, pistol in hand, his finger curling around the trigger. "Filthy, smelly old woman." She did not look nearly as old as she had when they entered the hut, perhaps not even old at all, and certainly not bent and crippled. "You have had a very narrow escape this afternoon."

"You have no idea who I am," the woman half sang, half moaned.

"*Scheisse*," Fischer spat. "Now we will go, and report you and your hovel."

"I am the scourge," she breathed. Her breath smelled like burning stone even three strides away. She backed into the hut but her voice did not diminish. "I am the visible hand, the pillar of cloud by day and the pillar of fire by night."

Fischer laughed. "You're right," he said to Von Ranke, "she isn't worth our trouble." He turned and stamped out the door. Von Ranke followed with one last glance over his shoulder into the gloom, the decay. *No one has lived in this hut for years,* he thought. Her shadow was gray and indefinite before the ancient stone hearth, behind the leaning, dust-covered table.

In the car, Von Ranke sighed. "You *do* tend toward arrogance, you know that?"

Fischer grinned and shook his head. "You drive, old friend. *I'll* look at the maps." Von Ranke ramped up the Mercedes's turbine until its whine was high and steady and its exhaust cut a swirling hole in the fog behind. "No wonder we're lost," Fischer said. He shook out the Pan-Deutschland map peevishly. "This is five years old—1979."

"We'll find our way," Von Ranke said.

From the door of the hut, the old woman watched, head bobbing. "I am not a Jew," she said, "but I loved them, too, oh, yes. I loved all my children." She raised her hand as the long black car roared into the fog.

"I will bring you to justice, whatever line you live upon, and all your children, and their children's children," she said. She dropped a twist of smoke from her elbow to the dirt floor and waggled her finger. The smoke danced and drew black figures in the dirt. "Into the time of your fathers." The fog grew thinner. She brought her arm down, and forty years melted away with the mist.

High above, a deeper growl descended on the road. A wide-winged shadow passed over the hut, wings flashing stars, invasion stripes, and cannon fire.

"Hungry bird," the shapeless figure said. "Time to feed."

# Tangents

The nut-brown boy stood in the California field, his Asian face shadowed by a hardhat, his short stocky frame clothed in a T-shirt and a pair of brown shorts. He squinted across the hip-high grass at the spraddled old two-story ranch house, whistling a few bars from a Haydn piano sonata.

Out of the upper floor of the house came a man's high, frustrated "Bloody hell!" and the sound of a fist slamming on a solid surface. Silence for a minute. Then, more softly, a woman's question, "Not going well?"

"No. I'm swimming in it, but I don't see it."

"The encryption?" the woman asked timidly.

"The tesseract. If it doesn't gel, it isn't aspic."

The boy squatted in the grass and listened.

"And?" the woman encouraged.

"Ah, Lauren, it's still cold broth."

The boy lay back in the grass. He had crept over the split-rail and brick-pylon fence from the new housing project across the road. School was out for the summer and his mother—foster mother—did not like him around the house all day. Or at all.

Behind his closed eyes, a huge piano keyboard appeared, with him dancing on the keys. He loved music.

He opened his eyes and saw a thin, graying lady in a tweed suit leaning over him, staring. "You're on private land," she said, brows knit.

He scrambled up and brushed grass from his pants. "Sorry."

"I thought I saw someone out here. What's your name?"

"Pal," he replied.

"Is that a name?" she asked querulously.

"Pal Tremont. It's not my real name. I'm Korean."

"Then what's your real name?"

"My folks told me not to use it anymore. I'm adopted. Who are you?"

The gray woman looked him up and down. "My name is Lauren Davies," she said. "You live near here?"

He pointed across the fields at the close-packed tract homes.

"I sold the land for those homes ten years ago," she said. She seemed to be considering something. "I don't normally enjoy children trespassing."

"Sorry," Pal said.

"Have you had lunch?"

"No."

"Will a grilled cheese sandwich do?"

He squinted at her and nodded.

In the broad, red-brick and tile kitchen, sitting at an oak

table with his shoulders barely rising above the top, he ate the slightly charred sandwich and watched Lauren Davies watching him.

"I'm trying to write about a child," she said. "It's difficult. I'm a spinster and I don't understand children."

"You're a writer?" he asked, taking a swallow of milk.

She sniffed. "Not that anyone would know."

"Is that your brother, upstairs?"

"No," she said. "That's Peter. We've been living together for twenty years."

"But you said you're a spinster... isn't that someone who's never married, or never loved?" Pal asked.

"Never married. And never you mind. Peter's relationship to me is none of your concern." She placed a bowl of soup and a tuna salad sandwich on a lacquer tray. "His lunch," she said. Without being asked, Pal trailed up the stairs after her.

"This is where Peter works," Lauren explained. Pal stood in the doorway, eyes wide. The room was filled with electronics gear, computer terminals, and bookcases with geometric cardboard sculptures sharing each shelf with books and circuit boards. She rested the tray precariously on a pile of floppy disks atop a rolling cart.

"Time for a break," she told a thin man seated with his back toward them.

The man turned around on his swivel chair, glanced briefly at Pal and the tray and shook his head. The hair on top of his head was a rich, glossy black; on the close-cut sides, the color changed abruptly to a startling white. He had a small thin nose and large green eyes. On the desk before him was a high-resolution computer monitor. "We haven't been introduced," he said, pointing to Pal.

"This is Pal Tremont, a neighborhood visitor. Pal, this is

Peter Tuthy. Pal's going to help me with that character we discussed this morning.''

Pal looked at the monitor curiously. Red and green lines shadowed each other through some incomprehensible transformation on the screen, then repeated.

''What's a 'tesseract'?'' Pal asked, remembering what he had heard as he stood in the field.

''It's a four-dimensional analog of a cube. I'm trying to teach myself to see it in my mind's eye,'' Tuthy said. ''Have you ever tried that?''

''No,'' Pal admitted.

''Here,'' Tuthy said, handing him the spectacles. ''As in the movies.''

Pal donned the spectacles and stared at the screen. ''So?'' he said. ''It folds and unfolds. It's pretty—it sticks out at you, and then it goes away.'' He looked around the workshop. ''Oh, wow!'' The boy ran to a yard-long black music keyboard propped in one corner. ''A Tronclavier! With all the switches! My mother had me take piano lessons, but I'd rather play this. Can you play it?''

''I toy with it,'' Tuthy said, exasperated. ''I toy with all sorts of electronic things. But what did you see on the screen?'' He glanced up at Lauren, blinking. ''I'll eat the food, I'll eat it. Now please don't bother us.''

''He's supposed to be helping *me*,'' Lauren complained.

Peter smiled at her. ''Yes, of course. I'll send him downstairs in a little while.''

When Pal descended an hour later, he came into the kitchen to thank Lauren for lunch. ''Peter's a real flake,'' he said confidentially. ''He's trying to learn to see in weird directions.''

''I know,'' Lauren said, sighing.

"I'm going home now," Pal said. "I'll be back, though...if it's all right with you. Peter invited me."

"I'm sure it will be fine," Lauren said dubiously.

"He's going to let me learn the Tronclavier." With that, Pal smiled radiantly and exited through the kitchen door, just as he had come in.

When she retrieved the tray, she found Peter leaning back in his chair, eyes closed. The figures on the screen were still folding and unfolding.

"What about Hockrum's work?" she asked.

"I'm on it," Peter replied, eyes still closed.


Lauren called Pal's foster mother on the second day to apprise them of their son's location, and the woman assured her it was quite all right. "Sometimes he's a little pest. Send him home if he causes trouble...but not right away! Give me a rest," she said, then laughed nervously.

Lauren drew her lips together tightly, thanked the woman, and hung up.

Peter and the boy had come downstairs to sit in the kitchen, filling up paper with line drawings. "Peter's teaching me how to use his program," Pal said.

"Did you know," Tuthy said, assuming his highest Cambridge professorial tone, "that a cube, intersecting a flat plane, can be cut through a number of geometrically different cross-sections?"

Pal squinted at the sketch Tuthy had made. "Sure," he said.

"If shoved through the plane the cube can appear, to a two-dimensional creature living on the plane—let's call him a 'Flatlander'—to be either a triangle, a rectangle, a trapezoid, a rhombus, or a square. If the two-dimensional being observes the cube being pushed through all the way, what he sees is one of more of these objects growing larger, changing shape suddenly, shrinking, and disappearing.''

"Sure," Pal said, tapping his sneakered toe. "That's easy. Like in that book you showed me."

"And a sphere pushed through a plane would appear, to the hapless flatlander, first as an 'invisible' point (the two-dimensional surface touching the sphere, tangential), then as a circle. The circle would grow in size, then shrink back to a point and disappear again.'' He sketched two-dimensional stick figures looking in awe at such an intrusion.

"Got it," Pal said. "Can I play with the Tronclavier now?''

"In a moment. Be patient. So what would a tesseract look like, coming into our three-dimensional space? Remember the program, now . . . the pictures on the monitor.''

Pal looked up at the ceiling. "I don't know," he said, seeming bored.

"Try to think," Tuthy urged him.

"It would . . .'' Pal held his hands out to shape an angular object. "It would look like one of those Egyptian things, but with three sides . . . or like a box. It would look like a weird-shaped box, too, not square. And if *you* were to fall through a flatland . . .''

"Yes, that would look very funny," Peter acknowledged with a smile. "Cross-sections of arms and legs and body, all surrounded by skin . . .''

"And a head!" Pal enthused. "With eyes and a nose."

The doorbell rang. Pal jumped off the kitchen chair. "Is that my mom?'' he asked, looking worried.

"I don't think so," Lauren said. "More likely it's Hockrum." She went to the front door to answer. She returned a moment later with a small, pale man behind her. Tuthy stood and shook the man's hand. "Pal Tremont, this is Irving Hockrum," he introduced, waving his hand between them. Hockrum glanced at Pal and blinked a long, cold blink.

"How's the work coming?" he asked Tuthy.

"It's finished," Tuthy said. "It's upstairs. Looks like your savants are barking up the wrong logic tree." He retrieved a folder of papers and printouts and handed them to Hockrum.

Hockrum leafed through the printouts. "I can't say this makes me happy. Still, I can't find fault. Looks like the work is up to your usual brilliant standards. Here's your check." He handed Tuthy an envelope. "I just wish you'd given it to us sooner. It would have saved me some grief—and the company quite a bit of money."

"Sorry," Tuthy said.

"Now I have an important bit of work for you . . ." And Hockrum outlined another problem. Tuthy thought it over for several minutes and shook his head.

"Most difficult, Irving. Pioneering work there. Take at least a month to see if it's even feasible."

"That's all I need to know for now—whether it's feasible. A lot's riding on this, Peter." Hockrum clasped his hands together in front of him, looking even more pale and worn than when he had entered the kitchen. "You'll let me know soon?"

"I'll get right on it," Tuthy said.

"Protégé?" he asked, pointing to Pal. There was a speculative expression on his face, not quite a leer.

"No, a young friend. He's interested in music," Tuthy said. "Damned good at Mozart, in fact."

"I help with his tesseracts," Pal asserted.

"I hope you don't interrupt Peter's work. Peter's work is important."

Pal shook his head solemnly. "Good," Hockrum said, and then left the house with the folder under his arm.

Tuthy returned to his office, Pal in train. Lauren tried to

work in the kitchen, sitting with fountain pen and pad of paper, but the words wouldn't come. Hockrum always worried her. She climbed the stairs and stood in the open doorway of the office. She often did that; her presence did not disturb Tuthy, who could work under all sorts of adverse conditions.

"Who was that man?" Pal was asking Tuthy.

"I work for him," Tuthy said. "He's employed by a big electronics firm. He loans me most of the equipment I use. The computers, the high-resolution monitors. He brings me problems and then takes my solutions back to his bosses and claims he did the work."

"That sounds stupid," Pal said. "What kind of problems?"

"Codes, encryptions. Computer security. That was my expertise, once."

"You mean, like fencerail, that sort of thing?" Pal asked, face brightening. "We learned some of that in school."

"Much more complicated, I'm afraid," Tuthy said, grinning. "Did you ever hear of the German 'Enigma,' or the 'Ultra' project?"

Pal shook his head.

"I thought not. Let's try another figure now." He called up another routine on the four-space program and sat Pal before the screen. "So what would a hypersphere look like if it intruded into our space?"

Pal thought a moment. "Kind of weird," he said.

"Not really. You've been watching the visualizations."

"Oh, in *our* space. That's easy. It just looks like a balloon, blowing up from nothing and then shrinking again. It's harder to see what a hypersphere looks like when it's real. Reft of us, I mean."

"Reft?" Tuthy said.

"Sure. Reft and light. Dup and owwen. Whatever the directions are called."

Tuthy stared at the boy. Neither of them had noticed Lauren in the doorway. "The proper terms are *ana* and *kata*," Tuthy said. "What does it look like?"

Pal gestured, making two wide wings with his arms. "It's like a ball and it's like a horseshoe, depending on how you look at it. Like a balloon stung by bees, I guess, but it's smooth all over, not lumpy."

Tuthy continued to stare, then asked quietly, "You actually see it?"

"Sure," Pal said. "Isn't that what your program is supposed to do—make you see things like that?"

Tuthy nodded, flabbergasted.

"Can I play the Tronclavier now?"

Lauren backed out of the doorway. She felt she had eavesdropped on something momentous, but beyond her. Tuthy came downstairs an hour later, leaving Pal to pick out Telemann on the synthesizer. He sat at the kitchen table with her. "The program works," he said. "It doesn't work for me, but it works for him. I've just been showing him reverse-shadow figures. He caught on right away, and then he went off and played Haydn. He's gone through all my sheet music. The kid's a genius."

"Musical, you mean?"

He glanced directly at her and frowned. "Yes, I suppose he's remarkable at that, too. But spacial relations—coordinates and motion in higher dimensions . . . Did you know that if you take a three-dimensional object and rotate it in the fourth dimension, it will come back with left-right reversed? So if I were to take my hand"—he held up his right hand—"and lift it *dup*"—he enunciated the word clearly, *dup*—"or drop it *owwen*, it would come back like this?" He held his left hand over his right, balled the right up into a fist, and snuck it away behind his back.

"I didn't know that," Lauren said. "What are *dup* and *owwen*?"

"That's what Pal calls movement along the fourth dimension. *Ana* and *kata* to purists. Like up and down to a flatlander, who only comprehends left and right, back and forth."

She thought about the hands for a moment. "I still can't see it," she said.

"I've tried, but neither can I," Tuthy admitted. "Our circuits are just too hard-wired, I suppose."

Upstairs, Pal had switched the Tronclavier to a cathedral organ and steel guitar combination and was playing variations on Pergolesi.

"Are you going to keep working for Hockrum?" Lauren asked. Tuthy didn't seem to hear her.

"It's remarkable," he murmured. "The boy just walked in here. You brought him in by accident. Remarkable."

"Can you show me the direction, point it out to me?" Tuthy asked the boy three days later.

"None of my muscles move that way," the boy replied. "I can see it, in my head, but . . ."

"What is it like, seeing that direction?"

Pal squinted. "It's a lot bigger. We're sort of stacked up with other places. It makes me feel lonely."

"Why?"

"Because I'm stuck here. Nobody out there pays any attention to us."

Tuthy's mouth worked. "I thought you were just intuiting those directions in your head. Are you telling me . . . you're actually *seeing* out there?"

"Yeah. There's people out there, too. Well, not people, exactly. But it isn't my eyes that see them. Eyes are like

212

muscles—they can't point those ways. But the head—the brain, I guess—can.''

"Bloody hell," Tuthy said. He blinked and recovered. "Excuse me. That's rude. Can you show me the people . . . on the screen?''

"Shadows, like we were talking about," Pal said.

"Fine. Then draw the shadows for me."

Pal sat down before the terminal, fingers pausing over the keys. "I can show you, but you have to help me with something."

"Help you with what?"

"I'd like to play music for them . . . out there. So they'll notice us."

"The people?"

"Yeah. They look really weird. They stand on us, sort of. They have hooks in our world. But they're tall . . . high dup. They don't notice us because we're so small, compared to them."

"Lord, Pal, I haven't the slightest idea how we'd send music out to them . . . I'm not even sure I believe they exist."

"I'm not lying," Pal said, eyes narrowing. He turned his chair to face a mouse on a black-ruled pad and began sketching shapes on the monitor. "Remember, these are just shadows of what they look like. Next I'll draw the dup and owwen lines to connect the shadows."

The boy shaded the shapes he drew to make them look solid, smiling at his trick but explaining it was necessary because the projection of a four-dimensional object in normal space was, of course, three-dimensional.

"They look like you take the plants in a garden, flowers and such, and giving them lots of arms and fingers . . . and it's kind of like seeing things in an aquarium," Pal explained.

After a time, Tuthy suspended his disbelief and stared in

open-mouthed wonder at what the boy was re-creating on the monitor.

"I think you're wasting your time, that's what I think," Hockrum said. "I needed that feasibility judgment by today." He paced around the living room before falling as heavily as his light frame permitted into a chair.

"I *have* been distracted," Tuthy admitted.

"By that boy?"

"Yes, actually. Quite a talented fellow—"

"Listen, this is going to mean a lot of trouble for me. I guaranteed the study would be finished by today. It'll make me look bad." Hockrum screwed his face up in frustration. "What in hell are you doing with that boy?"

"Teaching him, actually. Or rather, he's teaching me. Right now, we're building a four-dimensional cone, part of a speaker system. The cone is three-dimensional, the material part, but the magnetic field forms a fourth-dimensional extension—"

"Do you ever think how it looks, Peter?" Hockrum asked.

"It looks very strange on the monitor, I grant you—"

"I'm talking about you and the boy."

Tuthy's bright, interested expression fell slowly into long, deep-lined dismay. "I don't know what you mean."

"I know a lot about you, Peter. Where you come from, why you had to leave . . . It just doesn't look good."

Tuthy's face flushed crimson.

"Keep him away from here," Hockrum advised.

Tuthy stood. "I want you out of this house," he said quietly. "Our relationship is at an end."

"I swear," Hockrum said, his voice low and calm, staring up at Tuthy from under his brows, "I'll tell the boy's parents. Do you think they'd want their kid hanging around an old—

pardon the expression—queer? I'll tell them if you don't get the feasibility judgment made. I think you can do it by the end of this week—two days. Don't you?''

"No, I don't think so," Tuthy said. "Please leave."

"I know you're here illegally. There's no record of you entering the country. With the problems you had in England, you're certainly not a desirable alien. I'll pass word to the INS. You'll be deported."

"There isn't time to do the work," Tuthy said.

"Make time. Instead of 'educating' that kid."

"Get out of here."

"Two days, Peter."

Over dinner that evening, Tuthy explained to Lauren the exchange he had had with Hockrum. "He thinks I'm buggering Pal. Unspeakable bastard. I will never work for him again."

"We'd better talk to a lawyer, then," Lauren said. "You're sure you can't make him . . . happy, stop all this trouble?"

"I could solve his little problem for him in just a few hours. But I don't want to see him or speak to him again."

"He'll take your equipment away."

Tuthy blinked and waved one hand through the air helplessly. "Then we'll just have to work fast, won't we? Ah, Lauren, you were a fool to bring me here. You should have left me to rot."

"They ignored everything you did for them," Lauren said bitterly. "You saved their hides during the war, and then . . . They would have shut you up in prison." She stared through the kitchen window at the overcast sky and woods outside.

The cone lay on the table near the window, bathed in morning sun, connected to both the mini-computer and the Tronclavier. Pal arranged the score he had composed on a music stand before the synthesizer. "It's like Bach," he said, "but

215

it'll play better for them. It has a kind of over-rhythm that I'll play on the dup part of the speaker.''

"Why are we doing this, Pal?" Tuthy asked as the boy sat down to the keyboard.

"You don't belong here, really, do you, Peter?" Pal asked in turn. Tuthy stared at him.

"I mean, Miss Davies and you get along okay—but do you belong *here*, now?"

"What makes you think I don't belong?"

"I read some books in the school library. About the war and everything. I looked up 'Enigma' and 'Ultra.' I found a fellow named Peter Thornton. His picture looked like you. The books made him seem like a hero.''

Tuthy smiled wanly.

"But there was this note in one book. You disappeared in 1965. You were being prosecuted for something. They didn't say what you were being prosecuted for.''

"I'm a homosexual," Tuthy said quietly.

"Oh. So what?"

"Lauren and I met in England in 1964. We became good friends. They were going to put me in prison, Pal. She smuggled me into the U.S. through Canada.''

"But you said you're a homosexual. They don't like women.''

"Not at all true, Pal. Lauren and I like each other very much. We could talk. She told me about her dreams of being a writer, and I talked to her about mathematics, and about the war. I nearly died during the war.''

"Why? Were you wounded?"

"No. I worked too hard. I burned myself out and had a nervous breakdown. My lover—a man—kept me alive throughout the forties. Things were bad in England after the war. But he died in 1963. His parents came in to settle the estate, and

216

when I contested the settlement in court, I was arrested. So I suppose you're right, Pal. I don't really belong here."

"I don't, either. My folks don't care much. I don't have too many friends. I wasn't even born here, and I don't know anything about Korea."

"Play," Tuthy said, his face stony. "Let's see if they'll listen."

"Oh, they'll listen," Pal said. "It's like the way they talk to each other."

The boy ran his fingers over the keys on the Tronclavier. The cone, connected with the keyboard through the mini-computer, vibrated tinnily.

For an hour, Pal paged back and forth through his composition, repeating and trying variations. Tuthy sat in a corner, chin in hand, listening to the mousy squeaks and squeals produced by the cone. *How much more difficult to interpret a four-dimensional sound,* he thought. *Not even visual clues . . .*

Finally the boy stopped and wrung his hands, then stretched his arms. "They must have heard. We'll just have to wait and see." He switched the Tronclavier to automatic playback and pushed the chair away from the keyboard.

Pal stayed until dusk, then reluctantly went home. Tuthy sat in the office until midnight, listening to the tinny sounds issuing from the speaker cone.

All night long, the Tronclavier played through its pre-programmed selection of Pal's compositions. Tuthy lay in bed in his room, two doors down from Lauren's room, watching a shaft of moonlight slide across the wall. *How far would a four-dimensional being have to travel to get here?*

*How far have I come to get here?*

Without realizing he was asleep, he dreamed, and in his dream a wavering image of Pal appeared, gesturing with both arms as if swimming, eyes wide. *I'm okay,* the boy said without moving his lips. *Don't worry about me . . . I'm okay. I've been back to Korea to see what it's like. It's not bad, but I like it better here. . . .*

Tuthy awoke sweating. The moon had gone down and the room was pitch-black. In the office, the hyper-cone continued its distant, mouse-squeak broadcast.

Pal returned early in the morning, repetitively whistling a few bars from Mozart's Fourth Violin Concerto. Lauren let him in and he joined Tuthy upstairs. Tuthy sat before the monitor, replaying Pal's sketch of the four-dimensional beings.

"Do you see anything?" he asked the boy.

Pal nodded. "They're coming closer. They're interested. Maybe we should get things ready, you know . . . be prepared." He squinted. "Did you ever think what a four-dimensional footprint would look like?"

Tuthy considered for a moment. "That would be most interesting," he said. "It would be solid."

On the first floor, Lauren screamed.

Pal and Tuthy almost tumbled over each other getting downstairs. Lauren stood in the living room with her arms crossed above her busom, one hand clamped over her mouth. The first intrusion had taken out a section of the living-room floor and the east wall.

"Really clumsy," Pal said. "One of them must have bumped it."

"The music," Tuthy said.

"What in HELL is going on?" Lauren demanded, her voice starting as a screech and ending as a roar.

"Better turn the music off," Tuthy elaborated.

"Why?" Pal asked, face wreathed in an excited smile.

"Maybe they don't like it."

A bright filmy blue blob rapidly expanded to a yard in

diameter just beside Tuthy. The blob turned red, wriggled, froze, and then just as rapidly vanished.

"That was like an elbow," Pal explained. "One of its arms. I think it's listening. Trying to find out where the music is coming from. I'll go upstairs."

"Turn it off!" Tuthy demanded.

"I'll play something else." The boy ran up the stairs. From the kitchen came a hideous hollow crashing, then the sound of a vacuum being filled—a reverse-pop, ending in a hiss—followed by a low-frequency vibration that set their teeth on edge . . .

The vibration caused by a four-dimensional creature *scraping* across its "floor," their own three-dimensional space. Tuthy's hands shook with excitement.

"Peter—" Lauren bellowed, all dignity gone. She unwrapped her arms and held clenched fists out as if she were about to start exercising, or boxing.

"Pal's attracted visitors," Tuthy explained.

He turned toward the stairs. The first four steps and a section of floor spun and vanished. The rush of air nearly drew him down the hole. Regaining his balance, he knelt to feel the precisely cut, concave edge. Below lay the dark basement.

"Pal!" Tuthy called out.

"I'm playing something original for them," Pal shouted back. "I think they like it."

The phone rang. Tuthy was closest to the extension at the bottom of the stairs and instinctively reached out to answer it. Hockrum was on the other end, screaming.

"I can't talk now—" Tuthy said. Hockrum screamed again, loud enough for Lauren to hear. Tuthy abruptly hung up. "He's been fired, I gather," he said. "He seemed angry." He stalked back three paces and turned, then ran forward and leaped the gap to the first intact step. "Can't talk." He stumbled and scrambled up the stairs, stopping on the landing. "Jesus," he said, as if something had suddenly occurred to him.

"He'll call the government," Lauren warned.

Tuthy waved that off. "I know what's happening. They're knocking chunks out of three-space, into the fourth. The fourth dimension. Like Pal says: clumsy brutes. They could kill us!"

Sitting before the Tronclavier, Pal happily played a new melody. Tuthy approached and was abruptly blocked by a thick green column, as solid as rock and with a similar texture. It vibrated and ascribed an arc in the air. A section of the ceiling four feet wide was kicked out of three-space. Tuthy's hair lifted in the rush of wind. The column shrank to a broomstick and hairs sprouted all over it, writhing like snakes.

Tuthy edged around the hairy broomstick and pulled the plug on the Tronclavier. A cage of zeppelin-shaped brown sausages encircled the computer, spun, elongated to reach the ceiling, the floor, and the top of the monitor's table, and then pipped down to tiny strings and was gone.

"They can't see too clearly here," Pal said, undisturbed that his concert was over. Lauren had climbed the outside stairs and stood behind Tuthy. "Gee, I'm sorry about the damage."

In one smooth curling motion, the Tronclavier and cone and all the wiring associated with them were peeled away as if they had been stick-on labels hastily removed from a flat surface.

"Gee," Pal said, his face suddenly registering alarm.

Then it was the boy's turn. He was removed more slowly, with greater care. The last thing to vanish was his head, which hung suspended in the air for several seconds.

"I think they liked the music," he said, grinning.

Head, grin and all, dropped away in a direction impossible for Tuthy or Lauren to follow. The air in the room sighed.

Lauren stood her ground for several minutes, while Tuthy wandered through what was left of the office, passing his hand through mussed hair.

"Perhaps he'll be back," Tuthy said. "I don't even know . . ." But he didn't finish. Could a three-dimensional boy survive in a four-dimensional void, or whatever lay dup . . . or owwen?

Tuthy did not object when Lauren took it upon herself to call the boy's foster parents and the police. When the police arrived, he endured the questions and accusations stoically, face immobile, and told them as much as he knew. He was not believed; nobody knew quite what to believe. Photographs were taken. The police left.

It was only a matter of time, Lauren told him, until one or the other or both of them were arrested. "Then we'll make up a story," he said. "You'll tell them it was my fault."

"I will *not*," Lauren said. "But where *is* he?"

"I'm not positive," Tuthy said. "I think's he's all right, however."

"How do you *know*?"

He told her about the dream.

"But that was before," she said.

"Perfectly allowable in the fourth dimension," he explained. He pointed vaguely up, then down, and shrugged.

On the last day, Tuthy spent the early morning hours bundled in an overcoat and bathrobe in the drafty office, playing his program again and again, trying to visualize *ana* and *kata*. He closed his eyes and squinted and twisted his head, intertwined his fingers and drew odd little graphs on the monitors, but it was no use. His brain was hard-wired.

Over breakfast, he reiterated to Lauren that she must put all the blame on him.

"Maybe it will all blow over," she said. "They haven't got a case. No evidence . . . nothing."

"All blow *over*," he mused, passing his hand over his head and grinning ironically. "How *over*, they'll never know."

The doorbell rang. Tuthy went to answer it, and Lauren followed a few steps behind.

Tuthy opened the door. Three men in gray suits, one with a briefcase, stood on the porch. "Mr. Peter Thornton?" the tallest asked.

"Yes," Tuthy acknowledged.

A chunk of the door frame and wall above the door vanished with a roar and a hissing pop. The three men looked up at the gap. Ignoring what was impossible, the tallest man returned his attention to Tuthy and continued, "We have information that you are in this country illegally."

"Oh?" Tuthy said.

Beside him, an irregular filmy blue cylinder grew to a length of four feet and hung in the air, vibrating. The three men backed away on the porch. In the middle of the cylinder, Pal's head emerged, and below that, his extended arm and hand.

"It's fun here," Pal said. "They're friendly."

"I believe you," Tuthy said.

"Mr. Thornton," the tallest man continued valiantly.

"Won't you come with me?" Pal asked.

Tuthy glanced back at Lauren. She gave him a small fraction of a nod, barely understanding what she was assenting to, and he took Pal's hand. "Tell them it was all my fault," he said.

From his feet to his head, Peter Tuthy was peeled out of this world. Air rushed in. Half of the brass lamp to one side of the door disappeared.

The INS men returned to their car without any further questions, with damp pants and embarrassed, deeply worried

222

expressions. They drove away, leaving Lauren to contemplate the quiet. They did not return.

She did not sleep for three nights, and when she did sleep, Tuthy and Pal visited her, and put the question to her.

*Thank you, but I prefer it here,* she replied.

*It's a lot of fun,* the boy insisted. *They like music.*

Lauren shook her head on the pillow and awoke. Not very far away, there was a whistling, tinny kind of sound, followed by a deep vibration.

To her, it sounded like applause.

She took a deep breath and got out of bed to retrieve her notebook.

# Sisters

"**B**ut you're the only one, Letitia." Reena Cathcart lay a light, slender hand on her shoulder with a look of utmost sincerity. "You know none of the others can. I mean . . ." She stopped, the slightest hint of awareness of her faux pas dawning. "You're simply the only one who can play the old—the older—woman."

Letitia Blakely looked down at the hall floor, eyes and face hot, then circled her gaze up to the ceiling, trying to keep the fresh tears from spilling over. Reena tossed her long black hair, perfect hazel eyes imploring. A few stragglers sauntered down the clean and carpeted hall of the new school wing to their classes. "We're late for first period," Letitia said. "Why the

227

old woman? Why didn't you come to me when there was some other part to play?''

Reena was too smart not to know what she was doing. Smart, but not terribly sensitive. ''You're the type.''

''You mean frowsy?''

Reena didn't react. She was intent on a yes answer, the perfect solution to her problems.

''Or just dumpy?''

''You shouldn't be ashamed of how you look.''

''I look *frowsy* and *dumpy*! I'm perfect for the old woman in your lysing play, and you're the only one with the guts to ask me.''

''We'd like to give you a chance. You're such a loner, and we want you to feel like you're part—''

''Bullmusk!'' The moisture spilled over and Reena backed away. ''Leave me alone. Just leave me alone.''

''No need to swear.'' Petulant, offended.

Letitia raised her hand as if to strike. Reena swung her hair again defiantly and turned to walk away. Letitia leaned against the tile wall and wiped her eyes, trying to avoid damage to her carefully applied makeup. The damage was already done, however. She could feel the tear-tracks of her mother's mascara and the smudged eyeshadow. With a sigh, she walked off to the bathroom, not caring how late she was. She wanted to go home.

Coming into class fifteen minutes after the bell, Letitia was surprised to find the students in self-ordered discussion, with no sign of Mr. Brant. Several of Reena's drama group gave her frosty looks as she took her seat.

''TB,'' Edna Corman said beneath her breath from across the aisle.

''RC you,'' Letitia replied, head cocked to one side and tone matching Edna's precisely. She poked John Lockwood in the shoulder. Lockwood didn't care much for socializing; he seldom noticed the exchanges going on around him. "Where's Mr. Brant?"

"Georgia Fischer blitzed and he took her to the counselors. He told us to plug in and pursue."

"Oh." Georgia Fischer had transferred two months ago from a superwhiz class in Oakland. She was brighter than most but she blitzed about once every two weeks. "I may be fat and ugly," Letitia said for Lockwood's ears only. "But I never blitz."

"Nor I," Lockwood said. He was PPC, like Georgia, but not a superwhiz. Letitia liked him, but not enough to feel threatened by him. "Better pursue."

Letitia leaned back in her seat and closed her eyes to concentrate. Her mod activated and projections danced in front of her, then steadied. She had been cramming patient psych for a week and was approaching threshold. The little Computer Graphics nursie in whites and pillcap began discussing insanouts of terminal patient care, which all seemed very TB to Letitia; who died of disease now, anyway? She made her decision and cut to the same CG nursie discussing the shock of RoR— replacement and recovery. What she really wanted to study was colony medicine, but how could she ever make it Out There?

Some PPCs had been designed by their parents to qualify physically and mentally for space careers. Some had been equipped with bichemistries, one of which became active in Earth's gravity, the other in space. How could an NG compete with that?

Of the seven hundred adolescents in her high school training programs, Letitia Blakely was one of ten NGs—possessors of natural, unaltered genomes. Everyone else was the proud bearer of juggled genes, PPCs or Pre-Planned Children, all lovely and stable with just the proper amount of adipose tissue and just the proper infusion of parental characteristics and chosen features to be beautiful and different; tall, healthy, hair manageable, skin unblemished, well-adjusted (except for the occasional blitzer) with warm and sunny personalities. The old derogatory slang for PPCs was RC—Recombined.

Letitia, slightly overweight, skin pasty, hair frizzy, bulbous-nosed and weak-chinned, one breast larger than the other and already showing a droop pronounced enough to grip a stylus —with painful menstrual periods and an absolute indisposition to athletics—was the Sport. That's what they were called. NG Sports. TBs—Throwbacks. Neanderthals.

All the beautiful PPCs risked a great deal if they showed animosity toward the NGs. Her parents had the right to sue the system if she was harassed to the detriment of her schooling. This wasn't a private school where all parents paid astronomical tuitions; this was an old-fashioned public school, with public school programs and regulations. Teachers tended to nuke out on raggers. And, she admitted to herself with a painful loop of recrimination, she wasn't making it any easier for them.

Sure, she could join in, play the old woman—how much realism she would contribute to their little drama, with her genuine TB phys! She could be jolly and self-deprecating like Helen Roberti, who wasn't all that bad-looking anyway—she could pass if she straightened her hair. Or she could be quiet and camouflaged like Bernie Thibhault.

The CG nursie exited from RoR care. Letitia had hardly absorbed a thing. Realtime mod education was a bore, but she hadn't yet qualified for experience training. She had only one course of career study now—no alternates—and two aesthetic programs, individual orchestra on Friday afternoon and LitVid publishing on alternating weekends.

For pre-med, she was a washout, but she wouldn't admit it. She was NG. Her brain took longer to mature; it wasn't as finely wired.

She thought she was incredibly slow. She doubted whether she would ever be successful as a doctor; she was squeamish, and nobody, not even her fellow NGs, would want to be treated by a doctor who grew pale at the sight of blood.

Letitia silently told nursie to start over again, and nursie obliged.

Reena Cathcart, meanwhile, had dropped into her mod with a vengeance. Her blissed expression told it all. The realtime ed slid into her so smooth, so quick, it was pure joy.

No zits on her brain.

Mr. Brant returned ten minutes later with a pale and bleary-eyed Georgia Fischer. She sat two seats behind Letitia and over one aisle. She plugged in her mod dutifully and Brant went to his console to bring up the multimedia and coordinate the whole class. Edna Corman whispered something to her.

"Not a bad blitz, all in all," Georgia commented softly.

"How are you doing, Letitia?" the autocounselor asked. The CG face projected in front of her with some slight wirehash, which Letitia paid no attention to. CG ACs were the jams and she didn't appreciate them even in pristine perfection.

"Poorly," she said.

"Really? Care to elaborate?"

"I want to talk to Dr. Rutger."

"Don't trust your friendly AC?"

"I'd like some clear space. I want to talk to Dr. Rutger."

"Dr. Rutger is busy, dear. Unlike your friendly AC, humans can only be in one place at a time. I'd like to help if I may."

"Then I want program sixteen."

"Done, Letitia." The projection wavered and the face changed to a real-person simulation of Marian Tempesino, the only CG AC Letitia felt comfortable with.

Tempesino had no wirehash, which indicated she was a

231

seldom-used program, and that was just fine with Letitia. "Sixteen here. Letitia? You're looking cut. More adjustment jams?"

"I wanted to talk with Dr. Rutger but he's busy. So I'll talk to you. And I want it on my record. I want out of school. I want my parents to pull me and put me in a special NG school."

Tempesino's face didn't wear any particular expression, which was one of the reasons Letitia liked Program 16 AC. "Why?"

"Because I'm a freak. My parents made me a freak and I'd like to know why I shouldn't be with all the other freaks."

"You're a natural, not a freak."

"To look like any of the others—even to look like Reena Cathcart—I'd have to spend the rest of my life in bioplasty. I can't take it anymore. They asked me to play an old lady in one of their dramas. The only part I'm fit for. An old lady."

"They tried to include you in."

"That *hurt!*" Letitia said, tears in her eyes.

Tempesino's image wavered a bit as the emotion registered and a higher authority AC kicked in behind 16.

"I just want out. I want to be alone."

"Where would you like to go, Letitia?"

Letitia thought about it for a moment. "I'd like to go back to when being ugly was normal."

"Fine, then. Let's simulate. Sixty years should do it. Ready?"

She nodded and wiped away more mascara with the back of her hand.

"Then let's go."

It was like a dream, somewhat fuzzier than plugging in a mod. CG images compiled from thousands of miles of old films and tapes and descriptive records made her feel as if she were flying back in time, back to a place she would have loved to call home. Faces came to her—faces with ugly variations, growing old prematurely, wearing glasses, even beautiful faces which could have passed today—and the faces pulled away to become attached to bodies. Bodies out of shape, in good condition, overweight, sick and healthy, red-faced with high blood pressure: the whole variable and disaster-prone population of humanity, sixty years past. This was where Letitia felt she belonged.

"They're beautiful," she said.

"They didn't think so. They jumped at the chance to be sure their children were beautiful, smart, and healthy. It was a time of transition, Letitia. Just like now."

"Everybody looks alike now."

"I don't think that's fair," the AC said. "There's a considerable variety in the way people look today."

"Not my age."

"Especially your age. Look." The AC showed her dozens of faces. Few looked alike, but all were handsome or lovely. Some made Letitia ache just looking at them; faces she could never be friends with, never love, because there was always someone more beautiful and desirable than an NG.

"My parents should have lived back then. Why did they make me a freak?"

"You're developmentally normal. You're not a freak."

"Sure. I'm a DNG. Dingy. That's what they call me."

"Don't you invite the abuse sometimes?"

"No!" This was getting her nowhere.

"Letitia, we all have to adjust. Not even today's world is fair. Are you sure you're doing all you can to adjust?"

Letitia squirmed in her seat and said she wanted to leave. "Just a moment," the AC said. "We're not done yet." She knew that tone of voice. The ACs were allowed to get a little rough at times. They could make unruly students do grounds duty or detain them after hours to work on assignments usually given to computers. Letitia sighed and settled back. She hated being lectured.

"Young woman, you're carrying a giant chip on your shoulder."

"That's all the more computing capacity for me."

"Quiet, and listen. We're all allowed to criticize policy, whoever makes it. Dignity of office and respect for superiors has not survived very well into Century Twenty-one. People have to earn respect. That goes for students, too. The average student here has four major talents, each of them fitting into a public planning policy which guarantees them a job incorporating two or more of those talents. They aren't forced to accept the jobs, and if their will falters, they may not keep those jobs. But the public has tried to guarantee every one of us a quality employment opportunity. That goes for you, as well. You're DNG, but you also show as much intelligence and at least as many developable talents as the PPCs. You are young, and your maturation schedule is a natural one—but you are not inferior or impaired, Letitia. That's more than can be said for the offspring of some parents even more resistive than your own. You at least were given prenatal care and nutrition adjustment, and your parents let the biotechs correct your allergies."

"So?"

"So for you, it's all a matter of will. If your will falters, you won't be given any more consideration than a PPC. You'll have to choose secondary or tertiary employment, or even . . ." The AC paused. "Public support. Do you want that?"

"My grades are up. I'm doing fine."

"You are choosing career training not matching your developable talents."

"I like medicine."

"You're squeamish."

Letitia shrugged.

"And you're hard to get along with."

"Just tell them to lay off. I'll be civil . . . but I don't want them treating me like a freak. Edna Corman called me . . ." She paused. That could get Edna Corman into a lot of trouble. Among the students, TB was a casual epithet; to school authorities, applied to an NG, it might be grounds for a blot on Corman's record. "Nothing. Not important."

The AC switched to lower authority and Tempesino's face took a different counseling track. "Fine. Adjustment on both sides is necessary. Thank you for coming in, Letitia."

"Yeah. I still want to talk with Rutger."

"Request has been noted. Please return to your class in progress."


"Pay attention to your brother when he's talking," Jane said. Roald was making a nuisance of himself by chattering about the pre-flight training he was getting in primary. Letitia made a polite comment or two, then lapsed back into contemplation of the food before her. She didn't eat. Jane regarded her from the corner of her eye and passed a bowl of sugared berries. "What's eating you?"

"I'm doing the eating," Letitia said archly.

"Ha," Roald said. "Full load from this angle." He grinned at her, his two front teeth missing. He looked hideous, she thought. Any other family would have given him temporaries; not hers.

"A little more respect from both of you," said Donald. Her father took the bowl from Roald and scooped a modest portion into his cup, then set it beside Letitia. "Big fifteen and

235

big eight." That was his homily; behave big whether eight or fifteen.

"Autocounselor today?" Jane asked. She knew Letitia much too well.

"AC," Letitia affirmed.

"Did you go in?"

"Yes."

"And?"

"I'm not tuned."

"Which means?" Donald ask.

"It means she hisses and crackles," Roald said, mouth full of berries, juice dripping down his chin. He cupped his hand underneath and sucked it up noisily. Jane reached out and finished the job with a napkin. "She complains," Roald finished.

"About what?"

Letitia shook her head and didn't answer.

The dessert was almost finished when Letitia slapped both palms on the table. "Why did you do it?"

"Why did we do what?" he father asked, startled.

"Why are Roald and I normal? Why didn't you design us?"

Jane and Donald glanced at each other quickly and turned to Letitia. Roald regarded her with wide eyes, a bit shocked himself.

"Surely you know why by now," Jane said, looking down at the table, either nonplussed or getting angry. Now that she had laid out her course, Letitia couldn't help but forge ahead.

"I don't. Not really. It's not because you're religious."

"Something like that," Donald said.

"No," Jane said, shaking her head firmly.

"Then why?"

"Your mother and I—"

"I am *not* just their mother," Jane said.

"Jane and I believe there is a certain plan in nature, a plan we shouldn't interfere with. If we had gone along with most of the others and tried to have PPCs—participated in the boy-girl lotteries and signed up for the prebirth opportunity counseling— why, we would have been interfering."

"Did you go to a hospital when we were born?"

"Yes," Jane said, still avoiding their faces.

"That's not natural," Letitia said. "Why not let nature decide whether we'd be born alive or not?"

"We have never claimed to be consistent," Donald said.

"Donald," Jane said ominously.

"There are limits," Donald expanded, smiling placation. "We believe those limits begin when people try to interfere with the sex cells. You've had all that in school. You know about the protests when the first PPCs were born. Your grandmother was one of the protesters. Your mother and I are both NGs; of course, our generation has a much higher percentage of NGs."

"Now we're freaks," Letitia said.

"If by that you mean there aren't many teenage NGs, I suppose that's right," Donald said, touching his wife's arm. "But it could also mean you're special. Chosen."

"No," Letitia said. "Not chosen. You played dice with both of us. We could have been DDs. Duds. Not just dingies, but retards or spaz."

An uncomfortable quiet settled over the table. "Not likely," Donald said, his voice barely above a whisper. "Your mother and I both have good genotypes. Your grandmother insisted your mother marry a good genotype. There are no developmentally disabled people in our families."

Letitia had been hemmed in. There was no way she could see out of it, so she pushed back her chair and excused herself from the table.

237

As she made her way up to her room, she heard arguing below. Roald raced up the stairs behind her and gave her a dirty look. "Why'd you have to bring all that up?" he asked. "It's bad enough at school, we don't have to have it here."

She thought about the history the AC had shown her. Back then, a family with their income wouldn't have been able to live in a four-bedroom house. Back then, there had been half as many people in the United States and Canada as there were now. There had been more unemployment, much more economic uncertainty, and far fewer automated jobs. The percentage of people doing physical labor for a living—simple construction, crop maintenance and harvesting, digging ditches and hard work like that—had been ten times greater then than it was now. Most of the people doing such labor today belonged to religious sects or one of the Wendell Barry farming communes.

Back then, Roald and Letitia would have been considered gifted children with a bright future.

She thought about the pictures and the feeling of the past, and wondered if Reena hadn't been right.

She would be a perfect old woman.

Her mother came into her room while Letitia was putting up her hair. She stood in the door frame. It was obvious she had been crying. Letitia watched her reflection in the mirror of her grandmother's dressing table, willed to her four years before. "Yes?" she asked softly, ageless bobby pins in her mouth.

"It was more my idea than your father's," Jane said, stepping closer, hands folded before her. "I mean, I *am* your mother. We've never really talked about this."

"No," Letitia said.

"So why now?"

"Maybe I'm growing up."

"Yes." Jane looked at the soft and flickering pictures hung on the walls, pastel scenes of improbable forests. "When I was pregnant with you, I was very afraid. I worried we'd made the wrong decision, going against what everybody else seemed to think and what everybody was advising or being advised. But I carried you and felt you move . . . and I knew you were ours, and ours alone, and that we were responsible for you body and soul. I was your mother, not the doctors.''

Letitia looked up with mixed anger and frustration . . . and love.

"And now I see *you*. I think back to what I might have felt, if I were your age again, in your position. I might be mad, too. Roald hasn't had time to feel different yet; he's too young. I just came up here to tell you; I know that what I did was right, not for us, not for them''—she indicated the broad world beyond the walls of the house—"but right for you. It will work out. It really will.'' She put her hands on Letitia's shoulders. "They aren't having an easy time either. You know that.'' She stopped for a moment, then from behind her back revealed a book with a soft brown cover. "I brought this to show you again. You remember Great-Grandma? Her grandmother came all the way from Ireland, along with her grandpa.'' Jane gave her the album. Reluctantly, Letitia opened it up. There were real photographs inside, on paper, ancient black and white and faded color. Her great-grandmother did not much resemble Grandmother, who had been big-boned, heavy-set. Great-grandmother looked as if she had been skinny all her life. "You keep this,'' Jane said. "Think about it for a while.''

The morning came with planned rain. Letitia took the half-empty metro to school, looking at the terraced and gardened and occasionally neglected landscape of the extended suburbs through raindrop-smeared glass. She came onto the school grounds and went to one of the older buildings in the school, where there was a little-used old-fashioned lavatory. This sometimes served as her sanctuary. She stood in a white stall and breathed deeply for a few minutes, then went to a sink and washed her hands as if conducting some ritual. Slowly, reluctantly, she looked at herself in the cracked mirror. A janitorial worker went about its duties, leaving behind the fresh, steamy smell of clean fixtures.

The early part of the day was a numb time. Letitia began to fear her own distance from feeling, from the people around her. She might at any minute step into the old lavatory and simply fade from the present, find herself sixty years back . . .

And what would she really think of that?

In her third period class she received a note requesting that she appear in Rutger's counseling office as soon as was convenient. That was shorthand for immediately; she gathered up her mods and caught Reena's unreadable glance as she walked past.

Rutger was a handsome man of forty-three (the years were registered on his desk life clock, an affectation of some of the older PPCs) with a broad smile and a garish taste in clothes. He was head of the counseling department and generally well-liked in the school. He shook her hand as she entered the counseling office and offered her a chair. "Now. You wanted to talk to me?"

"I guess," Letitia said.

"Problems?" His voice was a pleasant baritone; he was probably a fairly good singer. That had been a popular trait in the early days of PPCs.

"The ACs say it's my attitude."

"And what about it?"

"I . . . am ugly. I am the ugliest girl . . . the only girl in this school who is ugly."

Rutger nodded. "I don't think you're ugly, but which is worse, being unique or being ugly?" Letitia lifted the corner of one lip in snide acknowledgment of the funny.

"Everybody's unique now," she said.

"That's what we teach. Do you believe it?"

"No," she said. "Everybody's the same. I'm..." She shook her head. She resented Rutger prying up the pavement over her emotions. "I'm TB. I wouldn't mind being a PPC, but I'm not."

"I think it's a minor problem," Rutger said quickly. He hadn't even sat down; obviously he was not going to give her much time.

"It doesn't feel minor," she said, anger poking through the cracks he had made.

"Oh, no. Being young often means that minor problems feel major. You feel envy and don't like yourself, at least not the way you look. Well, looks can be helped by diet, or at the very least by time. If I'm any judge, you'll look fine when you're older. And I *am* something of a judge. As for the way the others feel about you . . . I was a freak once."

Letitia looked up at him.

"Certainly. Bona fide. Much more of a freak than you. There are ten NGs like yourself in this school now. When I was your age, I was the only PPC in my school. There was still suspicion and even riots. Some PPCs were killed in one school when parents stormed the grounds."

Letitia stared.

"The other kids hated me. I wasn't bad-looking, but they knew. They had parents who told them PPCs were Frankenstein monsters. Do you remember the Rifkin Society? They're still around, but they're extreme fringies now. Just as well. They thought I'd been grown in a test tube somewhere and hatched out of an incubator. You've never experienced real hatred, I suspect. I did."

"You were nice-looking," Letitia said. "You knew somebody would like you eventually, maybe even love you. But what about me? Because of what I am, the way I look, who will ever want me? And will a PPC ever want to be with a Dingy?''

She knew these were hard questions and Rutger made no pretense of answering them. "Say it all works out for the worst," he said. "You end up a spinster and no one ever loves you. You spend the rest of your days alone. Is that what you're worried about?"

Her eyes widened. She had never quite thought those things through. Now she really hurt.

"Everybody out there is choosing beauty for their kids. They're choosing slender, athletic bodies and fine minds. You have a fine mind, but you don't have an athletic body. Or so you seem to be convinced; I have no record of you ever trying out for athletics. So when you're out in the adult world, sure, you'll look different. But why can't that be an advantage? You may be surprised how hard we PPCs try to be different. And how hard it is, since tastes vary so little in our parents. You have that built in."

Letitia listened, but the layers of paving were closing again. "Icing on the cake," she said.

Rutger regarded her with his shrewd blue eyes and shrugged. "Come back in a month and talk to me," he said. "Until then, I think autocounselors will do fine."

Little was said at dinner and less after. She went upstairs and to bed at an early hour, feeling logy and hoping for escape.

Her father did his usual bedcheck an hour after she had put on her pajamas and lain down. "Rolled tight?" he asked.

"Mmph," she replied.

"Sleep tighter," he said. Rituals and formulas. Her life had been shaped by parents who were comfortable with nightly rituals and formulas.

Almost immediately after sleep, or so it seemed, she came

abruptly awake. She sat up in bed and realized where she was, and who, and began to cry. She had had the strangest and most beautiful dream, the finest ever without a dream mod. She could not remember details now, try as she might, but waking was almost more than she could bear.

In the first period class, Georgia Fischer blitzed yet again and had to go to the infirmary. Letitia watched the others and saw a stony general cover-up of feelings. Edna Corman excused herself in second period and came back with red puffy eyes and pink cheeks. The tension built through the rest of the day until she wondered how anyone could concentrate. She did her own studying without any conviction; she was still wrapped in the dream, trying to decide what it meant.

In eighth period, she once again sat behind John Lockwood. It was as if she had completed a cycle beginning in the morning and ending with her last class. She looked at her watch anxiously. Once again, they had Mr. Brant supervising. He seemed distracted, as if he, too, had had a dream, and it hadn't been as pleasant as hers.

Brant had them cut mods mid-period and begin a discussion on what had been learned. These were the so-called integrative moments when the media learning was fixed by social interaction; Letitia found these periods a trial at the best of times. The others discussed their economics, Reena Cathcart as usual standing out in a class full of dominant personalities.

John Lockwood listened intently, a small smile on his face as he presented a profile to Letitia. He seemed about to turn around and talk to her. She placed her hand on the corner of her console and lifted her finger to attract his attention.

He glanced at her hand, turned away, and with a shudder looked at it again, staring this time, eyes widening. His mouth began to work as if her hand was the most horrible thing he had ever seen. His chin quivered, then his shoulder, and before Letitia could react he stood up and moaned. His legs went liquid beneath him and he fell to the console, arms hanging, then slid to the floor. On the floor, John Lockwood—who had never done such a thing in his life—twisted and groaned and shivered, locked in a violent blitz.

Brant pressed the class emergency button and came around his desk. Before he could reach Lockwood, the boy became still, eyes open, one hand letting go its tight grip on the leg of his seat. Letitia could not move, watching his empty eyes; he appeared so horribly *limp*.

Brant grabbed the boy by the shoulders, swearing steadily, and dragged him outside the classroom. Letitia followed them into the hall, wanting to help. Edna Corman and Reena Cathcart stood beside her, faces blank. Other students followed, staying well away from Brant and the boy.

Brant lowered John Lockwood to the concrete and began pounding his chest and administering mouth-to-mouth. He pulled a syringe from his coat pocket and uncapped it, shooting its full contents into the boy's skin just below the sternum. Letitia focused on the syringe, startled. Right in his pocket; not in the first-aid kit.

The full class stood in the hallway, silent, in shock. The medical arrived, Rutger following; it scooped John Lockwood onto its gurney and swung around, lights flashing. "Have you administered KVN?" the robot asked Brant.

"Yes. Five cc's. Direct to heart."

Room after room came out to watch, all the PPCs fixing their eyes on the burdened medical as it rolled down the hall. Edna Corman cried. Reena glanced at Letitia and turned away as if ashamed.

"That's five," Rutger said, voice tired beyond grimness. Brant looked at him, then at the class, and told them they were dismissed. Letitia hung back. Brant screwed up his face in grief and anger. "Go! Get out of here!"

She ran. The last thing she heard Rutger say was, "More this week than last."

Letitia sat in the empty white lavatory, wiping her eyes, ashamed at her sniveling. She wanted to react like a grown-up—she saw herself being calm, cool, offering help to whoever might have needed it in the classroom—but the tears and the shaking would not stop.

Mr. Brant had seemed angry, as if the entire classroom were at fault. Not only was Mr. Brant adult, he was PPC.

So did she expect adults, especially adult PPCs, to behave better?

Wasn't that what it was all about?

She stared at herself in the cracked mirror. "I should go home, or go to the library and study," she said. Dignity and decorum. Two girls walked into the lavatory, and her private moment passed.

Letitia did not go to the library. Instead, she went to the old concrete and steel auditorium, entering through the open stage entrance, standing in darkness in the wings. Three female students sat in the front row, below the stage level and about ten meters away from Letitia. She recognized Reena but not the other two; they did not share classes with her.

"Did you know him?"

"No, not very well," Reena said. "He was in my class."

"No ducks!" the third snorted.

"Trish, keep it *interior*, please. Reena's had it rough."

"He hadn't blitzed. He wasn't a superwhiz. Nobody expected it."

"When was his incept?"

"I don't know," Reena said. "We're all about the same

age, within a couple of months. We're all the same model year, same supplements. If it's something in the genotype, in the supplements . . .''

"I heard somebody say there had been five so far. I haven't heard anything," the third said.

"I haven't either," said the second.

"Not in our school," Reena said. "Except for the superwhizes. And none of them have died before now."

Letitia stepped back in the darkness, hand on mouth. Had Lockwood actually died?

She thought for a mad moment of stepping out of the wings, going into the seats and telling the three she was sorry. The impulse faded fast. That would have been intruding.

They weren't any older than she was, and they didn't sound much more mature. They sounded scared.

In the morning, at the station room for pre-med secondary, Brant told them that John Lockwood had died the day before. "He had a heart attack," Brant said. Letitia intuited that was not the complete truth. A short eulogy was read, and special hours for psych counseling were arranged for those students who felt they might need it.

The word "blitzing" was not mentioned by Brant, nor by any of the PPCs throughout that day. Letitia tried to research the subject but found precious few materials in the libraries accessed by her mod. She presumed she didn't know where to look; it was hard to believe that *nobody* knew what was happening.

The dream came again, even stronger, the next night, and Letitia awoke out of it cold and shivering with excitement. She saw herself standing before a crowd, no single face visible, for she was in light and they were in darkness. She had felt, in the dream, an almost unbearable happiness, grief mixed with joy, unlike anything she had ever experienced before. She *loved* and did not know what she loved—not the crowd, precisely, not a man, not a family member, not even herself.

She sat up in her bed, hugging her knees, wondering if anybody else was awake. It seemed possible she had never been awake until now; every nerve was alive. Quietly, not wanting anybody else to intrude on this moment, she slipped out of bed and walked down the hall to her mother's sewing room. There, in a full-length cheval mirror, she looked at herself as if with new eyes.

"Who are you?" she whispered. She lifted her cotton nightshirt and stared at her legs. Short calves, lumpy knees, thighs not bad—not fat, at any rate. Her arms were soft-looking, not muscular, but not particularly plump, a rosy vanilla color with strawberry blotches on her elbows where she leaned on them while reading in bed. She had Irish ancestors on her mother's side; that showed in her skin color, recessed cheekbones, broad face. On her father's side, Mexican and German; not much evidence in her of the Mexican. Her brother looked more swarthy. "We're mongrels," she said. "I look like a mongrel compared to PPC purebreds." But PPCs were not purebred; they were *designed*.

She lifted her nightshirt higher still, pulling it over her head finally and standing naked. Shivering from the cold and from the memory of her dream, she forced herself to focus on all of her characteristics. Whenever she had seen herself naked in mirrors before, she had blurred her eyes at one feature, looked away from another, special-effecting her body into a more acceptable fantasy. Now she was in a mood to know herself for what she was.

Broad hips, strong abdomen—plump, but strong. From her pre-med, she knew that meant she would probably have little trouble bearing children. "Brood mare," she said, but there was no critical sharpness in the words. To have children, she would have to attract men, and right now there seemed little chance of that. She did not have the "Attraction Peaks" so often discussed on the TV, or seen faddishly headlined on the LitVid mods; the culturally prescribed geometric curves allocated to so few naturally, and now available to so many by design. *Does Your Child Have the Best Design for Success?*

Such a shocking triviality. She felt a righteous anger grow—another emotion she was not familiar with—and sucked it back into the excitement, not wanting to lose her mood. "I might never look at myself like this again," she whispered.

Her breasts were moderate in size, the left larger than the right and more drooping. She could indeed hold a stylus under her left breast, something a PPC female would not have to worry about for decades, if ever. Rib cage not really distinct; muscles not distinct; rounded, soft, gentle-looking, face curious, friendly, wide-eyed, skin blemished but not so badly it wouldn't recover on its own; feet long and toenails thick, heavily cuticled. She had never suffered from ingrown toenails.

Her family line showed little evidence of tendency to cancer—correctible now, but still distressing—or heart disease or any of the other diseases of melting pot cultures, of mobile populations and changing habits. She saw a strong body in the mirror, one that would serve her well.

And she also saw that with a little makeup, she could easily play an older woman. Some shadow under the eyes, lines to highlight what would in thirty or forty years be jowls, laugh lines . . .

But she did not look old *now*.

Letitia walked back to her room, treading carefully on the carpet. In the room, she asked the lights to turn on, lay down on the bed, pulled the photo album Jane had given her from the top of her nightstand and gingerly turned the delicate black paper pages. She stared at her great-grandmother's face, and then at the picture of her grandmother as a little girl.

Individual orchestra was taught by three instructors in one of the older drama classrooms behind the auditorium. It was a popular aesthetic; the school's music boxes were better than most home units, and the instructors were very popular. All were PPCs.

After a half hour of group, each student could retire to box keyboard, order up spheres of countersound to avoid cacophony, and practice.

Today, she practiced for less than half an hour. Then, tongue between her lips, she stared into empty space over the keyboard. "Countersound off, please," she ordered, and stood up from the black bench. Mr. Teague, the senior instructor, asked if she were done for the day.

"I have to run an errand," she said.

"Practice your polyrhythms," he advised.

She left the classroom and walked around to the auditorium's stage entrance. She knew Reena's drama group would be meeting there.

The auditorium was dark, the stage lighted by a few catwalk spots. The drama group sat in a circle of chairs in one illuminated corner of the stage, reading lines aloud from old paper scripts. Hands folded, she walked toward the group. Rick Fayette, a quiet senior with short black hair, spotted her first but said nothing, glancing at Reena. Reena stopped reading her lines, turned, and stared at Letitia. Edna Corman saw her last and shook her head, as if this were the last straw.

"Hello," Letitia said.

"What are you doing here?" There was more wonder than disdain in Reena's voice.

"I thought you might still . . ." She shook her head.

"Probably not. But I thought you might still be able to use me."

"*Really,*" Edna Corman said.

Reena put her script down and stood. "Why'd you change your mind?"

"I thought I wouldn't mind being an old lady," Reena said. "It's just not that big a deal. I brought a picture of my great-grandmother." She took a plastic wallet from her pocket and opened it to a copy she had made from the photo in the album. "You could make me up like this. Like my great-grandmother."

Reena took the wallet. "You look like her," she said.

"Yeah. Kind of."

"Look at this," Reena said, holding the picture out to the others. They gathered around and passed the wallet from hand to hand, staring in wonder. Even Edna Corman glanced at it briefly. "She actually looks like her great-grandmother."

Rick Fayette whistled with wonder. "You," he said, "will make a really great old lady."

Rutger called her into his office abruptly a week later. She sat quietly before his desk. "You've joined the drama class after all," he said. She nodded.

"Any reason why?"

There was no simple way to express it. "Because of what you told me," she said.

"No friction?"

"It's going okay."

"Very good. They gave you another role to play?"

"No. I'm the old lady. They'll use makeup on me."

"You don't object to that?"

"I don't think so."

Rutger seemed to want to find something wrong, but he couldn't. With a faintly suspicious smile, he thanked her for her time. "Come back and see me whenever you want," he said. "Tell me how it goes."

The group met each Friday, an hour later than her individual orchestra. Letitia made arrangements for home keyboard hookup and practice. After a reading and a half hour of questions, she obtained the permission of the drama group advisor, a spinsterish non-PPC seldom seen in the hallways, Miss Darcy. Miss Darcy seemed old-fashioned and addressed all of her students as either "Mister" or "Miss," but she knew drama and stagecraft. She was the oldest of the six NG teachers in the school.

Reena stayed with Letitia during the audition and made a strong case for her late admittance, saying that the casting of Rick Fayette as an older woman was not going well. Fayette was equally eager to be rid of the part; he had another nonconflicting role, and the thought of playing two characters in this production worried him.

Fayette confessed his appreciation at their second Friday meeting. He introduced her to an elfishly handsome, large-eyed, slender group member, Frank Leroux. Leroux was much too shy to go on stage, Fayette said, but he would be doing their makeup. "He's pretty amazing."

Letitia stood nervously while Leroux examined her. "You've really got a *face*," he said softly. "May I touch you, to see where your contours are?"

Letitia giggled and abruptly sobered, embarrassed. "Okay," she said. "You're going to draw lines and make shadows?"

"Much more than that," Leroux said.

"He'll take a video of your face in motion," Fayette said. "Then he'll digitize it and sculpt a laserfoam mold—much better than sitting for a life mask. He made a life mask of *me* last year to turn me into the Hunchback of Notre Dame. No fun at all.''

"This way is much better," Leroux said, touching her skin delicately, poking under her cheeks and chin, pulling back her hair to feel her temples. "I can make two or three sculptures showing what your face and neck are like when they're in different positions. Then I can adjust the appliance molds for flex and give.''

"When he's done with you, you won't know yourself," Fayette said.

"Reena says you have a picture of your great-grandmother. May I see it?" Leroux asked. She gave him the wallet and he looked at the picture with squint-eyed intensity. "What a wonderful face," he said. "I never met my great-grandmother. My own grandmother looks about as old as my mother. They might be sisters.''

"When he's done with you," Fayette said, his enthusiasm becoming a bit tiresome, "you and your *great-grandmother* will look like sisters!''

When she went home that evening, taking a late pay metro from the school, she wondered just exactly what she was doing. Throughout her high school years, she had cut herself off from most of her fellow students; the closest she came to friendship had been occasional banter while sitting at the mods with John Lockwood, waiting for instructors to arrive. Now she actually liked Fayette, and strange Leroux, whose hands were thin and pale and strong and slightly cold. Leroux was a PPC, but obviously his parents had different tastes; was he a superwhiz? Nobody had said so; perhaps it was a matter of honor among PPCs that they pretended not to care about their classifications.

Reena was friendly and supportive, but still distant.

As Letitia walked up the stairs, across the porch into the

door of their home, setting her keyboard down by the closet, she saw the edge of a news broadcast in the living room. Nobody was watching; she surmised everybody was in the kitchen.

From this angle, the announcer appeared translucent and blue, ghostly. As Letitia walked around to the premium angle, the announcer solidified, a virtual goddess of Oriental-negroid features with high cheekbones, straight golden hair and copper-bronze skin. Letitia didn't care what she looked like; what she was saying had attracted her attention.

"—revelations made today that as many as one-fourth of all PPCs inceived between sixteen and seventeen years ago may be possessors of a defective chromosome sequence known as T56-WA 5659. Originally part of an intelligence enhancement macrobox used in ramping creativity and mathematical ability, T56-WA 5659 was refined and made a standard option in virtually all pre-planned children. The effects of this defective sequence are not yet known, but at least twenty children in our city have already died. They all suffered from initial symptoms similar to grand mal epilepsy. Nationwide casualties are as yet unknown. The Rifkin Society is charging government regulatory agencies with a wholesale coverup.

"The Parental Pre-Natal Design Administration has advised parents of PPC children with this incept to immediately contact your medicals and design specialists for advice and treatment. Younger children may be eligible to receive whole-body retroviral therapy. For more detailed information, please refer to our LitVid on-line at this moment, and call—"

Letitia turned and saw her mother watching with a kind of grim satisfaction. When she noticed her daughter's shocked expression, she suddenly appeared sad. "How unfortunate," she said. "I wonder how far it will go."

Letitia did not eat much dinner. Nor did she sleep more

than a couple of hours that night. The weekend seemed to stretch on forever.

Leroux compared the laserfoam sculptures to her face, turning her chin this way and that with gentle hands before the green room mirror. As Leroux worked to test the various molds on Letitia, humming softly to himself, the rest of the drama group rehearsed a scene that did not require her presence. When they were done, Reena walked into the green room and stood behind them, watching. Letitia smiled stiffly through the hastily applied sheets and mounds of skinlike plastic.

"You're going to look great," Reena said.

"I'm going to look *old*," Letitia said, trying for a joke.

"I hope you aren't worried about that," Reena said. "Nobody cares, really. They all like you. Even Edna."

"I'm not worried," Letitia said.

Leroux pulled off the pieces and laid them carefully in a box. "Just about got it," he said. "I'm getting so good I could even make *Reena* look old if she'd let me."

Letitia considered for a moment. The implication, rather than the meaning, was embarrassingly obvious. Reena blushed and stared angrily at Leroux. Leroux caught her stare, looked between them, and said, "Well, I could." Reena could not argue without sinking them all deeper. Letitia blinked, then decided to let them off this particular hook. "She wouldn't look like a grandmother, though. I'll be a much better old lady."

"Of course," Leroux said, picking up his box and the sculptures. He walked to the door, a mad headsman. "Like your great-grandmother."

For a long silent moment, Reena and Letitia faced each other alone in the green room. The old incandescent makeup lights glared around the cracked mirror, casting a pearly glow on the white walls behind them. "You're a good actress," Reena said. "It really doesn't matter what you look like."

"Thank you."

"Sometimes I wished I looked like somebody in my family," Reena said.

Without thinking, Letitia said, "But you're beautiful." And she meant it. Reena *was* beautiful; with her Levantine darkness and long black hair, small sharp chin, large hazel-colored almond eyes and thin, ever-so-slightly bowed nose, she was simply lovely, with the kind of face and bearing and intelligence that two or three generations before would have moved her into entertainment, or pushed her into the social circles of the rich and famous. Behind the physical beauty was a sparkle of reserved wit, and something gentle. PPCs were healthier, felt better, and their minds, on the average, were more subtle, more balanced. Letitia did not feel inferior, however; not this time.

Something magic touched them. The previous awkwardness, and her deft destruction of that awkwardness, had moved them into a period of charmed conversation. Neither could offend the other; without words, that was a given.

"My parents are beautiful, too. I'm second generation," Reena said.

"Why would you want to look any different?"

"I don't, I suppose. I'm happy with the way I look. But I don't look much like my mother or my father. Oh, color, hair, eyes, that sort of thing . . . Still, my mother wasn't happy with her own face. She didn't get along well with my grandmother . . . She blamed her for not matching her face with her personality." Reena smiled. "It's all rather silly."

"Some people are never happy," Letitia observed.

Reena stepped forward and leaned over slightly to face

Letitia's mirror image. "How do you feel, looking like your grandmother?"

Letitia bit her lip. "Until you asked me to join, I don't think I ever knew." She told about her mother giving her the album, and looking at herself in the mirror—though she did not describe being naked—and comparing herself with the old pictures.

"I think that's called an epiphany," Reena said. "It must have been nice. I'm glad I asked you, then, even if I was stupid."

"Were you . . ." Letitia paused. The period of charm was fading, regrettably; she did not know whether this question would be taken as she meant it. "Did you ask me to give me a chance to stop being so silly and stand-offish?"

"No," Reena said steadily. "I asked you because we needed an old lady."

Looking at each other, they laughed suddenly, and the charmed moment was gone, replaced by something steadier and longer-lasting: friendship. Letitia took Reena's hand and pressed it. "Thank you," she said.

"You're welcome." Then, with hardly a pause, Reena said, "At least *you* don't have to worry."

Letitia stared up at her, mouth open slightly, eyes searching.

"Got to go home now," Reena said. She squeezed Letitia's shoulder with more than gentle strength, revealing a physical anger or jealousy that ran counter to all they had said and done thus far. She turned and walked through the green room door, leaving Letitia alone to pick off a few scraps of latex and adhesive.

The disaster grew. Letitia listened to the news in her room late that night, whispers in her ear, projected ghosts of news-casters and doctors and scientists dancing before her eyes, telling her things she did not really understand, could only feel.

A monster walked through her generation, but it would not touch her.

Going to school on Monday, she saw students clustered in hallways before the bell, somber, talking in low voices, glancing at her as she passed. In her second period class, she learned from overheard conversation that Leroux had died during the weekend. "He was superwhiz," a tall, athletic girl told her neighbor. "They don't die, usually, they just blitz. But he died."

Letitia retreated to the old lavatory at the beginning of lunch break, found it empty, but did not stare into the mirror. She knew what she looked like and accepted it.

What she found difficult to accept was a new feeling inside her. The young Letitia was gone. She could not live on a battlefield and remain a child. She thought about slender, elfin Leroux, carrying her heads under his arms, touching her face with gentle, professional admiration. Strong, cool fingers. Her eyes filled but the tears would not fall, and she went to lunch empty, fearful, confused.

She did not apply for counseling, however. This was something she had to face on her own.

Nothing much happened the next few days. The rehearsals went smoothly in the evenings as the date of the play approached. She learned her lines easily enough. Her role had a sadness that matched her mood. On Wednesday evening, after rehearsal, she joined Reena and Fayette at a supermarket sandwich stand near the school. Letitia did not tell her parents she would be late; she felt the need to not be responsible to anybody but her immediate peers. Jane would be upset, she knew, but not for long; this was a *necessity*.

Neither Reena nor Fayette mentioned the troubles directly. They were fairylike in their gaiety. They kidded Letitia about having to do without makeup now, and it seemed funny, despite their hidden grief. They ate sandwiches and drank fruit sodas and talked about what they would be when they grew up.

"Things didn't used to be so easy," Fayette said. "Kids didn't have so many options. Schools weren't very efficient at training for the real world; they were academic."

"Learning was slower," Letitia said.

"So were the kids," Reena said, tossing off an irresponsible grin.

"I resent that," Letitia said. Then, together, they all said, "*I don't deny it, I just resent it!*" Their laughter caught the attention of an older couple sitting in a corner. Even if the man and woman were not angry, Letitia wanted them to be, and she bowed her head down, giggling into her straw, snucking bubbles up her nose and choking. Reena made a disapproving face and Fayette covered his mouth, snorting with laughter.

"You could paste rubber all over your face," Fayette suggested.

"I'd look like Frankenstein's monster, not an old woman," Letitia said.

"So what's the difference?" Reena said.

"Really, you guys," Letitia said. "You're acting your age."

"Don't have to act," Fayette said. "Just *be*."

"I wish we could act our age," Reena said.

Not once did they mention Leroux, but it was as if he sat beside them the whole time, sharing their levity.

It was the closest thing to a wake they could have.


"Have you gone to see your designer, your medical?" Letitia asked Reena behind the stage curtains. The lights were off. Student stagehands moved muslin walls on dollies. Fresh paint smells filled the air.

258

"No," Reena said. "I'm not worried. I have a different incept."

"Really?"

She nodded. "It's okay. If there was any problem, I wouldn't be here. Don't worry." And nothing more was said.

The night of dress rehearsal came. Letitia put on her own makeup, drawing pencil lines and applying color and shadow; she had practiced and found herself reasonably adept at aging. With her great-grandmother's photograph before her, she mimicked the jowls she would have in her later years, drew laugh lines around her lips, and completed the effect with a smelly old gray wig dug out of a prop box.

The actors gathered for a prerehearsal inspection by Miss Darcy. They seemed quite adult now, dressed in their period costumes, tall and handsome. Letitia didn't mind standing out. Being an old woman gave her special status.

"This time, just relax, do it smooth," said Miss Darcy. "Everybody expects you to flub your lines, so you'll probably do them all perfectly. We'll have an audience, but they're here to forgive our mistakes, not laugh at them. This one," Miss Darcy said, pausing, "is for Mr. Leroux."

They all nodded solemnly.

"Tomorrow, when we put on the first show, that's going to be for *you*."

They took their places in the wings. Letitia stood behind Reena, who would be first on stage. Reena shot her a quick smile, nervous.

"How's your stomach?" she whispered.

"Where's the bag?" Letitia asked, pretending to gag herself with a finger.

"TB," Reena accused lightly.

"RC," Letitia replied. They shook hands firmly.

The curtain went up. The auditorium was half filled with parents and friends and relatives. Letitia's parents were out there. The darkness beyond the stagelights seemed so profound it should have been filled with stars and nebulae. Would her small voice reach that far?

The recorded music before the first act came to its quiet end. Reena made a move to go on stage, then stopped. Letitia nudged her. "Come on."

Reena pivoted to look at her, face cocked to one side, and Letitia saw a large tear dripping from her left eye. Fascinated, she watched the tear fall in slow motion down her cheek and spot the satin of her gown.

"I'm sorry," Reena whispered, lips twitching. "I can't do it now. Tell. Tell."

Horrified, Letitia reached out, tried to stop her from falling, to lift her, paste and push her back into place, but Reena was too heavy and she could not stop her descent, only slow it. Reena's feet kicked out like a horse's, bruising Letitia's legs, all in apparent silence, and her eyes were bright and empty and wet, fluttering, showing the whites.

Letitia bent over her, hands raised, afraid to touch her, afraid not to, unaware she was shrieking.

Fayette and Edna Corman stood behind her, equally helpless.

Reena lay still like a twisted doll, face upturned to the flies, eyes moving slowly to Letitia, vibrating, becoming still.

"Not you!" Letitia screamed, and barely heard the commotion in the audience. "Please, God, let it be me, not her!"

Fayette backed away and Miss Darcy came into the light, grabbing Letitia's shoulders. She shook free.

"Not her," Letitia sobbed. The medicals arrived and surrounded Reena, blocking her from the eyes of all around. Miss Darcy firmly, almost brutally, pushed her students from the stage and herded them into the green room. Her face was stiff as a mask, eyes stark in the paleness.

"We have to *do* something!" Letitia said, holding up her hands, beseeching.

"Get control of yourself," Miss Darcy said sharply. "Everything's being done that can be done."

Fayette said, "What about the play?"

Everyone stared at him.

"Sorry," he said, lip quivering. "I'm an idiot."


Jane, Donald, and Roald came to the green room and Letitia hugged her mother fiercely, eyes shut tight, burying her face in Jane's shoulder. They escorted her outside, where a few students and parents still milled about in the early evening. "We should go home," Jane said.

"We have to stay here and find out if she's all right." Letitia pushed away from Jane's arms and looked at the people. "They're so frightened. I know they are. She's frightened, too. I saw her. She told me—" Her voice hitched. "She told me—"

"We'll stay for a little while," her father said. He walked off to talk to another man. They conversed for a while, the man shook his head, they parted. Roald stood away from them, hands stuffed into his pockets, dismayed, young, uncomfortable.

"All right," Donald said a few minutes later. "We're not going to find out anything tonight. Let's go home."

This time, she did not protest. Home, she locked herself in her bedroom. She did not need to know. She had seen it happen; anything else was self-delusion.

Her father came to the door an hour later, rapped gently. Letitia came up from a troubled doze and got off the bed to let him in.

"We're very sorry," he said.

"Thanks," she murmured, returning to the bed. He sat

beside her. She might have been eight or nine again; she looked around the room, at toys and books, knickknacks.

"Your teacher, Miss Darcy, called. She said to tell you, Reena Cathcart died. She was dead by the time they got her to the hospital. Your mother and I have been watching the vids. A lot of children are very sick now. A lot have died." He touched her head, patted the crown gently. "I think you know now why we wanted a natural child. There were risks—"

"That's not fair," she said. "You didn't have us ..." She hiccupped. "The way you did, because you thought there would be risks. You talk as if there's something wrong with these ... people."

"Isn't there?" Donald asked, eyes suddenly flinty. "They're defective."

"They're my friends!" Letitia shouted.

"Please," Donald said, flinching.

She got to her knees on the bed, tears coming again. "There's nothing wrong with them! They're people! They're just sick, that's all."

"You're not making sense," Donald said.

"I talked to her," Letitia said. "She must have known. You can't just say there's something wrong with them. That isn't enough."

"Their parents should have known," Donald pursued, voice rising. "Letitia ..."

"Leave me alone," she demanded. He stood up hastily, confused, and walked out, closing the door behind him. She lay back on the bed, wondering what Reena had wanted her to say, and to whom.

"I'll do it," she whispered.

In the morning, breakfast was silent. Roald ate his cereal with caution, glancing at the others with wide, concerned eyes. Letitia ate little, pushed away from the table, said, "I'm going to her funeral."

"We don't know—" Jane said.

"I'm going."

Letitia went to only one funeral: Reena's. With a puzzled expression, she watched Reena's parents from across the grave, wondering about them, comparing them to Jane and Donald. She did not cry. She came home and wrote down the things she had thought.

That school year was the worst. One hundred and twelve students from the school died. Another two hundred became very ill.

John Fayette died.

The drama class continued, but no plays were presented. The school was quiet. Many students had been withdrawn from classes; Letitia watched the hysteria mount, listened to rumors that it was a plague, not a PPC error.

It was not a plague.

Across the nation, two million children became ill. One million died.

Letitia read, without really absorbing the truth all at once, that it was the worst disaster in the history of the United States. Riots destroyed PPC centers. Women carrying PPC babies demanded abortions. The Rifkin Society became a political force of considerable influence.

Each day, after school, listening to the news, everything about her existence seemed trivial. Their family was healthy. They were growing up normally.

Edna Corman approached her in school at the end of one day, two weeks before graduation. "Can we talk?" she asked. "Someplace quiet."

"Sure," Letitia said. They had not become close friends,

but she found Edna Corman tolerable. Letitia took her into the old bathroom and they stood surrounded by the echoing white tiles.

"You know, everybody, I mean the older people, they stare at me, at us," Edna said. "Like we're going to fall over any minute. It's really bad. I don't think I'm going to get sick, but . . . It's like people are afraid to touch me."

"I know," Letitia said.

"Why is that?" Edna said, voice trembling.

"I don't know," Letitia said. Edna just stood before her, hands limp.

"Was it our fault?" she asked.

"No. You know that."

"Please tell me."

"Tell you what?"

"What we can do to make it right."

Letitia looked at her for a moment, and then extended her arms, took her by the shoulders, drew her closer, and hugged her. "Remember," she said.

Five days before graduation, Letitia asked Rutger if she could give a speech at the ceremonies. Rutger sat behind his desk, folded his hands, and said, "Why?"

"Because there are some things nobody's saying," Letitia told him. "And they should be said. If nobody else will say them, then . . ." She swallowed hard. "Maybe I can."

He regarded her dubiously for a moment. "You really think there's something important that you can say?"

She faced him down. Nodded.

"Write the speech," he said. "Show it to me."

She pulled a piece of paper out of her pocket. He read it carefully, shook his head—she thought at first in denial—and then handed it back to her.

*     *     *

Waiting in the wings to go on stage, Letitia Blakely listened to the low murmur of the young crowd in the auditorium. She avoided the spot near the curtain.

Rutger acted as master of ceremonies. The proceedings were somber, low-energy. She began to feel as if she were making a terrible mistake. She was too young to say these things; it would sound horribly awkward, even childish.

Rutger made his opening remarks, then introduced her and motioned for her to come on stage. Letitia deliberately walked through the spot near the curtain, paused briefly, closed her eyes and took a deep breath, as if to infuse herself with whatever remained there of Reena. She walked past Miss Darcy, who seemed to glare at her.

Her throat seized. She rubbed her neck quickly, blinked at the bright lights on the catwalk overhead, tried to see the faces beyond the lights. They were just smudges in great darkness. She glanced out of the corner of her eye and saw Miss Darcy nodding, *Go ahead*.

"This has been a bad time for all of us," she began, voice high and scratchy. She cleared her throat. "I've lost a lot a friends, and so have you. Maybe you've lost sons and daughters. I think, even from there, looking at me, you can tell I'm not . . . designed. I'm natural. I don't have to wonder whether I'll get sick and die. But I . . ." She cleared her throat again. It wasn't getting easier. "I thought someone like me could tell you something important.

"People have made mistakes, bad mistakes. But you are not the mistakes. I mean . . . they weren't mistaken to make you. I can only dream about doing some of the things you'll do. Some of you are made to live in space for a long time, and I can't do that. Some of you will think things I can't, and go places I won't . . . travel to see the stars. We're different in a lot

265

of ways, but I just thought it was important to tell you . . .''

She wasn't following the prepared speech. She couldn't. "I love you. I don't care what the others say. *We* love you. You are very important. Please don't forget that. And don't forget what it costs us all.''

The silence was complete. She felt like slinking away. Instead, she straightened, thanked them, hearing not a word, not a restless whisper, then bowed her head from the catwalk glare and the interstellar darkness beyond.

Miss Darcy, stiff and formal, reached her arm out as Letitia passed by. They shook hands firmly, and Letitia saw, for the first time, that Miss Darcy looked upon her as an equal.

Letitia stood backstage while the ceremonies continued, examining the old wood floor, the curtains, counterweights, and flies, the catwalk.

It seemed very long ago, she had dreamed what she felt now, this unspecified love, not for family, not for herself. Love for something she could not have known back then; love for children not her own, yet hers none the less. Brothers.

Sisters.

Family.

# The
# Machineries
# of Joy

Throughout my career, I've done occasional articles with a scientific slant for newspapers and magazines. I've covered all of the Voyager I and II flybys, and written about them for the San Diego *Union*. Fiction writing takes up most of my career now, but I still write nonfiction now and then.

In October of 1983, I traveled from San Diego to Los Angeles and San Francisco, researching a proposed article for *Omni* Magazine. What I saw astonished me . . . and influenced me heavily when I went on to write *Eon* and the novel-length *Blood Music*. Here was not the beginning of the computer graphics revolution, which had occurred decades earlier, but the beginning of the *flowering* of that revolution. I could hardly restrain my enthusiasm. I suspect the last few pages of this piece will date badly as time goes by, but they show my frame of mind. And the frame of mind of dozens of other authors, as well; the information age has taken science fiction by storm.

*Omni* never used this piece, although they paid me for it. Nor did they use the hundreds of pictures I gathered, a selection from which would have accompanied it. Many people gave generously of their time, yet never saw their names or ideas in print. I hope this publication pays them back in some small measure.

The circumstances described below have, of course, changed considerably. Digital Productions has changed hands and management; Robert Abel and Associates is no longer an independent company.

The revolution has become even more stimulating and promising. Its effects are everywhere.

This article was completed in early 1984.

"**D**inosaurs!" The artist spreads his arms as if to embrace them. "I need the exact specifications—gridwork layouts of bones, muscles, scale patterns." The artist's office is covered with drawings of spaceships and alien beings, strange landscapes and mechanical diagrams. "If I have those, I can put them into the computer. We can program each muscle, make the skin ripple over the muscles. Tell the computer how they took a step, how they fought . . ."

And once again, dinosaurs will walk and fight. The artist is living a childhood daydream: he has the power to bring dead creatures to life. Even more remarkable, he has the power—with the aid of dozens of technicians, programmers, and fellow artists—to film objects that have never existed in any material form and make them interact with live actors.

But dinosaurs are a future project. The matter immediately at hand is a space battle. At night, within a stark white-walled enclave, the artist, director, and technician sit before a video monitor, examining the progressive stages of a nonexistent spaceship's destruction. Highly detailed ships—complete with crew—are dueling to the finish. One spaceship is destined not to survive; its hull is disassembled in the first of six boxes on the monitor. The early stages of an expanding blast are overlaid in subsequent boxes.

The artist describes an explosion in space. "I'd like the whole screen to flash white for one frame. Next we see an opaque fireball—fuzzy at the edges—surrounding the debris." He demonstrates an expanding sphere with hand gestures. "Then we ramp it down to transparency as the fireball grows." (To "ramp" is to smoothly increase or decrease any function.) "When the shockwave passes, all the little stuff—gases and tiny fragments—fly past and then we see the big scraps, moving a little slower." His grin is gleeful now. The director nods in agreement; this is, indeed, an explosion in space, not your usual smoke-and-fireworks exhibit.

The stages of the explosion are being fed into powerful computers, isolated beyond glass walls at the opposite end of the studio in a pristine white-floored environment. Artist, director, and technician are playing god games in an unreal universe.

Ultimately, it is all numbers, points charted in a space of three dimensions within a computer. Each number represents part of the position of a pixel, or picture element, millions of which go together to form a shape. It is the computer's duty to keep track of the numbers, and the shapes they represent. Perspective, color, shadow, motion, must all be processed with scrupulous accuracy or the apparent reality will collapse.

The numbers are then converted to signals which can be displayed on a monitor. The pixels assemble, and a spaceship is destroyed, frame by frame. When the result is printed onto film, it will be indistinguishable from very high-grade special effects accomplished with painstaking model work.

It will look as real as anything else in the finished motion picture.

The artist, director, and technician are, of course, fictitious, and the scenario is a technological fantasy, not to be realized for years, perhaps decades to come—

And if you believe *that*, you haven't been keeping track of recent advances in the incredible field of computer graphics.

It is happening now.

The artist is veteran production designer Ron Cobb (*Alien, Conan the Barbarian*); the director is Nick Castle (*Tag, Skatetown U.S.A.*), and the motion picture is *The Last Starfighter*, a joint Universal-Lorimar production. Under the auspices of Los Angeles–based Digital Productions, headed by John Whitney Jr., all of the special effects for *The Last Starfighter* are being done by digital scene simulation—computer graphics designed to match reality. Using two powerful Cray supercomputers and a phalanx of other machines, Digital Productions is taking a gamble—some say a big gamble—by committing itself wholeheartedly to the future.

The future of computer graphics will be extraordinary. Most of the experts in the field—the best can still be numbered on two hands—agree that we are on the verge of a revolution perhaps more basic and disruptive than Gutenberg's movable type. Communications and education will be fundamentally reshaped. The entertainment industry will experience changes far more drastic than the transition from silent movies to talkies, and talkies to TV.

The power that presently resides in the hands of a knowledgeable few will soon be available to all.

But first, back to the numbers.

The world of the computer is a very simple one. Everything is broken down into bits, a bit being the information required to answer any question with yes or no; in binary, yes equals 1, and no equals 0. Binary numbers consists of chains of ones and zeros. (In binary, 01 equals one, but 10 equals two.) More elaborate codes have been created to relate letters and symbols to certain numbers—thus allowing computers to display both numbers and text. Other codes relate the positions of glowing dots on a video screen using coordinates much like those on a map. A picture can be "digitized"—broken down into these numbered positions—and put into a computer, which can then manipulate the picture in a wide variety of ways.

A picture can also be formed within the computer by charting key elements on a graph, feeding the computer coordinates, and instructing it to draw lines or curves between the points. Mathematical equations which determine fixed geometric figures or curves can simplify the process; the computer can be instructed to draw a circle of a certain diameter around a point, or an ellipse; to trace out a square and expand it into a cube, and so on.

In fact, a "space" is determined within the computer, having three or more dimensions, and any object can be described within that space, given sufficiently detailed coordinates. If the object is simple, like a cone, a "lathe" program can rotate a triangle around an axis to form a cone, or a circle can be turned around any diameter to create a sphere, much as a shape is spun from a block of wood on a lathe. More complex, irregular shapes take more complicated instructions, and much more time.

Once the object is constructed in a simple line drawing, or "wireframe," additional programs can add a light source to give it highlight and cast a shadow. Colors and textures can be "mapped" on its surface. A point of view can be established, and what is not seen from that point of view—the back of the object—can be clipped, making it appear opaque and solid.

The process seems simple enough, but in reality the work involved in creating real-seeming objects on today's machines is extensive. The most complicated methods of creating objects in a computer—such as a technique called "ray tracing"—can take weeks of computer time. Simpler techniques can reduce the time to fractions of a second, but with a corresponding loss of color, shadow, and detail.

Once the object's numbers have been fed into the computer, the computer knows what the object looks like from all sides, at any distance, in relation to any other object or perspective within the machine's memory. A nonexistent spaceship can be made to zoom past a simulated planet, approach a much larger "mother ship," and dock inside a highly detailed landing bay, all in perfect perspective.

The computer can then display the objects in two dimensions on a video screen, or send signals to a printer to transfer images to film. Since the object has actually been mapped in more than two dimensions, the computer can be instructed to project two points of view, creating a parallax similar to that between our two eyes. The slightly separated images can be combined stereoscopically for a realistic feeling of depth.

If the film image needs to be "squeezed" anamorphically onto 35mm stock for later projection on a wide screen, the computer can do that, as well. Any required lens can be simulated within the machine.

In the 1950s, artists and programmers began to pioneer the techniques still being elaborated upon today. John Whitney Sr. was among the earliest, starting in the late 1940s. He later received the first IBM grant to study computer graphics in detail, and was installed in a ground-floor corner window of the IBM building in New York, displaying images for passersby.

Bill Fetter began exploring the possibilities of wireframe animation at Boeing in the late 1950s, and assembled the first computer-generated commercial in the late 1960s.

In the early seventies, Ken Knowlton and Michael Noll came on the scene—Knowlton working for Bell Labs, and Noll arranging for the first gallery showing of computer art. Noll's specialty was simulating "clay paintings" using computer images. Many viewers couldn't tell which were pictures of real clay paintings, and which were simulated.

In the last ten years, the progress has been astonishing; around the world, computers are helping to create images for scientific research, education, fine art, and entertainment.

Sometimes the divisions between these categories are erased; the enchanting beauty of a moving computer image can turn a prosaic enterprise—such as stress analysis of pipe joins—into art.

The most extensive use of computer animation has been in advertising. Already familiar to TV viewers are the plethora of "neon"-look commercials for banks, airlines, and automobile manufacturers.

Generically, computer animation relying on line graphics is known as "vector" animation. Using various animation techniques—inside and outside the computer—the lines of these "wireframe" drawings can be made to glow like neon tubes. This look has become so widespread that within the industry it is becoming a cliché, to be avoided if possible.

Filling in a wireframe object with color, shadow, and texture is called "raster graphics" or "raster" animation. This requires a more powerful computer, such as the Evans and Sutherland, or the Digital Equipment Corporation VAX machines commonly found in commercial studios.

Some interesting effects can be obtained by fudging (not a technical term). The surface of an object to be vector-animated can be covered with "crossthatching," using more lines instead of full raster graphics. This is known as "pseudo-raster" animation and can be charming, even though it falls in a middle range likely to be used less often as equipment and programming improve.

Crude raster graphics can be judged by "aliasing"—the appearance of the "jaggies" along an object's edges. Each pixel stands out against a contrasting color, and when the object moves, the pixels can appear to march along the edge. These can be eliminated by coloring alternating edge pixels in shades between the contrasting colors. The border is softened slightly, and the graphics are said to be "anti-aliased."

The most powerful computers available to animators—the Cray series (the Cray 1, an expanded version called the Cray XMP, and a much smaller, even faster Cray 2) usually reside in defense establishments and major research laboratories. Digital Productions is the only private effects studio that owns Crays. The Cray Corporation is reluctant to release the locations of all its machines, but it is well known that the Sandia Labs and Lawrence Livermore National Laboratory have a number on hand.

By time-sharing—having the computers process their work when not otherwise busy—researchers in several such establishments have done important work programming computers to "understand" and draw transparent objects, lenses, and realistic landscapes.

Two of the most prolific of these researchers are James F. Blinn at the Jet Propulsion Laboratory in Pasadena and Nelson Max at Lawrence Livermore National Laboratories. Blinn's group at JPL animated the striking computer simulations of the Voyager probes' journeys to the outer planets, widely shown on network and public television. Nelson Max has worked largely on graphic representations of biological processes. Using his graphics programs, he has been able to predict how molecules will interact before lab tests have been made. Max has also investigated the effects of mutagens on DNA, and modeled the structure of very tiny viruses.

After months or years of painstaking labor, computer artists display their wares at annual SIGGRAPH conventions. (SIGGRAPH stands for Special Interest Group, Graphics, a division of the Association of Computing Machinery, or ACM.) Private individuals, employees of giant research establishments, and commercial film studios gather to compare notes and keep up on the latest developments.

Not since Leonardo da Vinci have so many technical disciplines been required of working artists. Not only must they have basic drawing and drafting skills, but they must know at least the rudiments of programming. They must understand how light reflects, refracts, and diffuses—and be able to translate their knowledge into terms the computer can digest. The artist can no longer stand aloof from science and math.

New techniques can take him to the frontiers of theory. Recent work in the texturing of surfaces has used fractals, mathematical entities capable of generating very complex patterns. Perhaps the most familiar example of computer animation with fractal-generated landscape is the "Genesis" sequence from *Star Trek II: The Wrath of Khan*, made for Paramount Pictures by Sprockets, the computer division of Lucasfilm's Industrial Light and Magic.

One of the focal points for computer animators was the Walt Disney production of *Tron*. Information International, Inc. (known as triple-I), Mathematical Applications Group, Inc. (MAGI), Robert Abel and Associates, and Digital Effects all contributed their expertise; yet *Tron* contained only ten to fifteen minutes of full computer animation. The rest was accomplished with more conventional special effects and animation techniques.

A great many of the people who worked on *Tron* have now moved on to positions in companies around the country. A few, such as Richard Taylor, are still involved with feature-length motion pictures. Taylor is reportedly hard at work on a film called *Dreamer* for Paramount.

In advertising, two of the biggest film companies have made a major commitment to computer graphics. Robert Abel in Hollywood—long renowned for the beautiful combinations of live action and back-lit animation in his Levi's and Seven-Up commercials—assembled a computer graphics division while assigned to do special effects for *Star Trek: The Motion Picture*. Unlike Digital Productions, however, Abel kept all his other special effects techniques, considering computer graphics as another tool, not an end in itself. "A lot of the stuff we do is combination," Abel explains, "where we combine miniatures and live action with computer images." Pure computer animation, at present, is more expensive than many other techniques, and in Abel's view, flexibility and variety are necessary to the production of commercial advertising films.

Bo Gehring, in charge of Bo Gehring Associates in Venice, California, originally came to the West Coast to do computer animation tests for Steven Spielberg's *Close Encounters of the Third Kind*. The tests proved unsatisfactory but Gehring stayed on to found his own company—again, with a complete spectrum of techniques at his disposal. Unlike Abel, who began as a documentary film maker, Gehring's roots are in computer graphics, but he agrees with Abel that commitment to one technique is risky. As for getting involved in feature films: "Ninety million dollars is spent *each day* on advertising in the United States," Gehring says. "Feature films can't begin to match that level of financing. I'm secure where I am."

Both Gehring and Abel believe that computer graphics is still in its infancy, and will probably have a major effect on all forms of visual communication. For the moment, however, neither is willing to make the leap of faith required for an operation such as that being conducted at Digital Productions. And truthfully, Gehring admits that his financial backing is not equal to Digital Productions', which is supported by Ramtek, a major computer company. "I am a bit envious of what John Whitney Jr. and Gary Demos have come into at Digital—all that [computing] power. But I'm happy with my situation, and just can't see taking that kind of risk right now."

Gehring also expresses an interest in digital *sound* synthesis. "I'm one of those people who has to pull off the road when something really intriguing comes on the car radio. I firmly believe that sound is at least the equal of sight in bandwidth—complexity of information—and synthetic sound is a fascinating area that's barely been explored."

Another of the Big Three companies, R. Greenberg in New York, is rapidly building its computer graphics division.

Computers have revolutionized the film industry in many more ways than computer graphics. Virtually all commercial studios, whether producing advertising or feature films, use computers to control complex camera movements or integrate different elements of photography.

At Robert Abel, slit-scan photography is a staple item. The process was originally invented by John Whitney, Sr., and was developed by Con Pedersen and Douglas Trumbull while working for Stanley Kubrick on *2001: A Space Odyssey*. Pedersen now works at Abel, where he supervises other aspects of special effects production, including computer graphics. (Trumbull, interestingly, seems to eschew full computer animation. In his recent film *Brainstorm*, even sequences which appeared to be computer-generated were done using other techniques.)

In slit-scan, a camera is mounted at the end of a long track, at the opposite end of which a piece of flat artwork is masked to reveal only a narrow horizontal slit. As the camera moves forward very slowly, a computer coordinates the motion of the slit up or down on the artwork. The result is a drawn-out image of the artwork, stretched in perspective by the camera's approach.

Computers are also responsible for the many forms of motion-control used to photograph space battles at Lucasfilm and elsewhere. Signals from a camera mount are fed into a computer, which memorizes the camera positions and can then control the camera for repeated passes. Different models, mattes, and other special effects elements can be added with great precision.

Computers are even involved in stop-motion puppet animation at Industrial Light and Magic. The "Go-Motion" computerized system was used in *Dragonslayer* to memorize the motions of an armatured miniature dragon as it was manually "walked through" its sequences.

All these elaborations—from slit-scan to Go-Motion puppet animation—are likely to become passé before the end of the century. Whatever the risks, Digital Productions is obviously where the field is moving.

But computers have one major hurdle to leap before they dominate. Character animation—whether it be the fluid motions of a Disney cel-animated deer, or a human being—is still very difficult for computers.

Computers are happiest when dealing with shapes defined by simple mathematics—planes in perspective, spheres, cones, polygons, and polyhedrons. Humans (not to mention Bambi or dragons) are not composed of these objects, at least not at first glance. Living characters are lumpy, bumpy, and in constant motion—all parts of them. Muscles shift beneath skin and skeletal angles change. Facial expression is a nightmare of complexity, with hundreds of muscles providing a bewildering variety of shapes—all of them familiar to the viewer, and therefore difficult to fake convincingly.

For the artist, years of study are required to convincingly replicate human and animal shapes. The human mind is enormously more complicated than any modern computer, with millions of "algorithms" all smoothly blending in unconscious processes. How can a computer hope to match the work of a skilled cartoon animator, much less the reality of a human being?

Tim Heidmann, at R&B EFX in Glendale, believes character animation is the stumbling block of computer graphics. "When you think of all the expertise required to get a Disney-type character on film—including the distortion of reality, stretching characters to add life, exaggerating expressions—the problem seems insurmountable." Heidmann does computer graphics for R&B EFX using a much smaller Hewlett-Packard business computer. The HP manipulates wireframe images which are then photographed and enhanced by hand in R&B's own small animation studio. The entire system costs under $25,000. "What computers do best," he explains, "is what human animators do with the most difficulty—changing perspective, drawing geometric shapes. And what humans do best is most difficult for computers—especially a small system like ours: coloring, shading, characters." R&B combines the two with ingenuity instead of massive number-crunching.

Digital Productions is hard at work using both ingenuity and brute computing power to overcome the difficulties of animating characters in a computer. Most of this work is under tight wraps of security, but it appears they are building up human and humanlike figures by creating "intelligent shapes" which will mimic muscles on fixed skeletal frames. These "intelligent shapes" will be programmed to interact with other shapes—other muscles—around a skeleton, within the constraints of skin.

Motion studies of animals and humans are programmed into their machines to give them parameters within which to work. Ron Cobb explains: "A computer doesn't know where to stop. If you have a character's arm swinging, the arm in the machine isn't *real*. It doesn't have an elbow or a shoulder to stop it. It just keeps swinging in a circle until you tell it what the limits are. Then it has the limits in memory, but you have to be very specific, very careful."

The computer cannot intuit anything. It is literal. Everything must be described in detail. Consequently, the computing capacity and time required to control these figures will be enormous—at first. But the cost of the early stages in labor and money can be compared to research and development costs in any industry. The initial outlay is always greater than the cost of later work.

One small hint of the coming revolution is provided by the locations of two major companies relying on computer graphics. Cranston-Csuri, founded by pioneer computer artist Charles A. Csuri, is located in Columbus, Ohio. Computer Creations takes pride in being based in South Bend, Indiana—far from the advertising capitals of New York and Los Angeles. Electronics can deliver messages and products around the world; in the future, location will be less and less important.

Size will also become less important. With computers, a commercial studio can begin operations with only a handful of creative people. Pacific Data Images (PDI), in Sunnyvale, California, has only four employees, yet has already landed major advertising and promotional contracts. With initial costs of less than a million dollars, entrepreneurs like PDI's Carl Rosendahl are already taking advantage of the built-in flexibility of the computer. Costs are dropping and software is improving, albeit more slowly than hardware. Within ten years, the big advertising companies will be surrounded by smaller, tougher firms with equal capabilities. The bottom line will then be not money, but creativity.

There is no lack of creativity. The computer images and motion pictures produced by artists around the world are dizzying in variety and quantity. California's David Em is well known for his architectural fantasies and abstractions. Paul Allen Newell has animated M.C. Escher–inspired tessellated designs that transform with enchanting smoothness and precision.

Nancy Burson of New York (profiled in *Omni*, "The Arts," June 1983) uses computers to digitally combine photographic images of people and animals. She was responsible for the portrait of Big Brother commissioned for CBS's tribute to Orwell's *1984*. By digitizing and melding the portraits of the twentieth century's worst tyrants, she came up with a hauntingly familiar, somehow benevolent, and yet very unsettling hybrid. Much more charming is her mix of woman and cat.

Em, Burson, and Newell highlight the successes and problems of presenting computer graphics on the printed page. Em's and Burson's images are static, suitable for magazine reproduction, but the charm of Newell's work lies in motion.

Even more difficult to convey is the wonder of a live computer art performance, where performer and audience are one. Ed Tannenbaum of Raster Master in San Francisco has installed a performance art center in his city's public-access science center, Exploratorium. A video camera photographs people in a room as they move about and then feeds their images to a computer. The result is projected in real-time (that is, live) on a large screen, allowing infinite varieties of human-machine artwork. Children can dance and paint with their bodies, becoming their own kaleidoscopes.

Educators inevitably become more involved with computer

graphics as classroom computers proliferate. Simple graphics programs can teach even very young children how to work (and play) with computers. Today's youngsters will find computers and computer art a part of their lives.

This is where the revolution truly becomes powerful.

In one or two decades, at the present rate of progress, computers cheap enough for home use will be capable of graphics even more sophisticated than those being produced by today's major studios. Graphics buffs will be creating, trading, and selling programs to generate different kinds of images—including images of realistic characters.

Eventually, perhaps by the end of this century, a kind of visual typewriter will be possible. Any scene the programmer/artist/writer can imagine will be brought to life using computer animation. As software and hardware advance and become cheaper, and as information and image networks expand, virtually anybody can become a Cecil B. De Mille. The major requirements will be time and talent—*not* money.

The greatest handicap to cinema at the moment is the dominance of accounting over creativity. Faced with budgets of tens of millions of dollars, studio executives are justifiably concerned that their products should appeal to large numbers of people. The result is often pablum. Primary creativity is endlessly ignored or second-guessed.

Commercial television networks are even more handicapped; to satisfy advertisers, incredible numbers of people must tune in to their programs. Few artists or writers have ever made anything worthwhile by pandering to the lowest common denominator, yet this is the current state of most of network television.

The printed word allows more freedom. A pencil and a piece of paper are all that is required for expression in print. The production of a book is measured in tens of thousands of dollars for an average press run, not millions. Publishing—for the moment—still allows a great many writers to create personal works. A writer can establish a reputation with only a few hundred or a few thousand steady readers.

Yet only ten to twenty percent of Americans regularly read books. Newspapers and magazines fare better—but less than half of all Americans receive any of their information from the printed word. What we have is a colossal failure of a communications medium—print—to reach the masses.

For many people, print is difficult to assimilate. It has many uses and advantages, but often it cannot convey information as quickly and efficiently as other media.

The dilemma is clear. Print offers diversity and individual expression—as well as the active participation of the reader, in imagining and fleshing out what the words convey—but cannot reach as many people as television or motion pictures.

Television and motion pictures appeal to the masses, but more often than not spoon-feed pablum to a barely conscious viewer.

By combining both print and vision, computers will break the money monopoly and allow many more people to work with "pictorial narratives," a catch-all phrase for the multitude of art forms which will inevitably develop.

Robert Abel sees a future society with individuals becoming more and more isolated, physically, as the electronics revolution allows them to work at home. With increasingly sophisticated entertainment forms, there will be less need to leave home for recreation. With more leisure time, the public will demand more entertainment. And with more artists able to produce complicated pictorial narratives, the demand could well be met with an explosion of creativity—if the audience isn't already conditioned to textureless drivel. If it isn't too late even now . . .

Take a deep breath.

We're going to enter a possible future, and it will take some effort to get used to it.

You're on a street. A woman approaches you. She appears to be wearing a jungle. You stare in amazement as she passes; to a distance of about six inches, all around her, you can see gnarled trees, vines and creepers, exotic birds, even a leopard lying in wait.

She walks along a wall and the building suddenly smiles at her—the entire wall one massive pair of lips in three dimensions. "Good morning, Miss Andrews," it says. "How may we serve you today? Shopping for apparel, or just out for a stroll?" AdWalls are formal and slightly stodgy by design. Virtually everyone is known, on sight, by ad companies who use computers to target not just groups of consumers but individuals.

The woman pays no attention and continues on. The smile disintegrates into a flight of wildly colored butterflies as you approach.

"Distinguished sir," the AdWall says. Butterflies flitter around you. "I don't have your name in memory at this moment. How may Freepic serve you today?"

You mumble something about wanting to find a computer store.

"Chips'n'disks, the city's oldest computer store, lies but two blocks away." A map appears in front of your face, then transforms into a speeded-up visual tour. You see yourself walking two blocks south, turning left, and entering the store. The image ends with a large-scale projection of the storefront. Symbols conveying hours of business, product lines available, and even clerks' faces are overlaid on each side of the map.

You make your way through parti-robed citizens and find the store. Inside, you marvel at the systems available. There are computers for computing, and for just about anything else imaginable. You can rent information networks, even gain access to a worldwide library system for a low monthly fee. ("Less than one percent of the average household income!" a display enthuses. There are two billion subscribers.)

Your domicile can be turned into any environment you wish, complete with sounds and smells. You can even create your own environment, using the Apple 89 Worldmaker.

"Occupation?" the clerk asks. The clerk grins and fades to transparency, then opacifies again, as required by law in the first few minutes of service. You realize you are being served by a very realistic hologram.

"Writer," you say.

"Oh, then you need a minezeye." It takes you a few minutes to realize the clerk means "Mind's Eye." The unit is quite small, the size of a cigarette case, and comes complete with plugs to hook directly into the cerebral cortex.

"The Mind's Eye is a Hair Trigger unit, taking instruction in basic Brainwave, spoken language, or even Touchcode, rather like typing. If you wish, it has a translator which can turn a videotext into a visual experience. Plug the Mind's Eye into a Page Turner and you can interactively turn your favorite classic into a motion picture, just as *you* visualize it; you coordinate the action through the cerebral cortex plugs. Some training required," the clerk informs you cheerfully.

Videotext combines visual and aural information with high-density symbols—symbols which both inform and trigger intellectual and emotional cues in the adept viewer. Some videotexts compress a hundred flashing signals within a few seconds' time. The symbols are distant relatives of Egyptian hieroglyphs—and modern road signs. Some are based on the logos of famous businesses. Some are as stylish as Japanese calligraphy.

Realtime units will soon be available. If you think it takes too long to imagine a scene, Realtime can supplement your brainwaves. If a jungle in required, Realtime has seventy different jungles in memory, and soon will have cable connections with real jungles, which can be digitized and reshaped at will.

All computers in Chips'n'disks are, or course, Child Easy. In fact, the 1-Thru-5 unit is designed to be used by an infant. It comes complete with Sensual Crib and access to the Sesame Net.

If you're a fiction writer, you can peddle your creation on the Lie Wire (stet!). If you're a philosopher, your works can find their audience (for a fee, or course) on the Mindbender cable. Historians frequently sell to the Pasttime Cable.

On any of these networks, you can start out on the Low Rung and gradually, through jury selection or User Acceptance (the ratings, that is), move up step by step to the very height of success. A single work might reach as many people as, say, the Britannica Visual.

Peripherals include MovieLife, a chip which can be dropped into your home computer to turn any 20th century film into a living experience for you and your family. If you'd prefer to see Humphrey Bogart star in *The Man Who Would Be King*, instead of Michael Caine, that can be arranged.

Live actors are still in great demand. They frequently license their images for computer generation, making a substantial second income—but virtually everyone acknowledges that a real actor is better than a simulation. Some actors have ruined promising careers by selling rights to less reputable retailers, who place their images in all sorts of compromising products.

But be warned—if you get *too* involved in all this, and happen to Drop Out—leave the real world and zip along the underground nets, where all sort of unsavory simulations are available—the Bug Police are tapping the wires every day. There are many legitimate adult services, such as FantaFem and

Woman of Your Dreams, but many more balance precariously on the borders of the law, or fall completely offsides.

"Bookstores?" The clerk responds to your question with some surprise. "We've heard of a few shops catering to the collector's market—and of course, there's always the Winston Smith Society. It meets once a month to trade crumbling paperbacks."

You look around the shop, at the profusion of systems that serve more to supplement or replace creativity than enhance it. "Don't you have anything for someone who just wants to tell his own story, with his own images?" you ask, frowning.

"Sir," the clerk says indignantly, "that's where this all *begins*. Not everyone is as privileged as you must be, however."

You are reminded of electronic musical instruments, decades in the past. Some became so elaborate that you barely had to touch a key to produce a tune. Distasteful to the concert pianist, perhaps, but a great deal of fun for the dabbler.

"Come with me," the clerk says, taking you in his ghostly hand. "Let me show you some basic models. For the person who wants to create, rather than simply consume."

You are led into a simply and tastefully furnished room. A boy and girl, no older than ten, are sitting before an extensive keyboard. Colors and vague shapes flicker in a cleared area beyond the machine. "Did we get all the numbers right this time?" the girl asks. "We want it to be as accurate as possible."

"They're right," the boy assures her.

"Let's see it, then."

The boy pushes a display key.

In the cleared area, a tyrannosaurus rex appears in horrible, fascinating detail, tail swishing back and forth, walking on its six clawed toes. It opens its mouth and emits a curious, birdlike squawk.

"Oh, they didn't sound like *that*," the girl says, shaking her head vigorously.

"How do you know?" the boy asks.

"Let's make it roar."

With a few nimble keyboard touches, they make the beast change its tune and roar.

"Don't you just *love* dinosaurs?" the girl asks, clapping her hands.

Your fingers twitch. Where was this kind of machine when you were a child? You step forward and politely ask, "Here. May I play with that?

"I've always fancied sea monsters, myself..."

(The author, by the way, is highly enamored of books and other print media. All letters of protest should be addressed to people not yet born.)